Applied Business
for GCSE

Malcolm Surridge

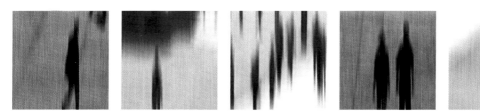

Collins

CONTENTS

Acknowledgements

To Jackie, a very special person, with all my love.

I am grateful to those who supported me in writing this book. The text was improved by Richard Thompson's constructive comments; his ideas improved the book in many ways. Mike March's careful editing helped to adapt the text to the format of the book and eliminated a number of errors, inconsistencies and ambiguities.

At Collins Educational, Graham Bradbury and Kay Wright were hugely supportive. Kay's good humour, patience and advice proved invaluable. In spite of all these contributions, any errors that remain are my responsibility.
Malcolm Surridge

The author and publisher would like to thank the following for permission to reproduce photographs and other material:

ACE Photo Agency: David Kerwin (page 83); Kevin Phillips (pages 63, 188); Malcolm Burkett (page 110); Gabe Palmer (page 123); SMP Assocs (page 205)
Acestock.com: Chris Middlebrook (page 39); Jigsaw 2 (page 124)
Advertising Archives (page 133)
AstraZeneca (page 59)
Bank of England (page 208)
BBC Picture Library (page 136)
Capital Radio (page 76)
Collections: Eric Lewis (page 10); Roger Scruton (page 17, 89); Paul Watts (page 28)
Curry's (page 69)
Elizabeth Smith (page 155)
Environmental Images: Leslie Garland (page 86); Toby Adamson (page 137); Alex Olah (page 212)
Equal Opportunities Commission (page 103)
GlaxoSmithKline (page 50)
Honda (page 99)
Impact: Gavin Milverton (page 183); Chris Moyse (page 195)
Kwik-Fit (page 79)

lastminute.com (page 100)
Marks & Spencer (pages 85, 129, 185)
Multiyork/Studio 5 (page 126)
PA Photos Ltd (page 43)
Popperfoto: Anthony Upton (page 100); Adrian Dennis (page 105); Chris Helgren (page 107); Jeff J Mitchell (page 109)
Rex Features: (page 44); SIPA (pages 81, 153); GRW (page 171); Nils Joregensen (page 173); Clive Dixon (page 210)
Robert Harding: Dennis Firminger (page 145); PBI (page 147); Hans-Peter Merten (page 149); Jean-Luc Brouard (page 193)
Roger Scruton (pages 19, 25, 83, 97, 113, 131, 135, 168, 174, 175, 179, 187, 197)
Rover (page 35)
Sainsbury (pages 41, 207)
Science Photo Library (page 77)
Tesco (pages 49, 97, 133)
UK Coal (page 30)

Every effort has been made to contact copyright holders, but if any have been inadvertently overlooked, the publishers will be pleased to make the necessary arrangements at the first opportunity.

The purpose of this book

The purpose of this book is to help you to develop the knowledge and understanding that you'll need to complete a GCSE Applied Business course. The book has been written specifically to cover the topics in each of the three units that make up your GCSE course.

GCSE Applied Business units

Unit 1   Investigating business

Unit 2   People and business

Unit 3   Business finance

This book aims to help you gain a good, clear understanding of important topics in business. Hopefully, it might also encourage you to consider a career in business. Taking a GCSE Applied Business course will introduce you to the wide range of careers that are included under the heading "business". Perhaps one of the topics you will study will catch your attention, and may lead you to an interesting and rewarding job.

How does the book work?

The book is organised in the same way as your GCSE Applied Business course. There are three main units and these are divided into double-page topics. For example, the topic 'Changing working arrangements' is covered on pages 94 to 97 (pages 96 and 97 are shown opposite). The topics covered in each unit are listed on the contents page at the start of the unit. You can also find the topics that you're looking for by using the index at the end of the book.

Every double-page topic spread has a number of features. These include the topic information (often given as bullet points to make your learning easier), as well as **Case Study**, **Stop & Think** and **Over To You** activities. You should try to complete the activities as you come to them because they are designed to help you learn and understand the topic information more clearly. Each of the units also includes a number of revision pages. These provide you with an opportunity to look again at what you have studied and help you to test your understanding of the topics.

Completing the Stop & Think activities and the Revision pages won't always be easy, but it will help you to learn more. It's worth making the effort if you want to achieve the best grade that you can.

Towards the end of the book you will find a lengthy list of websites that will help you to prepare the evidence needed to complete units 1 and 2.

What is different about this GCSE?

GCSE Applied Business is a **vocational qualification**. This means that it is work-related. It aims to provide the basic knowledge, skills and understanding that you will be able to use in a business. It can also lead to further education or training in business subjects. The content of the course and the work that you do will all be related to the world of business in some way. For example, you'll look at the types of businesses that exist in the United Kingdom, the range of job roles that exist in them and discover the different skills and knowledge that are needed to run even the smallest business successfully. You will also be introduced to the external factors that affect how businesses work. The rate of interest and laws protecting consumers are just two of these.

What will my GCSE Applied Business course cover?

All GCSEs in vocational subjects are composed of three compulsory units. The titles and a brief description of your three compulsory units are set out below.

The content of each unit is set out in detail in a course specification. Your teacher will have copies of this.

How will my GCSE Applied Business course be assessed?

This GCSE requires you to work at the same level as any other non-vocational GCSE, such as history or mathematics. The qualification that you'll receive when you complete the course will be graded on an A* to G scale. However, GCSE Applied Business is a double award. This means that you will receive the equivalent of two GCSEs at the grade you are awarded when you complete the course. Your grade will therefore be somewhere between A*A* and GG.

GCSE Applied Business Units

Unit title	what's it about?
1. Investigating business	■ What is a business? ■ The types of businesses in Britain ■ The different parts (or functions) that make up a business. ■ External influences on business such as the government and protecting the environment.
2. People and business	■ The different individual and groups who are interested in businesses. ■ The experience of working in businesses. ■ Employment laws and disputes at work. ■ How to apply for a job successfully. ■ How businesses look after customers.
3. Business finance	■ Financial documents used by businesses. ■ Planning business finance. ■ Sources of business finance. ■ Costs, revenues and profits. ■ Making and receiving payments.

To gain a graded GCSE qualification you will need to complete an assessment of your learning in each of the three course units. You will have to complete assignments set by your teachers for units 1 and 2 and you must also sit a test set by the Awarding Body (examination board) for unit 3. You will need to complete each of these three assessments to be awarded an Applied GCSE in business.

What can I do with my GCSE Applied Business?

A GCSE Applied Business qualification can help you progress into further education, training or employment. Your choices are shown below.

Alongside other GCSEs, your Applied Business qualification could give you access to AS and A level courses at your school or at a local college. You might choose to develop your knowledge of business by progressing to an AS or A level course.

You may also use it to gain entry to an Advanced Vocational Certificate in Education, with Business an obvious choice! These awards are assessed mainly through coursework. About a third of the assessment will be through examinations – exactly the

same as your GCSEApplied Business.

Alternatively, GCSE Applied Business could help you to access an NVQ training course in a range of business subjects such as Administration, Accounting or Marketing.

The final option could be to use it to gain employment in one of a wide range of careers as shown below. This shows just a small selection of jobs that it is possible to have in business. Most jobs will require further training.

Whatever your career plans, a GCSE Applied Business course should provide you with an opportunity to explore and develop your knowledge and understanding of the world of business. I hope that this is an enjoyable experience and that the book helps you to achieve the best possible grade.

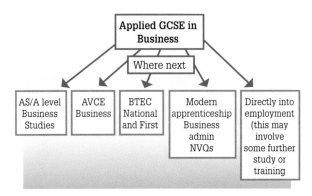

Possible routes from your Applied GCSE in Business

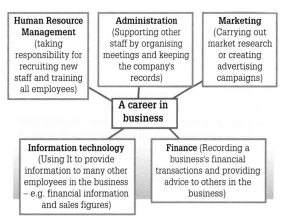

Careers in business

Investigating business

This unit introduces you to the different types of businesses found in the UK. It also prepares you to study the other two units that make up your GCSE in Applied Business. You will learn about:

- business aims and objectives
- business ownership, which may be public sector (owned and run by central or local government) or private sector (owned and run by just one individual or a partnership of individuals or a large company with many owners)
- business ownership by co-operatives or franchises
- how a business chooses its location
- the different sectors in which businesses operate
- the patterns of consumer spending and the changes in production and employment
- the different functions of a business, including research and development, human resources, marketing and sales, finance, administration and customer service
- how businesses communicate internally and with other businesses
- using information technology in a business
- external influences on businesses.

If you are thinking of working in the world of business, studying this unit will help you to develop a good understanding of how businesses work. Studying business will be of benefit to you in whatever career you eventually choose.

Unit 1 of this book covers Unit 1, Investigating business, of the GCSE Applied Business award.

Prontaprint!

A question...

Read the list of familiar organisations set out below and decide which of them are businesses:

- Marks & Spencer plc
- the National Health Service
- your local corner shop
- Cadbury Schweppes plc
- your school or college
- the London Underground
- Nissan's car factory in Sunderland
- a neighbour who works at home designing websites for individuals and companies.

KEY CONCEPTS

A **business** is any organisation that produces or supplies goods or services.

A **good** is any product that can be seen or felt. Examples include mobile telephones, houses and CDs.

A **product** is a more general term, covering both goods and services.

A **service** is a business that does not produce goods but involves some action being taken on behalf of an individual or a firm. Examples include hairdressing and health care.

Profit is the amount of money a firm has left from selling its products, after it has paid all its expenses, such as employees' wages.

BBC Broadcasting House, London

STOP & THINK

The BBC aims to 'inform, educate and entertain' through its television and radio programmes. It does not aim to make huge profits.

Think of five businesses that do not aim to make profits. Are there any similarities between them?

And the answer...

They all are! A business is any organisation that:

- produces goods (cars or cream cakes, for example)
- supplies services (such as health care, education)
- distributes or sells these products (businesses such as haulage (transport) firms and shops).

We use a number of terms to describe businesses.

- A firm or an organisation is any type of business – these are general words for businesses.
- A company is a special type of business, which we will look at in more detail on pages 20–1.

Businesses can be huge. Vodafone is a very large business employing thousands of people. However, many businesses are made up of just one person. Your window cleaner or hairdresser may be an example of a one-person business.

The word 'business' comes from 'busy-ness'. 'Busyness' is a good description of firms. Most firms are busy carrying out activities such as:

- producing goods
- supplying services
- selling and transporting their products
- training and managing their workers
- communicating with suppliers.

We will investigate the various functions that make up a business. Businesses have to

- employ people
- look after the business's money (and keep careful records of spending and earnings)
- produce goods or supply services
- inform people of their products through advertising
- make sure customers are happy with the goods and services supplied
- research new products.

We will find out how businesses decide on where to locate. They do not always choose the cheapest property they can find. Often they want to be near their customers or close to firms that supply raw materials.

Communication is very important to businesses. Communication might be internal between employees or external with suppliers and customers. We will look at how and why firms communicate.

Businesses can be affected by many factors that are beyond their control. For example, Vodafone faces tough competition from other firms such as Orange and might lose customers if its competitors decide to lower their prices.

Vodafone might be affected by other external factors, such as:

- changes in interest rates
- a rise in the value of the pound, making it worth more dollars or more euros
- laws that stop the business causing pollution.

We will consider these and other external factors that affect businesses in the centre of this unit.

OVER TO YOU

Vodafone provides mobile phone services for 93 million customers in 28 different countries. Vodafone is one of the largest businesses in Europe.

Discover more about Vodafone by looking at its website (www.vodafone.co.uk). Can you find out:

- how many people it employs?

- how much money the business receives from selling its products?

What are aims?

Aims are the long-term goals of the business. Businesses try to achieve one or more aims. The list below sets out the most important business aims.

- **Make a profit.** This means that the firm's earnings from selling its goods or services should be greater than its running costs.
- **Provide goods or services.** Many businesses do not aim to make profits. They may have the goal of providing goods or services to larger groups of people. For example, The UK's Blood Transfusion Service aims to provide supplies of blood to people in hospital in all parts of the country.
- **Survival.** This means making sure that the business continues to trade and is not forced to close down. Survival is an important aim for:
  - recently set up businesses
  - businesses that have lost large numbers of customers.
- **Growth or expansion.** Once a business is well established and looks likely to survive, its aim may change to growth. A business might grow by:
  - joining with another business to form a new, larger business
  - increasing sales of its products.
- **Maximise sales.** Some businesses aim to sell as many products as possible. They may deliberately sell their products at low prices. This helps them to become well known and to win new customers.
- **Improve the quality of the product.** One aim of a business might be to produce high-quality products. This may mean making sure that customers are very happy with the firm's products. Kwik-Fit, who replace tyres and exhausts for thousands of the UK's motorists, have the aim of 'customer delight', not just customer satisfaction.

STOP & THINK

Businesses draw up mission statements and aims before deciding on objectives. Why is it important that aims are set before objectives?

A Aims and objectives

BUSINESS AIMS
May be written in a mission statement.

BUSINESS OBJECTIVES
Help a business to achieve its aims.

SHORT-TERM TARGETS
These might be set for individuals or departments in a business and help to achieve objectives.

KEY CONCEPTS

A **mission statement** sets out the general purpose of a business. It helps employees work towards a common goal. For example, Microsoft's mission statement (1999) is 'to give people great software anytime, any place...'

A **business aim** is an organisation's long-term goal. For example, Shell might aim to make large amounts of profit.

Business objectives are targets pursued by a firm to help it achieve its aims. Thus, Shell might seek to increase its sales of oil products in eastern Europe.

Managers are the people who run businesses on a day-to-day basis. They take decisions on matters such as prices to charge and amounts to produce. In a small business the manager might also be the owner.

STOP & THINK

Some important aims for businesses are shown in **B**. Which of these aims do you think would match the following businesses:
1 the Salvation Army
2 Apple Computers
3 BP Amoco
4 your local college
5 Ryan Air (the low price airline)?

■ **Be highly competitive.** A competitive business is one that provides good-quality products (perhaps better than those sold by rival firms) at prices that consumers think are good value.
■ **Provide charitable or voluntary services.** In the UK, charities and voluntary organisations aim to help the elderly, the homeless, animals and poor people, rather than make profits.
■ **Be environmentally friendly.** For many businesses it important not to damage the environment. Body Shop is famous for refusing to sell products that have been tested on animals.

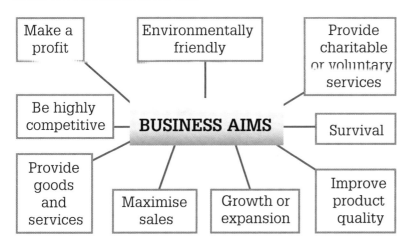

B A summary of business aims

All businesses have aims. One measure of the success of a business is if it achieves its aims. Businesses should:

■ set aims once they are established
■ review aims regularly to check whether these are still appropriate.

JOINED-UP THINKING

Once a business has decided what its aims are it can decide on its objectives. A firm's objectives should help it to achieve its overall aims. Business objectives are looked at in detail on pages 14–15.

The aims of a business will vary according to its size and type. For example, large companies have very different aims from those of smaller businesses that employ only a handful of people. We look at types of businesses on pages 16–27.

Visit the website of a large, well-known business and find out its aims. Firms that you might try include:

■ Cadbury Schweppes – www.cadburyschweppes.com
■ Coca-Cola – www.coca-cola.com
■ ICI – www.ici.com
■ Nestlé – www.nestle.com
■ Nokia – www.nokia.com
■ Sainsbury's – www.sainsburys.co.uk

Write down the aims of your chosen company.

Visit a small, local business. It is useful if you know the owner. Ask the owner what his or her aim is in running the business.

Very likely the aims of the two businesses will be quite different. Why is this so? Were you surprised by your answers?

What are objectives?

Business objectives are goals that a firm sets itself for the next three to five years. Objectives should:

- have a timescale over which they should be achieved
- be stated in numerical terms (be measurable)
- contribute to the business achieving its aims.

Tesco, the UK's biggest retailer, has two aims:

- increase its share of the UK grocery market
- develop its non-food business.

In 2000, Tesco said that that one of its objectives was to be the leading internet grocer in the world by the end of that year. By selling more of its products over the internet, the company hoped to increase its food sales and share of the UK grocery market.

KEY CONCEPTS

Business objectives are goals or targets that a firm pursues to help it achieve its aims. Thus, Shell might seek to increase its sales of oil products in eastern Europe by 10 per cent over the next two years.

STOP & THINK

Visit the Tesco website (www.tesco.com/). What activities is Tesco involved in that may help it to achieve its aim of increasing its non-food business?

Can you think of any objectives that the company may have that will help it fulfil this aim?

What objectives might businesses pursue?

Objectives are targets and challenges for all businesses. Examples of some of the objectives that businesses pursue are:

1 **Selling more than a competitor**. Tesco's aim for many years was to grow. One of its objectives was to overtake Sainsbury's in terms of grocery sales. In 1997 Tesco met this objective and became the UK's leading supermarket.

2 **Selling more products than in the previous year**. Firms may seek to increase sales each year if they have business aims such as growth or becoming more competitive. If firms set an objective to increase sales, they will expand and might take customers from competitors. Nokia, the mobile phone manufacturer, has an objective of increasing its sales of phones each year. This helps it to achieve its aim of making profits.

3 **Producing new goods or providing new services**. This objective can help firms to achieve their aims, for example, making large amounts of profit. In 1999 Levi's, famous for manufacturing denim jeans, was suffering from falling profits. The firm introduced its Stayprest range of trousers, followed, in 2001, by twisted denim jeans. Levi's profits have risen thanks to these new products.

4 **Improving a product.** Some businesses have the objective of improving a good or service as a means of achieving their overall aims. Improving the product may make it more attractive to customers. This should lead to higher sales and more profits for the business.

Lastminute.com

Lastminute.com sells a wide range of products via the internet. It is ideal for people who need to buy urgently. The firm can provide lots of products, including theatre tickets and restaurant bookings, at a moment's notice. In October 2001 the company started supplying sandwiches to office workers in London. Hungry workers can order online for immediate delivery.

Lastminute.com has not yet made a profit. Its main aim must be survival. The objectives that it sets will help to achieve this aim.

1 Look at the list of business objectives opposite. Which ones do you think might help Lastminute.com to fulfil its aim of surviving?

2 If Lastminute.com survives and grows, how do you think its aims might change?

Public and private sector businesses

In the UK there are two groups of businesses. Some of these are owned and run by the government or local councils. Others are privately owned and run by individuals or groups of people.

The various types of business are summarised in ▲ . We will look in detail at each of these types over the next few pages.

BUSINESS IN THE UK

PRIVATE SECTOR
(Owned by individuals or other businesses)

PUBLIC SECTOR
(Owned by local councils or government)

Sole trader e.g. Corner shop Hairdresser

Companies e.g. Virgin Group, ICI

Co-operatives e.g. Shops Travel agents

Partnerships e.g. Solicitors Accountants

Public corporations e.g. BBC

Others e.g. National Health Service, Customs and Excise

Government departments e.g. Department for Education and Skills

▲ Examples of the different types of business found in the UK

KEY CONCEPTS

A **sole trader** (or sole proprietorship) is a business that is owned by one person.

Capital is the money invested into a business by its owners, either when it is set up or at some later date.

The **private sector** is made up of businesses that are owned by individuals or groups of individuals. It is possible for businesses in the private sector to be owned by other businesses.

The **public sector** is made up of businesses that are owned and run by the government or local councils.

Unlimited liability means that the owners of the business are responsible for its debts, however large these may be.

Unincorporated businesses are those that have unlimited liability. Sole traders and partnerships are examples of unincorporated businesses.

Sole traders

A person who is the sole owner and manager of a business is called a sole trader. Sole traders are common in businesses that are simple to run and do not need many workers. A sole trader may employ other people, but the owner takes all the decisions. Sole traderships are the most common type of business in the UK. It is normal to find that plumbers, decorators, hairdressers, shop owners and even writers set up as sole traders.

STOP & THINK

For each of the categories shown in ▲ , can you think of another example?

Advantages of setting up as a sole trader

- It is simple and cheap to start a business as a sole trader. The business can start immediately and there are no complicated forms to fill in.
- The sole trader is the boss and takes all the decisions about the business. Many people enjoy having control of their business and being involved in all aspects of running it.
- The sole trader keeps all the profits from the business (if it makes any!). Many sole traders feel they are justly rewarded for working long hours.
- Sole traders do not need large amounts of money (known as capital) to start trading. It may not be necessary to borrow large sums to start the business.

Disadvantages of setting up as a sole trader

- The major disadvantage is unlimited liability. A sole trader is not regarded as being legally separate from his or her business. This means that he or she is liable for all the debts of the business should it fail. Sole traders may be forced to sell their homes or other valuable possessions to settle their business debts.
- Sole traders frequently work very long hours. They often do not employ other people to share the burden of the business and have to do most jobs themselves. It can be very difficult for them to take a holiday.
- Sole traders may find it difficult to raise the capital to start the business. They often use savings or borrow from friends and family. However, these methods are unlikely to provide the business with large sums of capital, which may mean that the business cannot grow.
- The range of skills possessed by sole traders is limited. No matter how hard-working and enthusiastic a sole trader may be, it is unlikely that he or she will have all the knowledge and skills needed by the business. For example, a sole trader running a building firm may be good at laying bricks, but know little about keeping financial records.

C A S E   S T U D Y

Home-cooking restaurant

Paul Hills is about to open a restaurant in Norwich as a sole trader. He plans to stay open seven afternoons and six evenings each week and to provide inexpensive home-cooked food. He wants to offer low prices to attract customers.

Paul has rented an attractive property in a quiet street in Norwich for his restaurant and has decorated it. He is fitting the kitchen with new cookers and other equipment. He intends to open in four weeks' time.

Tasks

1 Make a list of the personal qualities that Paul might need in order to succeed. The first one on the list could be 'prepared to work hard'!

2 What problems do you think Paul might face in starting his business?

3 Who might be able to advise him on how to run the restaurant successfully?

JOINED-UP THINKING

Many, but not all, of the disadvantages of running a business as a sole trader can be overcome by forming a partnership. You should read pages 18–25 on partnerships and compare the benefits of running a business as a partnership with those of being a sole trader.

Partnerships

Partnerships have more than two owners – known as partners. The partners normally all contribute capital to establish the business and they take a share of the profits. Partnerships are very common in the professions, such as among accountants, doctors and estate agents.

KEY CONCEPTS

Partnerships are businesses having more than two owners, who normally contribute money and expertise.

Deed of Partnership is a document stating the arrangements for running a partnership.

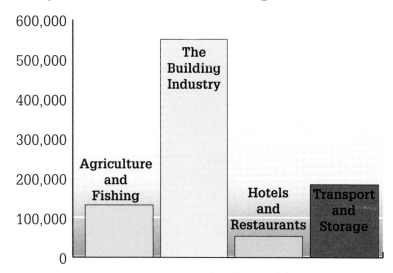

A Graph showing numbers of businesses in the UK owned by one person or by a partnership in 2000

STOP & THINK

Why do you think partnerships and sole trader businesses are so common in the building industry and in hotels and restaurants?

A solicitor draws up a document called a Deed of Partnership. This states:

- the amount of capital put in by each partner
- the share of profits each should receive
- how decisions will be taken
- how arguments between partners might be settled.

Advantages of a partnership

- Having partners can be less stressful than being a sole trader. Partners are available to cover for holidays and during periods of illness.
- Partnerships normally find it easier to raise capital than sole traders do. There are more owners to invest money, and banks may be more willing to lend to partnerships. Some partnerships have sleeping partners, who invest money but take no part in the management of the business.
- It can be comforting for partners not to have sole responsibility for a business, especially when major decisions have to be made.
- Partnerships are less likely to suffer from a lack of specialist skills than a sole trader. For example, a doctors' practice run as a partnership may mean that doctors can specialise in certain areas of medicine, giving patients a better service.

STOP & THINK

Visit your high street and write down the names of all the businesses that appear to be partnerships. What types of businesses are they?

A firm of solicitors run as a partnership

Disadvantages of a partnership

- Most partnerships have unlimited liability. As with sole traders, if the business fails, the partners' personal possessions may be sold to settle its debts.
- Partners often disagree. Discussions can be helpful when new ideas are being considered, but disputes can be destructive and lead to the break-up of the business. Some people enjoy having complete control over a business and find it difficult to work with partners.
- Many partnerships still find it difficult to raise the capital they need. Because of unlimited liability, it can be difficult to attract new partners. Banks may be unwilling to lend money because they regard small businesses as risky and fear that the loan will not be repaid.

STOP & THINK

In the case study on page 17 we met Paul Hills, who is planning to open a restaurant. Read this case study again and think of the benefits Paul might get from taking a partner into his business.

CASE STUDY

The Milton Brewery

In 2000 the Milton Brewery was voted the 'Small Business of the Year' for the East Anglia region. The brewery employs just one person and produces 14 different beers, one of which won an award recently.

The brewery is a partnership, owned by Richard Naisby, Clive Fussell and Mike Morley. The partners had been keen to start a brewing business for many years. Only Richard runs the brewery; the other two are what are known as sleeping partners.

Before starting the business, the partners visited over fifty other breweries to look at how they ran their businesses. The partners chose to start their business in Cambridge, as there are few other small breweries in the area.

The business was profitable almost from the outset and sales reached £100,000 in the first year of trading.

Source: www.cambridge-news.co.uk

Tasks

Investigate the Milton Brewery's website on the internet (www.miltonbrewery.co.uk) and answer the questions below:

1 Why do you think the Milton Brewery has been so successful?

2 The Milton Brewery is expected to grow quite quickly. What difficulties might this cause for the business?

Companies

A company is a special type of business. It has two or more owners (called shareholders) and the largest companies can have many thousands of owners. In law, a company and its owners are separate – unlike sole traders and most partnerships.

What is limited liability?

Companies have the protection of limited liability. The owners of companies do not put at risk their personal possessions such as houses. If the company fails, shareholders lose only the money that has been invested. Shareholders and the company are legally separate: shareholders are not responsible for all the debts of the business.

Private and public companies

In the UK two types of companies exist: private and public.

Name	Private limited companies	Public limited companies
	All private limited companies have the word Limited or Ltd after their name.	Public limited companies have the letters plc after the company name.
Features	• Tend to be relatively small • Shareholders and directors are often the same people • Cannot sell their shares on the Stock Exchange • Shares sold to founders, relatives and friends	• Much larger than most private limited companies • Founders of company lose control • Can advertise their shares freely • Shares sold on the Stock Exchange • Have to publish financial information each year
Examples	Family businesses are often run as private companies. More famous examples of private companies include the Virgin Group.	Most of the UK's best-known businesses are public limited companies, including Marks & Spencer, Cadbury Schweppes and Next.

A Differences between private and public limited companies

STOP & THINK

Public limited companies have many benefits. Why do some businesses decide to trade as private limited companies?

As a company becomes larger, it is less likely that all the owners will have a say in how the business is run. Compare, for instance, Norwich Kitchens with Pizza Express.

Norwich Kitchens Ltd

- Based in Norfolk, this is a small, private limited company that designs and fits kitchens.
- The company has two shareholders who work as directors of the business.
- The shareholders are closely involved in the running of the business.

Pizza Express

- Pizza Express is a public limited company running 300 restaurants in the UK and Ireland.
- It has several thousand shareholders and has sold nearly 80 million shares.
- The shareholders do not really have a say in how the business is run. They elect directors at the company's Annual General Meeting (AGM) to manage the company on their behalf.

Advantages and disadvantages of companies

Forming a company gives several advantages:

- The owners of the business (the shareholders) benefit from limited liability. Reducing risk to shareholders makes it easier for the company to raise capital.
- Public limited companies can sell their shares on the Stock Exchange and this allows them to raise capital to develop new products and purchase new buildings and machinery.
- Companies benefit from continuity. If a shareholder dies, the shares are sold to someone else and the business carries on.

But companies have drawbacks too:

- Companies have to fulfil a number of legal formalities. For example, they are required to publish an Annual Report containing financial information about the business. Competitors are able to study this information.
- Companies, and especially public limited companies, have their business affairs discussed in newspapers and on television. It is easy for them to attract bad publicity.
- It is much more expensive to start a company than to set up as a sole trader. The company has to go through the process shown in **B** . This can be expensive, especially if the business has to hire a solicitor and an accountant.

MEMORANDUM OF ASSOCIATION
Contain the following details:
- company's purpose in trading
- amount of capital it will raise
- name and address

ARTICLES OF ASSOCIATION
State the internal arrangements of the business
- shareholders' rights
- directors' power
- rules for company meetings

sent to

REGISTRAR OF COMPANIES
- keep records of all British companies

issues

CERTIFICATE OF INCORPORATION
- allows the company to start trading

B Forming a company

CASE STUDY

The flotation of easyJet

easyJet is a British airline that offers cheap flights to destinations throughout Europe. The company was started by one of Europe's richest men – the Greek millionaire Stelios Haji-Ioannu. It was set up in 1995 and has grown rapidly. The company recently bought 32 new aircraft.

In 2000, the business took the decision to change from being a private limited company to becoming a public limited company – a process known as floating the company on the Stock Exchange, or flotation.

Tasks

1 Use either the internet or your school library to find the following information.
   a) Is easyJet flying more planes?
   b) Is the company making larger profits?
   c) Is easyJet flying on new routes?

2 Explain two advantages easyJet might get from becoming a public limited company (plc).

3 Explain why someone should buy shares in easyJet.

Co-operatives

Co-operatives are owned by their members. Co-operatives' members contribute to the capital of the business and share any profits that are made.

The key features of a co-operative society are:

- It has limited liability protection.
- Shares can only be bought from or sold to the society.
- Individuals who purchase shares in a co-operative are called members.
- Co-operatives are democratic – each member is permitted one vote regardless of the size of his her shareholding.

There are three types of co-operative operating in the UK: retail co-operatives, worker co-operatives and marketing co-operatives.

RETAIL CO-OPERATIVE SOCIETIES
Over 40 retail Co-operative Societies operate throughout the UK.

WORKER CO-OPS
Businesses owned and managed by their employees. Over 1,500 exist in the UK.

THE CO-OPERATIVE WHOLESALE SOCIETY (CWS)
Buys products in bulk and supplies Co-op Retail Societies. Is also Britain's largest farmer.

MARKETING CO-OPS
Small scale producers work together to sell their products.

THE CO-OPERATIVE MOVEMENT

NATIONAL CO-OPERATIVE SERVICES

TRAVELCARE
The Co-operative Travel Agency organises holidays and business trips.

THE CO-OPERATIVE BANK
The Co-operative Bank provides banking services to businesses and individuals.

CO-OPERATIVE INSURANCE SOCIETY
The Co-operative provides insurance cover for nearly 5 million customers.

 **A** The Co-operative Movement

Retail co-operatives

Most towns and cities in the UK have retail co-operatives, whose members include the customers. The Heart of England Co-operative Society has 1,000 employees working in 11 supermarkets and 24 smaller stores in Coventry and elsewhere in Warwickshire. The Society has invested in opening new stores and has refitted others. The Society also provides travel centres, funeral services and post offices.

Co-operative retail societies pass their profits on to members by:

1 offering stamps that can be exchanged for products or money
2 paying interest to members on their shares.

KEY CONCEPTS

Co-operatives are businesses that are owned and run by groups of people called members, who invest capital and take decisions together.

Members are the sole owners of co-operatives.

Worker co-operatives are businesses that are owned and managed by all the employees.

Marketing co-operatives are formed when groups of small producers join together to advertise, distribute and sell their products.

STOP & THINK

Why do you think co-operatives are successful at supplying services?

STOP & THINK

What benefits might co-operative retail societies gain from merging to create larger organisations?

Worker co-operatives

Worker co-operatives are businesses that are owned and managed by the employees. All employees:

- are members of the co-operative
- have an equal say in the running of the business
- have equal share in the ownership of the business.

Worker co-operatives can give great job satisfaction, as members are working for themselves.

In the 1970s, several large worker co-operative businesses in the UK failed because of poor management and difficulties in raising capital. Modern worker co-operatives are smaller.

Marketing co-operatives

Producers form marketing co-operatives to sell and distribute products. This can be helpful to small businesses that may not be able to afford to advertise their products or distribute them widely. Marketing co-operatives are common in agriculture, particularly among organic farmers who, by joining together, can often persuade supermarkets to pay higher prices for their produce.

Advantages and disadvantages of co-operatives

Co-operatives have a number of advantages:

- Some people are attracted by becoming members and receiving a share of the profits of their business.
- Co-operative employees are normally well-motivated. Worker co-operatives give employees a say in business decisions.
- Co-operatives allow small businesses some of the advantages of larger businesses. Marketing co-operatives, for example, help small farmers to negotiate good prices when selling foodstuffs.

But there are drawbacks too:

- Co-operatives do not pay the highest wages and often struggle because they do not have top-quality managers.
- Co-operatives are frequently short of capital, as members invest only small amounts in the business. This makes it difficult for retail co-operatives to succeed against large supermarkets such as Sainsbury's.
- Many consumers think that co-operatives provide second-class products, although the success of the Co-operative Bank has helped to change opinions.

CASE STUDY

The Edinburgh Bicycle Workers' Co-operative

The Edinburgh Bicycle Workers' Co-operative started in 1977 as a bicycle repair business with three employees. Gradually the co-operative changed to selling bicycles and cycling equipment. By 2001, the Co-operative had 20 full-time employees and owned workshops, shops and an office.

The members run the workers' co-operative. All workers at the co-operative take part in planning and in major decisions. For day-to-day matters, such as ordering new bicycles to sell, the workers are divided into teams. Each team has different responsibilities.

Anyone who completes the training successfully becomes a member and has a say in how the business is managed. Employees are committed to the business and few leave. Every member of the co-operative has a say in which bicycles are sold.

Tasks

1 How might the working day of a member of a workers' co-operative differ from that of an employee in a company?

2 Why do you think this workers' co-operative is successful?

Franchises

Franchising is an arrangement by which the owner of a business idea gives other individuals or groups the right to trade using its name or idea. Franchises are common in many industries, including public houses, shops, fast food outlets, driving schools and hairdressing.

A franchise is not a type of business organisation. It is a way of managing and expanding a business.

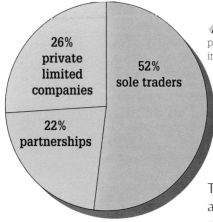

A Types of business ownership as percentages of franchises in the UK in 2000

26% private limited companies

52% sole traders

22% partnerships

The types of business ownership used by franchises in 2000 are shown in **A**. The form of business ownership chosen to operate a franchise will depend on:

- the amount of capital needed
- the number of people starting the franchise
- whether they want to have the benefit of limited liability.

How do franchises work?

Someone choosing to start a business as a franchise will be given a licence by the original business. This licence gives the right to run an identical business in a particular area or location. The firm selling the right is called the franchisor, and the person or business buying it is the franchisee.

STOP & THINK

What types of business ownership shown in **A** could be chosen by someone setting up a business to provide limited liability? What benefits would someone running a franchise gain from having limited liability?

STOP & THINK

What types of businesses are easiest to franchise? The logos opposite should give you a clue.

CASE STUDY

McDonald's franchises

McDonald's sells the right to operate its fast food restaurants in locations throughout the UK. On 31 December 2000, about one-third of McDonald's 1,116 restaurants in the UK were franchises.

Franchisees get the following benefits:

- the rights to operate a particular restaurant for 20 years
- the right to use the company's trademarks, signs and menus
- the use of McDonald's systems to order supplies and keep financial records
- advice on managing the franchise.

McDonald's franchisees must agree to:

- run the business as a sole trader
- complete a nine-month training programme before starting the business
- operate McDonald's standards: food must be properly prepared and the restaurant must be hygienic

- raise at least £85,000 to operate a McDonalds's franchise
- pay a proportion of profits to the company.

Task

Imagine you are opening a McDonald's restaurant as a franchise. Why might this be more likely to succeed than a non-franchise restaurant?

Advantages and disadvantages of operating a franchise

Advantages:

- The business has been successful elsewhere and is less risky than a new business idea.
- Many franchises such as the British School of Motoring already have an established name, so that less advertising is needed.
- Franchisors often provide initial training and further advice once the franchise is trading.
- The franchisor frequently develops new products that enable franchisees to keep ahead of competitors.

Disadvantages:

- A franchisee is not really his or her own boss. Franchisees are under the control of the franchisor.
- Franchises are an expensive way of starting a business. An initial payment is expected and the franchisor will expect a share of the profits.
- If some franchises run their businesses badly, they may all suffer as a result.

B Growth in franchises 1990–2000

	1990	1999	2000
Annual sales (£m)	4,800	8,928	9,300
Number of franchise businesses	18,260	34,010	35,600
% franchises making a profit	70	92	95

Do you think that the data in B would encourage someone to start up a franchise?

The public sector

The public sector is made up of organisations owned and controlled by local authorities or the government. The objective of public sector businesses is to provide high-quality services in equal measure across the UK. These businesses are not expected to make a profit.

THE PUBLIC SECTOR

CENTRAL GOVERNMENT — LOCAL AUTHORITIES

PUBLIC CORPORATIONS — GOVERNMENT DEPARTMENTS — DEPARTMENTS

Post Office
BBC — ORGANISATIONS — Department of Health — LOCAL SERVICES — Trading Standards, Housing

Inland Revenue, Customs and Excise

schools libraries parks

A The public sector

Businesses run by the government

The government runs many major organisations that are important to many people.

- Channel 4 and the Post Office are run by organisations called public corporations.
- A public corporation is owned by the government and has limited liability.
- Public corporations aim to provide a high-quality service to people in all parts of the country.
- Some public corporations are paid for through taxation whereas others, such as the Post Office, are self-financing.

Since 1980, the government has sold off many businesses to the private sector. This process is called privatisation.

KEY CONCEPTS

The **public sector** consists of organisations owned by the state and run by local councils or the government.

The **private sector** is made up of businesses owned by individuals or groups of individuals. Some private sector businesses are owned by other businesses.

Privatisation is the selling of state-owned businesses to the private sector.

Public corporations are bodies set up by the government to run large public sector enterprises such as the BBC.

STOP & THINK

Why do you think that local governments run services such as schools, but national government looks after organisations such as the BBC?

STOP & THINK

The Post Office delivers mail to remote areas such as the Isle of Skye in Scotland. How do the people who live on Skye benefit from having their mail delivered by a public sector business?

B A selection of main UK public sector enterprises

Public sector enterprise	No. of employees	Sales turnover (£m)
BBC	23,119	2,847
Civil Aviation Authority	6,158	611
Channel Four	674	590
London Transport	19,000	1,338
Post Office	201,000	6,759
Royal Mint	994	91

Source: HM Treasury

Businesses run by local authorities

Local authorities provide many services for communities. Local councils run leisure centres, parks and libraries. Although charges are made for some of these services, the businesses are not expected to make a profit.

Some private sector enterprises have been taken out of the hands of the local councils. For example, trust hospitals are run by separate organisations but they remain in the public sector.

Advantages and disadvantages of public sector businesses

Public sector businesses offer a number of advantages to customers and employees.

- Because they do not aim to make a profit they concentrate on supplying high-quality products.
- They supply products when it is unprofitable. Private sector organisations would not do this.
- Public sector organisations also tend to offer more secure employment.

But public sector businesses have attracted a number of criticisms.

- Public sector businesses sometimes do not manage their costs very well as they are not expected to make a profit.
- Some public sector businesses that do not have any competitors may offer customers a poor-quality service.
- Public sector businesses can charge high prices because they have no competitors.

Public–private partnerships: a foot in both camps

Recently the government has attempted to bring together the private and the public sector to run businesses. The government plans to use public private partnerships (PPPs) in schools and hospitals. For example, some private hospitals are being paid by the government to treat National Health Service patients who have been waiting a long time for treatment.

What might be the advantages and disadvantages of working in a public sector business?

To increase your understanding of the public sector, choose one of the following public sector organisations:

- Channel 4
- Royal Mint
- Post Office
- BBC
- London Transport.

Find out the following about your chosen organisation:

- the full range of goods and services that it supplies
- how the business is organised
- who is in charge of the organisation
- how decisions are taken
- where the business is located
- how it earns the money needed to run as a business.

CHOOSING A BUSINESS LOCATION

Where to locate

One of the first decisions to be made when starting a business is where to locate. Some businesses will be looking for factories and others for offices. A number of businesses may be seeking land or other natural resources.

- **Factories.** Manufacturing businesses will be looking for a factory where they can produce their goods ready for sale. For example, in 2001 the car manufacturer Nissan chose Sunderland as a location for a factory to build the new Nissan Micra.
- **Offices and shops.** Businesses providing services will try to find a suitable shop or office, depending on the type of business. A hairdresser would want a shop convenient to customers while a solicitor would seek out a suitable office.
- **Natural resources.** Some businesses require land, or other natural resources, as well as buildings. Imagine you were setting up a fish farm to breed salmon for local shops and restaurants. A nearby lake or river might be the most important factor to you when deciding on a location. Similarly, English wine producers look for sunny, well-drained land for growing grapes.

What do businesses take into account?

A good location can help to make a business successful. A location that has the lowest possible costs helps the firm to make the largest possible profit.

Not all businesses would regard the same factor as the most significant. However, generally, the factors that influence the choice of location of businesses are labour, finance, competitors and transport links.

Labour. Businesses look for:

- areas with low wages and salaries
- locations where people are available to work
- employees with the right skills.

An English vineyard

Finance. Businesses try to find low-cost locations:

- factories or shops with low rents
- financial help from the government or the EU
- low taxation levels

Customers. A good location will:

- have plenty of customers nearby
- be in area where people have enough money to buy the firm's products.

Competitors and transport links. Businesses choosing a location also:

- avoid sites close to competitors
- look for good transport links, such as nearby motorways and airports
- choose areas close to suppliers.

CASE STUDY

Locating in Grimsby

Grimsby is on the east coast of England and is famous as a fishing port. In recent years the town has become the location for a wide range of industries, and in 2001 was recognised as the UK's most profitable business location.

Grimsby has a workforce of 90,000 people living within a 15-minute drive of the town. Lorries from Grimsby have access to a market of over 40 million people less than a four-hour drive away. The town boasts the Europarc Innovation Centre, which offers local businesses access to the latest technology as well as staff who speak several languages.

Tasks

1 Explain three reasons why Grimsby has proved to be a popular location for many businesses.

2 This case study contains much information about Grimsby. What additional information might a firm thinking about locating in Grimsby need?

3 ProntoPak is a company that manufactures boxes and other packaging. The company sells its products to firms throughout the UK and is planning to sell to European firms. What are the advantages and disadvantages of Grimsby as a location for ProntoPak?

Data influencing business decisions to locate to Grimsby

	Grimsby	UK
Unemployment (unemployed in June 2001)	7.8%	4.9%
Weekly earnings before tax (2001)	£393.20	£444.30
House prices (detached houses, 2000)	£79, 285	£134, 585 (England and Wales)

Transport (all distances from Grimsby)

Airports

Humberside	16 km
East Midlands	165 km

Motorway

| M180 | 19 km |

Sea

Grimsby is a major seaport.

Lincolnshire and East Yorkshire, showing position of Grimsby, key transport links and other important nearby towns

The primary sector

Businesses in the primary sector grow crops or extract raw materials. This sector includes agriculture, fishing, forestry, mining and quarrying.

Many firms in the primary sector are relatively small, particularly in agriculture and fishing. Often, farms and fishing boats belong to family businesses passed down through the generations.

It is more common for firms in fuel extraction, mining and quarrying to be large. For example, the mining company UK Coal:

- produces over 20 million tonnes of coal a year
- employs 8,000 people at 40 locations throughout the UK
- supplies mining consultancy services to other companies.

JOINED-UP THINKING

Many small firms in the primary sector form co-operatives to improve the marketing of their products and to gain higher prices. Co-operatives, including marketing co-operatives, were explained on pages 22–3.

STOP & THINK

Does UK Coal operate entirely within the primary sector of the British economy? Explain your answer.

STOP & THINK

Into which of the categories in **A** would firms producing the following be placed:
- washing machines
- dyes for use in making clothes
- televisions?

KEY CONCEPTS

The **primary sector** comprises those industries concerned with growing natural products and extracting mineral resources.

The **secondary sector** includes businesses involved in manufacturing and construction, often using products from the primary sector.

The **tertiary sector** is made up of businesses providing services.

One of UK Coal's opencast coal mines

The secondary sector

Secondary production covers manufacturing and construction. Manufacturing involves converting raw materials into finished goods, such as in the making of mobile phones. Construction includes, for example, building houses.

A Producer and consumer goods

Producer goods	Consumer goods
Goods that are used in the production of other goods	Goods that are bought by individuals for their own use
Example Rolls Royce supplies producer goods in the form of aircraft engines, which it sells to firms such as Boeing.	***Example*** British Bakeries Ltd manufactures a range of bread products including Hovis, which are bought by consumers.

The secondary sector has changed, as foreign manufacturing firms like Sony and Nissan have moved to the UK. New technology has also transformed manufacturing. It has caused the decline of some traditional industries while creating new ones, such as computer manufacturing.

The tertiary sector

Tertiary production is also called the services sector. It includes banking, insurance and finance – industries in which the UK is recognised as a world leader. London is one of the major financial centres in the world.

Tertiary industry	Examples
Retailing (the sale of goods)	Next, Waterstones, Littlewoods (mail order), Amazon.com
Client services (for example, financial services, health care, leisure and sport, internet access)	Abbey National, BUPA, David Lloyd Leisure centres, Virgin Net (an internet service provider or ISP)
Other services (for instance, transport and communications)	Anglia Railways, London Transport, Orange, British Telecommunications

B The tertiary sector

Other examples of tertiary sector industries include travel agents and fast food restaurants.

Integrating the sectors

Some businesses cannot simply be classified as belonging to one or other of the primary, secondary or tertiary sectors. Balfour Beatty, for example, operates in both the secondary and tertiary sectors. As a large business with a number of activities it:

- provides advice on the design and maintenance of buildings
- takes on major construction projects. For example, building a road linking the A1 and M1 south of Leeds.

A chain of production links primary, secondary and tertiary businesses. For example, many farmers in the east of England grow barley. Some of this barley is sold to Greene King, a brewery in Bury St Edmund's. In turn, Greene King sells its beer to Sainsbury's. So a product of the primary sector eventually is sold as part of a service industry.

OVER TO YOU

Choose two areas in a nearby town, one a main street in the centre of the town, the other an industrial estate. Visit the two locations and select 15 businesses in each. For the 30 businesses you have chosen, write down the following information:

- the full name of the business
- a brief description of the products supplied by the business
- the ownership of the business.

Use the information you have gathered to complete the following tasks.

1 Classify the businesses according to whether they are primary, secondary or tertiary.
2 Draw a map or chart to show where the three categories of business are located.
3 Explain possible reasons for the locations of the various types of businesses.

STOP & THINK

What are the benefits to Balfour Beatty of being in more than one sector of the economy?

Changes in businesses

Businesses in the UK are continually changing. Some of the major reasons for this change include:

- new technology creating new products
- new methods of production such as the use of robots on production lines
- new products wanted by consumers.

Technological developments

Improvements in technology are having a huge impact. Some industries, in particular, have seen very rapid change.

1 **Retailing.** Although selling on the internet has not grown as swiftly as some people predicted, it is nevertheless becoming increasingly important. All major retailers and most small businesses sell via the internet.

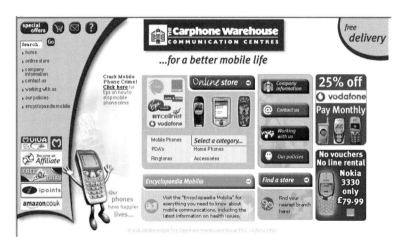

2 **Telecommunications.** Because of mobile phones, people are making less use of telephone boxes. BT has removed many of them, but is developing a new range of mobile telephones.

3 **Banking.** Great changes have taken place in banking due to the increasing popularity of the internet. New banks, such as Smile, have appeared but many branches have closed, as the banks seek to cut costs.

Consumers' expenditure

The increase and changes of pattern in consumer spending in recent years are shown in **A** and **B**.

What are the benefits to Carphone Warehouse and its customers of selling products on the internet?

Carphone Warehouse employs fewer people than it would if it sold its products through traditional shops. Why is this? What different skills might an employee working for an internet retailer need?

Carphone Warehouse website home page

As consumers have become richer, they have spent more on certain items.

- Businesses producing and supplying consumer durables, such as televisions and household furniture, have seen a rise in sales.
- Sales of vehicles (cars, vans and lorries) have fluctuated, but have increased overall.
- In 1991, 11.7 per cent of expenditure was on food (£47, 51 million); by 2000 this had risen to £56,123 million, but was only 10.4 per cent of consumers' spending. Sales had risen, but incomes had grown more quickly.
- Consumers spent their extra income on other goods and, particularly, services.

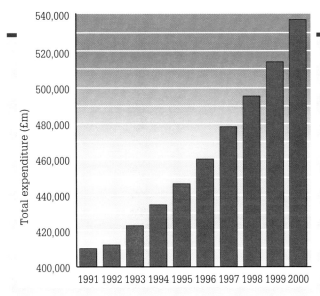

A Total consumers' expenditure 1991–2000

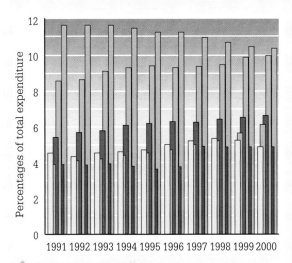

B Consumers' expenditure on selected goods and services as percentages of total expenditure

Source: Adapted from www.statistics.gov.uk

Vehicles
Consumer durables
Clothing and footwear
Transport and communications
Financial services
Food

OVER TO YOU

Using **A** and **B**, answer the following questions.

1 Which industries have had the quickest growth in consumer expenditure during the 1990s?

2 What other products can you think of that have become more popular over this period?

3 How much did consumers actually spend on clothing and footwear in 1991 and 2000?

4 The percentage of income spent on financial services (banking and insurance, for example) has stayed constant. Does this mean that consumer expenditure on these services is unchanged?

5 Would firms in the clothing and footwear industry have been encouraged by these figures? Explain your answer.

CASE STUDY

SMILE: The Internet Bank

The Co-operative Bank launched Smile, its Internet Bank, in October 1999. To open an account, you complete an online form. Smile does not have any branches, but money can be paid in and cheques cashed at Post Offices.

Because all its business is conducted online, Smile is very cheap to operate. The internet offers customers advantages but it also has its drawbacks.

Tasks

1 Visit a branch of a well-known bank near to you. Gather information on their accounts and other services.

2 Use the internet to research the services offered by Smile.

3 Compare the two banks using the following headings:

a) interest rates paid
b) ease of paying in and withdrawing money
c) the range of services available to customers.

4 Which bank do you think offers the best service? You should justify your answer.

New products and new skills

Businesses have responded to changes in consumer spending and technology by introducing new products. They have also employed different numbers of workers with different skills.

Changes in production

The quantities and types of goods produced by UK firms have changed in recent years for a number of reasons.

- Consumers have demanded different goods and services. For example, in 1990 relatively few people had a mobile telephone but by 2000, over 25 million owned one.
- Advances in technology have meant that new products become available and others become outdated. For instance, traditional postal services have been affected by the widespread use of e-mail.
- Overseas businesses are better at supplying certain goods and services, which has resulted in the closure of some UK firms. In 1999 Corus, one of the few remaining producers of steel in the UK, announced that it was closing several factories. They blamed increased competition from overseas for the decision.

Several industries in the primary and secondary sectors have increased their production levels, but have employed fewer people.

- Many industries are using more technology and are replacing people with machines. For example, in agriculture large tractors can do the work of many men. Robots on the production lines in factories have replaced assembly workers. Even in the tertiary sector, automated switchboards have resulted in the loss of jobs among receptionists.
- Improved techniques of production have increased output without requiring more employees. Thus improved strains of wheat, for example, have increased production of these crops dramatically.

KEY CONCEPTS

Production is all the activities needed to change raw materials and labour services into saleable products.

Employment is the use of people (as managers and secretaries, for example) in production.

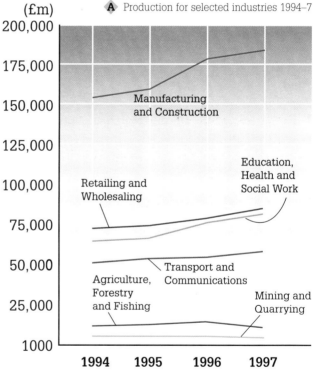

A Production for selected industries 1994–7

STOP & THINK

Which of the industry groups in **A** is the fastest-growing? Are all the firms in that industry likely to be growing as quickly?

Robots working on a production line

STOP & THINK

Machines such as robots can replace many employees. What are the benefits to businesses of replacing labour with technology in this way? Can you think of any problems that might occur?

OVER TO YOU

Use the government's statistics website or The Annual Abstract of Statistics to find the most recent figures for the industries shown in **A**.

Select two of these industries that show significant changes and explain why these changes may have taken place.

■ Better management of employees has resulted in fewer workers producing more output. Honda has given employees much greater responsibility and car production per worker has risen as a result.

Changes in employment

The percentage of the workforce employed in the primary, secondary and tertiary sectors over the last century is shown in **B**. A number of important trends can be identified.

■ The proportion of employees in the primary and secondary sectors has fallen steadily, but output has not fallen as much.
■ The decline in employment in the primary sector is most noticeable.
■ Employment in the tertiary sector has risen to create new jobs for those leaving the other sectors.
■ Today, the tertiary sector is easily the largest employer.

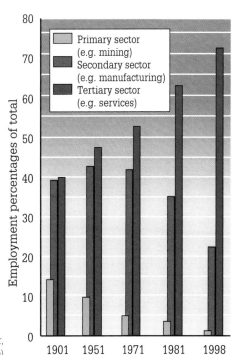

B Employment by industrial sector, 1901–98 (percentages of total workforce)

Primary sector (e.g. mining)
Secondary sector (e.g. manufacturing)
Tertiary sector (e.g. services)

Employment percentages of total

1901 1951 1971 1981 1998

The first 26 pages of Unit 1 have introduced you to some important business ideas. You should now be able to answer the questions that follow.

10 revision questions

Check your knowledge of the first part of Unit 1 by tackling these questions.

1 What is the difference between an aim and an objective? (4 marks)

2 BP Amoco is one of the UK's largest businesses. Write down **four** objectives that the company might want to achieve. (4 marks)

3 Describe **three** differences between a private limited company and a public limited company. (6 marks)

4 A sole trader is thinking about taking on a partner and forming a partnership. Explain **two** advantages and **two** disadvantages that might result from forming a partnership. (8 marks)

5 Name **four** businesses that are part of the public sector. (4 marks)

6 Explain three factors that might cause businesses to locate in the area in which you live. (6 marks)

7 Give **one** example of a business in each of the primary, secondary and tertiary sectors. (3 marks)

8 People spend more money on some goods and products as they become richer. List **three** goods or services that consumers will buy more of as their incomes rise. (3 marks)

9 The number of people employed in manufacturing in Britain has fallen steadily for many years. Give **two** reasons why this change has taken place.(6 marks)

10 Explain **one** way in which changing technology has affected how bookshops sell their products. (6 marks)

Total = 50 marks

Visit the BP Amoco website and answer the following questions.

- What are the company's activities?

- In what sectors of the economy (for example, primary, tertiary) is BP Amoco involved? Explain your answer.

PUTTING IT INTO PRACTICE

Choosing your businesses

The following advice may help you decide which two businesses to investigate for your assignment for this unit.

Look at two businesses that are very different. You could choose one in the secondary and one in the tertiary sector (for example, a car manufacturer and a shop).

Choose a business on which you can find plenty of information. There are several ways in which you might do this:

- use the business's website

- choose a local business, which you can visit to ask for information

- select a business where friends or relatives work, who may be able to help you to collect information.

What you need to find out

By this stage of Unit 1, you should have selected the businesses you will investigate for your assignment for this unit ('Putting it into Practice' gives advice on how to make your choice). You will need to know the following about each of your chosen businesses:

- what each business does: its aims and objectives, the type of ownership, the liabilities of its owners and its location
- how the business is organised and the areas (or functions) that make up the business
- methods of communication used inside and outside the business

- external influences on the business (for example, the business's competitors, its location and environmental issues).

Starting to write your portfolio evidence

So far in Unit 1 you will only have learnt about the topics covered by the first bullet point (shown in bold type) in the list just given. But you should be able to write the first part of your evidence for your portfolio giving an overview of the two businesses. Make sure you know which Awarding Body (AQA, Edexcel or OCR) you are following. Once you know this, choose the correct column from the chart below to guide you in writing the first part of your portfolio evidence.

AWARDING BODY			
	AQA	Edexcel	OCR
What you have to do Describe	• the most important activities of the businesses • the main aims and objectives of the businesses • the ownership of the business • the location or locations of the business	• the business's activities and how they help the business to achieve its aims and objectives • the differences between aims and objectives for each of the businesses. • the type of ownership, the liabilities of the owners and the businesses'	• locations the main activities of the businesses • the location or locations of the businesses • the businesses' aims and objectives • the ownership of the businesses

Explain	• how objectives can help the businesses to judge their success
	
	• why the types of ownership are suited to each of the businesses.
		• how the businesses' activities allow aims and objectives to be met
		
		• how objectives can help the businesses to judge their success
		
		• the reasons for the type of ownership and the choices of locations
			• the similarities and differences between the:
			  • activities
			  • location
			  • ownership
			  • aims and objectives of the two businesses.

Evaluate (this may mean making judgements or offering and justifying suggestions)	• how the number of other businesses involved in the same activity might affect the aims and objectives of the business in the future	• how the activities of the businesses may need to change over time to make sure they continue to be successful
		
		• why the type of ownership is appropriate and how the locations help to achieve the businesses' aims
			• Suggest and justify changes in:
			  • activities
			  • location
			  • ownership
			  • aims and objectives of the businesses that might make them more successful

Human resources

To be successful, any business has to carry out a range of functions. The human resources department of a business exists to recruit the best employees and to make sure that they work effectively and safely in assisting the firm to achieve its objectives. The human resources department within a business carries out a number of activities. The key role of human resource planning is summarised below.

WHAT EMPLOYEES DO WE NEED?
- Number of workers?
- Skills required?
- Where do we need them?

WHAT EMPLOYEES HAVE WE ALREADY GOT?
- Existing workers?
- Less those leaving/retiring?
- Any hidden skills?

THE PLAN
- How many (and what types) of workers we need to RECRUIT
- What TRAINING we need to offer
- The REDUNDANCIES (if any) we need to make
- Improvements in WORKING CONDITIONS that may be needed

Activities of the human resources department

1 Recruiting, keeping and dismissing employees

A major task of the human resources department is to ensure that the business has the right employees for future success. This may involve a number of activities:

- recruiting new employees – whether hiring people from outside the firm or promoting people from within. Firms like to recruit from outside the firm as new employees sometimes bring with them fresh ideas and enthusiasm.

- keeping existing employees. Firms do not want to lose experienced and highly trained staff. Recruiting new workers and training them to the required level can be a very expensive process.

- dismissing employees. Sometimes this occurs because an employee cannot carry out his or her job effectively. However, more often employees are made redundant, because their jobs no longer exist. The fall in demand for mobile phones during 2001 led to firms such as Motorola making large numbers of staff redundant.

STOP & THINK

What are the advantages to a firm of recruiting employees to senior positions from within the firm?

STOP & THINK

What difficulties might a firm face after making a large number of employees redundant?

Working in a call centre

2 Providing good working conditions

Working conditions include issues such as:

- the warmth and cleanliness of the workplace
- the provision of rest areas and leisure facilities
- hours of work and holiday entitlement.

Working conditions have an impact on how well workers carry out their jobs. They are normally a subject for negotiation between trade unions and the human resources department.

Working conditions in call centres have received a great deal of criticism. In some call centres, employees are not given sufficient breaks. A number of call centre staff have gone on strike to win improved conditions. Why might a business allow poor working conditions to exist?

3 Training, developing and promoting employees

The human resources department can use a number of techniques to provide workers with the necessary skills:

- training employees at the workplace or through courses at local colleges or training centres
- planning jobs so that employees enjoy new experiences and develop new skills
- promoting employees to more senior positions to give the firm the skills and experience it needs.

4 Negotiating with trade unions

The human resources department discusses and agrees pay and working conditions with trade unions or other representatives of the workforce. This process is called collective bargaining.

5 Health and safety

Health and safety is an important responsibility for the human resources department. The Health and Safety Act requires firms to provide all employees with a secure and risk-free working environment. Employees working in such an environment are also likely to work more effectively.

OVER TO YOU

Search one or more of the newspaper websites for a recent article about a firm that has recruited a large number of employees. You might try, for example:

- *Daily Telegraph* – www.telegraph.co.uk
- *Financial Times* – www.globalarchive.ft.com
- *Guardian* – www.guardianunlimited.co.uk
- *Independent* – www.independent.co.uk

Once on the website, follow links saying 'archive' or 'search'.

Choose a story that describes the train of events leading up to recruitment and what happened afterwards. Print out the article.

You should prepare a brief presentation for the rest of your class, including the following:

- the reason for the recruitment in this case
- the benefits the business might gain from receiving new employees.

Finance

The finance department of a business manages money for the business. The department records the financial transactions of a business and helps managers to plan for the future. The workings of a finance department are summarised in **A** .

Activities of the finance department

1 Recording all the financial matters of a business

Businesses are constantly spending money or receiving it from the sale of goods and services. It is vital that the business keeps records of all its activities in order to:

- calculate whether the business is profitable
- assess how much tax the business will have to pay
- help managers to take the right decisions.

2 Preparing accounts

All businesses prepare accounts to summarise their financial affairs during a year. Companies and other large businesses are legally obliged to publish detailed accounts. The most important parts of these accounts are:

- the balance sheet, which states both what a business owns and its debts
- the profit and loss account, which records the profit or loss the business made over a one-year period.

Accounts are useful to different people for different reasons.

- The Inland Revenue can confirm that the business has paid the correct amount of tax.
- Suppliers can see whether the business is able to pay its debts.
- Shareholders can decide whether or not to invest in the business.

KEY CONCEPTS

A **balance sheet** is a financial document recording both the items owned by the business and its debts.

Capital is the money invested in a business by its owners, either when it is set up or at some later date.

Income tax is a charge paid on the earnings of employees.

National Insurance is a payment made by employers and employees to the government to provide for retirement pension, sick pay and unemployment benefits.

A **profit and loss account** is a financial statement recording the income, expenses and profits or losses made by a business over a period of time, usually one year.

STOP & THINK

The finance department works with people and groups outside the business, such as suppliers. Name two other groups who might work with the finance department.

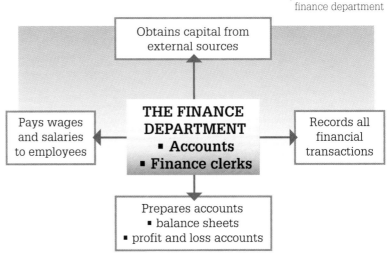

A The activities of a finance department

Obtains capital from external sources

Pays wages and salaries to employees

THE FINANCE DEPARTMENT
- Accounts
- Finance clerks

Records all financial transactions

Prepares accounts
- balance sheets
- profit and loss accounts

A Sainsbury's superstore

STOP & THINK

In 2001, Sainsbury's announced its intention to move to new head offices in Holborn, in London. The offices will be built above a major new superstore. The cost is expected to be £50 million. From where might Sainsbury's raise this capital?

CASE STUDY

The Finance Department at the University Of York

York University offers a wide range of courses to 6,000 students. The finance department has 40 staff and manages millions of pounds.

York University's finance department carries out important roles within the University.

- It pays the salaries and wages of all the teaching and support staff.
- It collects fees from students.
- It pays all the other bills incurred by the University, for example heating and lighting.
- It produces the University's Annual Report and Accounts.

Task

Draw a chart to show the links between the finance department and other areas and departments within York University.

3 Paying wages and salaries

Wages and salaries (monthly pay) involve the finance department in a number of activities.

- The business has to deduct income tax and national insurance from employees' pay.
- It may be required to operate a pension scheme for its employees.
- It will need to keep very accurate records of wages and salaries.

4 Obtaining capital and other resources

All businesses need some resources in order to start up and to trade successfully. To purchase these resources, businesses might need to raise large sums of money, known as capital.

A business has two main sources of capital:

- **loan capital**. This is raised by borrowing money, normally from a bank or other business.
- **retained profits**. If the business has been profitable, it may be able to keep some of these profits to purchase the resources that it needs.

Companies can sell shares in the business to raise more capital. The people who buy these shares (known as shareholders) give money to the business in exchange for owning a part of it.

Finance and other business functions

The work of the finance department affects other parts of the business. The finance department:

- places orders and pays bills on behalf of other departments within the business
- advises other areas of the business as to the amount of money available to them
- helps senior managers to make major decisions.

Administration

The administration department provides important support services to other departments in the business. Not all administration departments are the same. In a small business, the administration department might take responsibility for human resources or finance. In a larger organisation, it is likely to be more specialised and to have responsibilities such as those shown in **A**. All administration departments make considerable of use of information technology (IT).

Activities of the administration department

1 Clerical services

The main role of an administration department is clerical. The department may provide clerical services to all other departments within the business. These services include:

- word-processing letters, making telephone calls and booking accommodation for staff
- sorting and delivering incoming mail and posting outgoing mail
- organising meetings and keeping records of what is said and agreed at these meetings, such as at the important Annual General Meeting for a company's shareholders
- taking responsibility for the company's reception area, dealing with general inquiries and welcoming visitors
- creating and keeping records about the company.

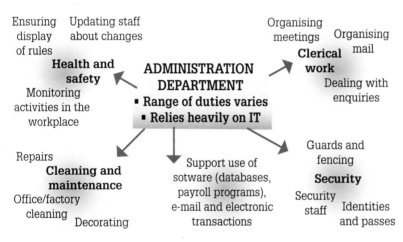

2 Cleaning and maintenance

All business premises require regular cleaning. This is especially true of a business where hygiene is important, such as a restaurant. The administration department also organises the maintenance of a firm's buildings and other resources. This may include decorating the inside and outside of buildings and maintaining machinery.

Five main activities that an administration department might carry out are shown in **A**. How might IT be used in each of these activities?

A The activities of an administration department

Machines have replaced many switchboard operators. In what other ways might technology be used to carry out some of the administration department's functions?

3 Health and safety

Health and safety issues include:

- providing safety clothing for workers, for example on building sites
- ensuring there are no dangers in the workplace, for instance by providing toughened glass in doors
- providing regular medical checks for those working in risky environments, such as in a chemicals firm.

We saw on page 39 that the human resources department takes responsibility for setting health and safety policies. The administration department makes sure that these are implemented and work effectively. We will consider health and safety more fully in Unit 2

The administration department will oversee the operation of health and safety within a business. It ensures that health and safety notices are displayed clearly and that health and safety representatives are appointed to look out for problems.

4 Security

Security is an increasingly important issue for businesses. Security duties include:

- signing visitors in and out of the premises, and issuing them with identification badges
- ensuring that unauthorised people are kept out, perhaps by use of patrols or guard dogs
- protecting computer systems from hackers
- in shops, patrolling to prevent shoplifting (many shops employ security guards in uniforms).

5 Support for software applications

Information technology is used by businesses to provide:

- spreadsheets to record financial data, such as sales figures
- databases for customer, employee and supplier records
- payroll systems to calculate employees' wages and salaries and to produce pay slips
- e-mail for communicating with groups such as suppliers
- web-based systems for selling goods and services on the internet and taking payment from credit cards securely.

The administration department in a large business will also support other departments in the business using software, by:

- providing training for new employees or training in the use of new software
- advising on what software should be purchased for other departments.

STOP & THINK

Why do many firms prefer to hire security guards from other companies rather than recruit their own?

Talk to your teacher and find out who in your school or college is in charge of administration. Arrange a meeting with this person to find out what his or her responsibilities are. Compare your findings with the duties set out in **A** . Is your school's administration department typical in terms of its responsibilities and the way that it carries them out?

Operations/production

The operations function within a business is sometimes called the production department. The task of those responsible for operations is to bring together all the resources needed to produce the firm's goods or services. This process is illustrated in **A** .

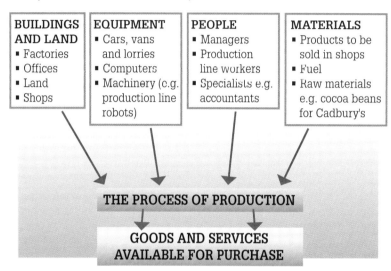

BUILDINGS AND LAND	EQUIPMENT	PEOPLE	MATERIALS
▪ Factories ▪ Offices ▪ Land ▪ Shops	▪ Cars, vans and lorries ▪ Computers ▪ Machinery (e.g. production line robots)	▪ Managers ▪ Production line workers ▪ Specialists e.g. accountants	▪ Products to be sold in shops ▪ Fuel ▪ Raw materials e.g. cocoa beans for Cadbury's

THE PROCESS OF PRODUCTION

GOODS AND SERVICES AVAILABLE FOR PURCHASE

On pages 30–1, we looked at the three industrial sectors – primary, secondary and tertiary – in which all firms in the UK can be classified. The resources used by a business depend on the type of business.

- Primary sector businesses, such as farms and quarries, rely heavily on natural resources.
- Firms in the secondary sector depend on buildings and equipment. For example, Cadbury's needs factories and machinery for making chocolate.
- Tertiary sector businesses rely on people. Health care requires highly skilled professionals to supply services. Buildings may also be important to service industries; for example, retailers need shops.

Producing high-quality goods and services

High-quality goods and services fully satisfy customers' needs. Customers expect high-quality products.

Businesses use two main techniques to make sure their products are of high quality.

1. **Quality-control** systems involve checks carried out on products to ensure they meet agreed standards. Quality control takes place after the production process, to establish whether products are of sufficient standard to meet the needs of consumers.

Operations management is the task of using resources of land, labour and materials to produce goods and services.

Quality control and **quality assurance** measure the extent to which goods and services meet consumers' needs.

Resources are the natural products, people, raw materials, components and machinery used to provide goods and services.

A Bringing resources together in production

STOP & THINK

What are the differences between the resources used in a brewery and those used in a hospital? (Use the four types of resources in **A** as a guide to your answer.)

CAM in use on a production line

2 **Quality assurance** systems are designed to prevent poor-quality products slipping through. At each stage of production, employees check that the product meets quality standards and is free from defects. Other features of quality assurance include purchasing high-quality raw materials and components and delivering products on time.

Businesses can improve quality in a number of ways:

- training employees to help them carry out their jobs more effectively
- giving employees responsibility for checking the quality of production, as in quality assurance systems
- inviting all employees to suggest ways of improving quality.

Technology and production

Technology is a feature of production in many businesses.

Computer-Aided Design (**CAD**) uses modern technology in the design stage of the production process. CAD allows businesses to:

- produce accurate, three-dimensional drawings on computers
- store and edit drawings as required
- overcome any design problems before manufacturing takes place
- convey designs electronically to customers and manufacturers.

In 1999, the aircraft manufacturer Boeing designed and tested a new aeroplane, using a computer – avoiding many of the teething problems associated with building and testing a model.

Computer-Aided Manufacture (**CAM**) uses computers as part of the production process. Computers are used in production to:

- manage the delivery of materials and components to the production line
- control the operation of robots carrying out production activities
- offer improvements in productivity and quality.

How might using a quality assurance system help a firm to reduce costs?

CASE STUDY

The K Shoes Factory in Kendal, Cumbria

K Shoes employs 400 people at its shoe factory in Kendal. Twenty years ago, 2,500 people worked in the factory, but fierce foreign competition caused job losses. Since 1994, to compete with shoe manufacturers in Poland and China, who pay much lower wages, K Shoes has used robots on its production line. In 2000, the company bought more up-to-date robots. These can carry out boring tasks that human workers usually hate doing. Managers at K Shoes believe robots help them to fight off competition from cheap, imported shoes. Robots are able to work without a rest and they produce consistently high-quality products.

Tasks

1 Why might the shareholders of K Shoes support the use of robots on the company's production line?

2 Explain the problems that K Shoes might have faced in 1994 when it introduced robots to the production line.

Marketing and sales

Marketing and sales involve businesses in many activities. Marketing is the process that helps businesses to discover and meet the needs of consumers. Marketing activities are illustrated in **A** .

Researching the market

Market research might be carried out locally throughout the UK, or sometimes internationally. It enables businesses to discover:

- consumers' reactions to the firm's existing products
- what new goods and services consumers want
- whether new products will prove popular
- the prices consumers are prepared pay for particular goods and services
- how satisfied consumers are with the service provided by its employees.

There are two major types of market research: primary and secondary, as shown in **B** .

E-commerce is buying and selling products using the internet.

Market research is a series of cost-effective ways of finding out what consumers want and what they think.

Promotion is a range of techniques, such as advertising and special offers, aimed at encouraging consumers to buy a particular product.

A Marketing activities: meeting customers' needs through marketing

1 Discover customer's needs through market research, for example:
- Telephone interviews
- Questionnaires

2 Advise customers of products through promotion:
- Advertising
- Special offers
- Public relations

3 Achieve sales:
- Customers buy products to meet their needs

B Primary and secondary market research

Primary market research	However, it is slower and more expensive.
Primary research gathers data for the first time, normally by asking for people's views.	
The main techniques of primary market research are: ■ asking possible customers to complete questionnaires ■ conducting telephone interviews ■ carrying out in-depth interviews with customers, ■ observing customers shopping.	
Primary market research gives more detail and is relevant to the business carrying it out.	

Promotion

Perhaps the best-known marketing activity is promotion, which can include:

- advertising on television, radio, the internet and billboards – as well as in newspapers and magazines
- sales promotions, such as giving free samples and 'buy one get one free' offers
- public relations – attempting to influence the public's opinions of the business and its products through sponsorship, attending trade fairs and press releases.

Businesses use a combination of promotion techniques (types) best suited to their products and customers. This is known as the promotional mix.

STOP & THINK

Many businesses use specialist market research agencies for market research. What are the advantages of doing so?

Beltain is a small business making candles on the Shetland Islands, off the northern coast of Scotland. Visit Beltain's website at http://sites.ecosse.net/beltain/. Look around the site and research answers to the following questions:

1 What is unique about the products sold by Beltain?

2 What information does the website give about Beltain's products?

3 In what ways does Katrina Semple, the owner of Beltain, find out her customers' opinions?

4 Can you suggest any ways in which Beltain might make it easier for customers to buy its products online?

5 Why do you think that this website is very important to the marketing of Beltain's products?

Sales

Businesses try to achieve sales using a variety of techniques.

- Selling their products through shops. Some businesses have their own shops (farm shops are an example) though most sell through separate retailing businesses.
- Personal selling, such as when sales representatives encourage customers to buy their products. This is common in the insurance industry, where salespeople contact potential customers either in person or by telephone.
- Internet selling is an increasingly important sales method for a variety of businesses. A wide range of products can be bought on the web, including holidays and new cars.

Information technology

IT can assist businesses in their marketing activities in many ways.

- Collecting information about customer spending. Supermarkets use loyalty cards to collect a great deal of information about their customers.
- E-commerce – that is, using the internet to help small businesses sell products nationally, or even internationally
- Using internet advertising to sell products
- Using computer programs to select people at random for market research purposes.

STOP & THINK

Thomson Holidays pays millions of pounds to promote its name on Tottenham Hotspur football team shirts.

What benefits might Thomson expect to receive from this sponsorship? Why do you think they chose to sponsor a football club?

Customer service

Customer service involves businesses in a number of duties.

- Offering fair prices, good-quality products and reliable delivery.
- Providing customers with detailed information and advice about products before they buy them.
- Operating efficient ordering systems, so that products can be ordered quickly and easily and customers can find out when delivery is due.
- Offering efficient after-sales services, such as repair and maintenance and the replacement of faulty products or parts.
- Responding to enquiries about the business and/or its products
- Dealing with written complaints from customers promptly and fairly
- Offering customers credit. Many businesses arrange loans to help customers buy their products. This can often be done immediately, allowing customers to have their goods straightaway.
- Delivering goods. It is normal for businesses to deliver bulky or heavy items, but delivery of goods as a customer service has become more important now that consumers buy more on the internet.

How is customer service organised?

1 Traditional methods of customer service

Some businesses run a separate department to provide the highest possible standards of customer service. Staff employed in customer service will need:

- high levels of training to deal with a wide range of customer enquiries
- the ability to communicate easily and provide customers with advice and information
- a wide knowledge of the business so as to be able to deal effectively with customers' questions
- excellent interpersonal skills with the ability to calm upset customers and keep them satisfied.

KEY CONCEPTS

Credit is an arrangement that allows an individual to borrow money, such as when a firm lends money to a customer to buy its products.

Customer service is the methods used by a firm to deliver the product or service that a customer wants or needs. It includes after-sales support for the customer.

STOP & THINK

Some of the functions of customer service are likely to involve staff from the marketing department of the business. Which of those functions do you consider to be marketing activities?

A The functions of customer service

OVER TO YOU

The customer services department will need to work closely with people working in other areas of the business. These include:

- the marketing department, to provide feedback of customers' views and opinions (an informal type of market research)
- the operations (production) department, to advise on any faults or problems that may arise with the firm's products
- the finance department, as part of the function of offering customers credit
- the personnel department, for the training of customer service staff.

Customer service is an important part of marketing. In many businesses, the marketing department has responsibility for the customer service function.

2 Modern methods of customer service

A more recent approach to customer service is to stress the role played by all employees in ensuring that consumers are satisfied. Every member of staff is expected to provide customer service to an equally high standard. Staff are all trained in customer service and given the opportunity to gain qualifications in this aspect of the job.

In some industries such as retailing, a high standard of customer service is a way of gaining a competitive advantage. Tesco, the UK's largest retailer, has acknowledged that one way that it competes with other supermarkets is by offering higher standards of customer service.

Supermarkets consider high-quality customer service to be very important. Visit a local supermarket and walk around, paying particular attention to all the signs and posters.

1 Make a note of the types of customer services that are advertised or available.

2 See if you can find a copy of the supermarket's customer services charter. Does it mention all the functions shown in **A** ?

3 Why do you think that good customer services are so important to supermarkets?

A supermarket counter devoted to customer services

Research and development

Research and development (R&D) is big business. Firms in the UK spent £10,231 million on R&D in 1998. In that year, the pharmaceutical industry spent £2,238 million researching and developing new drugs. However, new ideas do not always lead to new products being made available to consumers. Between 1986 and 2001, the pharmaceutical industry in the UK spent thousands of millions of pounds researching 1,900 new drugs, but only 137 of these led to new products becoming available.

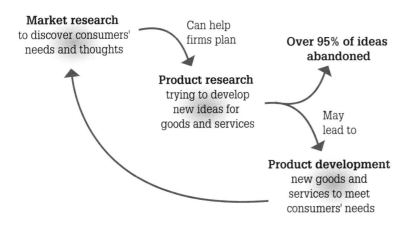

Market research to discover consumers' needs and thoughts

Can help firms plan

Product research trying to develop new ideas for goods and services

Over 95% of ideas abandoned

May lead to

Product development new goods and services to meet consumers' needs

The processes of market research, product research and product development are all linked, as shown above. But it is important not to confuse market research with product research. We looked at market research on page 46. Now we will focus on product research and the development that normally follows this.

Reasons for research and development

Research and development is very expensive and can take a long time to produce any results. In spite of this, businesses invest in research and development for many reasons.

■ They can gain an advantage over rival firms. Businesses investing in R&D hope to offer products that are better designed and more technologically advanced.
■ Research can be used to improve existing products so as to extend their lives. For example, Microsoft has updated its software regularly after continuous technical research.

GlaxoSmithKline's research and development centre in Harlow, Essex

STOP & THINK

GlaxoSmithKline is a huge pharmaceutical company formed as a result of a merger. Which companies joined together to form GlaxoSmithKline? What benefits might the new company gain from the merger?

- Businesses may discover cheaper ways of producing current products, which will result in higher profits. McDonald's have developed high-technology kitchen equipment so that their restaurants can serve food quickly and efficiently. This also improves customer satisfaction.
- Research and development can eventually lead to new products. Higher prices can be charged for new products, enabling firms to make large profits.

Risk in research and development

Research and development can result in new and profitable products. However, there is no guarantee that even the most brilliant invention will result in a successful new product. Research and development is risky.

- Over 90 per cent of new ideas fail during the development stage. Businesses may invest heavily in new ideas, yet receive no money in return.
- Other businesses can copy ideas, reducing the profits for the firm that conducted the research. It is possible to prevent rivals copying new products, by applying for a patent. However, patents only last for a maximum of 20 years.
- Even when UK businesses have discovered new ideas, they have not always been successful in using them to produce new goods and services. For example, UK firms invented the hovercraft and the drug Viagra, but did not exploit these ideas commercially.

A Research and development spending by selected UK industries for 1988 and 1998

Industry	1988 (£m)	1998 (£m)
Chemicals	642	688
Pharmaceuticals	843	2,238
Engineering	424	730
Transport	536	983
Aerospace	725	1,039
All Services	**1,587**	**2,359**

Source: www.dti.gov.uk/ost/setstats/data/4

STOP & THINK

Which two industries shown in **A** have increased their spending on research and development by the greatest amount? Why do you think this has happened?

CASE STUDY

James Dyson is one of the UK's best-known inventors. Not only has he come up with some brilliant ideas, but he has also managed to turn his ideas into successful products. His 'bagless' vacuum cleaner is his most famous product. The extract from his website shows that he has also invented a new type of washing machine.

Tasks

1 Visit the Dyson website at www.dyson.com and read 'The Dyson Story' to understand the risks and benefits entailed in investing in research and development.

2 Why do you think that so many good ideas never get to become successful products?

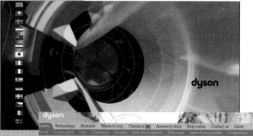

Information technology

Information technology (IT) is sometimes called information and communications technology, or ICT. Businesses have experienced a revolution in information technology over recent years. IT can take many forms, including:

- personal computers and networks of computers
- the internet and intranets
- mobile phones
- bar code scanners, such as those used in shops
- relatively simple technology, such as faxes.

Modern businesses rely on information technology to carry out a range of functions within the business, from administration to production.

KEY CONCEPTS

Information technology (**IT**) is the use of electronic equipment such as computers for storing and exchanging information.

The **internet** is a worldwide system of linked computer networks that facilitates communication and commercial activities throughout the world.

STOP & THINK

Looking at **A**, do you think information technology is as useful to small businesses as it is to larger ones?

A Uses of information technology within businesses

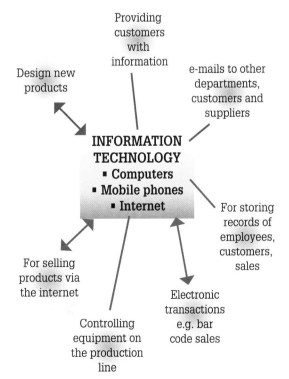

Providing customers with information

Design new products

e-mails to other departments, customers and suppliers

INFORMATION TECHNOLOGY
- **Computers**
- **Mobile phones**
- **Internet**

For selling products via the internet

For storing records of employees, customers, sales

Controlling equipment on the production line

Electronic transactions e.g. bar code sales

Using information technology within businesses

Businesses use information technology in many ways.

- It is common practice for larger businesses to set up an **intranet** – a system of linking computers within a business, allowing information to be exchanged and shared. Intranets are valuable in businesses trading on many different sites; they can be used for:
  - sending orders from the sales team to the production department
  - keeping important central records (employee records, for example) for access by authorised personnel
  - keeping records of stock held.

- When marketing products, firms may invite customers to complete online questionnaires as part of a market research programme, or they may advertise their products on the internet.

- Firms are selling more and more on the internet. Travel tickets and books are two products that are commonly bought online. But information technology has a wider role in sales: for example, it is used in bar code systems at checkouts.

- Information technology can be used to design products. It can create easily altered three-dimensional drawings, and is used on production lines to control robots and other high-technology equipment.

- Computers can store sales records, process orders and automatically print invoices requesting payment from customers.
- Information technology plays an important role in security for businesses. It might:
  - operate closed-circuit televisions
  - protect business records against computer viruses
  - control access to sensitive company records through a system of passwords.

Benefits of information technology

All businesses can benefit from using information technology in a number of functional areas.

- It allows businesses to communicate immediately and to keep permanent records. E-mail can be sent any distance in a few seconds. The combination of speed and written or visual information is very valuable.
- Businesses can cut costs. For example, information technology allows manufacturers to order more raw materials as and when they are needed. This saves storage costs and fewer staff will be required to look after warehouses and manage stocks.
- Selling on the internet saves the costs of running a shop. Carphone Warehouse, for example, sells many of its mobile phones through its website.
- Information technology offers new business opportunities. For example, with the introduction of the internet, many businesses offered services designing websites.
- Information technology has helped some businesses to improve their goods and services. For instance, photographers using computer software can digitally enhance their pictures to achieve the desired effect. Also, customers ordering online can check on the progress of their order and know when to expect delivery.

STOP & THINK

List as many costs as you can that Carphone Warehouse might have to pay when it opens a shop in a high street near to you, rather than relying on its internet sales.

CASE STUDY

SNA EpoS system

The SNA Electronic Point of Sale (EpoS) shop management system is a comprehensive system offering many advantages for businesses:

- a till that records sales and calculates change
- automatic generation of orders to replace goods that have been sold
- the creation of financial accounts to help manage the business
- efficient stock control – managers know how much stock they have and orders can be made automatically.

Tasks

1 What advantages might this EpoS system offer to someone who is running a shop for the first time?

2 Visit a local shop where they use electronic point of sale systems. Ask what the advantages and disadvantages of the systems are.

3 Do you think that all shops should operate these systems? Explain your answer.

The SNA is designed to offer a complete management solution to shopkeepers.

How businesses communicate

Good communication is essential for businesses. Without it, employees do not know what they are supposed to do and managers will not know what customers want. Good communication means that the right people get the right information at the right time.

The communication process

There are common elements in any communication.

- A sender decides to communicate with another person or group (the audience).
- The sender decides on the information to be transmitted.
- A decision is made on which medium to use; that is, how the information will be communicated.
- The audience for the information is determined.
- The audience may send feedback to confirm that the message has been received and understood.

This process is shown in **A**.

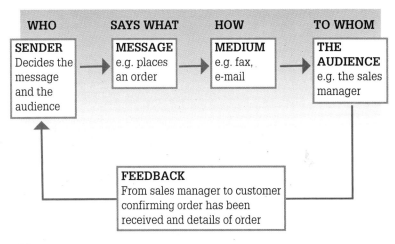

WHO	SAYS WHAT	HOW	TO WHOM
SENDER Decides the message and the audience	**MESSAGE** e.g. places an order	**MEDIUM** e.g. fax, e-mail	**THE AUDIENCE** e.g. the sales manager

FEEDBACK
From sales manager to customer confirming order has been received and details of order

A The process of communication

KEY CONCEPTS

Communication is the process of exchanging information or ideas between two or more individuals or groups.

Feedback is the response stage within the communication process. Criticism of an advertising campaign is an example of feedback.

The **paperless office** is an office in which traditional communication methods have been replaced by electronic ones.

STOP & THINK

How might a company's suppliers, its customers and its shareholders be affected by poor communication? In each case, try to think of two problems that might occur.

STOP & THINK

Explain why feedback is an important part of the process of communication.

Methods of communication

1 **Oral communication** (the spoken word) can be by several methods:
   - a telephone conversation placing an order with a business
   - telephone conferencing, allowing several people to hold a conversation without needing to travel to a meeting
   - meetings, a common form of oral communication; for example a meeting of the board of directors of a large company or a meeting of two sales representatives to decide how to deal with a difficult customer.

2 **Video communication** relies on information technology. It is of particular value to businesses whose employees do not work near to each other. Techniques such as video conferencing and video links on the internet allow people to see and hear one another. Many people can speak together, and seeing one another improves the quality of communication.

JOINED-UP THINKING

On pages 52–3 we looked in detail at information technology.

Information technology and communication are closely related. Good-quality communication in a modern business depends to a great extent on information technology.

STOP & THINK

Can you think of any ways in which information technology might harm the process of communication either within or outside a business?

3 **Written communication** is still used in all types of businesses, despite the widespread use of information technology. It can take several forms.

- A memorandum (or memo) is used within a business for many communication purposes, for example, to inform employees of the appointment of a new member of staff.
- Letters are generally used to communicate with people and organisations outside the business. A business might write to its customers announcing a new product.
- Companies are required by law to publish financial details in their annual report.
- Advertisements in magazines and newspapers are further examples of written communication.
- E-mails often contain attachments that include written communications. These can be lengthy documents, such as the records from recent meetings.

4 **Graphical communication**. Businesses frequently send and receive graphical information, for example the design of the front cover of a new book. This may be done on an intranet or the internet.

Communication within and between businesses

Employees of businesses are involved in two main types of communication

- With other people in the same business. For example, the customer services department might advise operations (production) of complaints regarding the quality of a particular product.
- With individuals and organisations outside the business, which is equally essential. For example, the finance department of a business is likely to communicate with Customs and Excise over the payment of Value Added Tax.

Communication within the business

Businesses use a number of techniques for internal communication.

- Newsletters inform employees of matters relating to the business, such as sales figures, social events and new members of staff.
- Notice boards can be used to provide some information to small groups of employees, as long as they read the notices!
- Team briefings are intended to inform staff of recent happenings, such as receiving a new order. In small businesses the whole staff may attend a team briefing; in large companies different departments might hold their own briefings.
- Some large companies operate their own business television systems, giving detailed information about all the company's activities.
- Other methods include memos and meetings.

Communications outside the business

External communication is vital for a business. It is a major influence on how the business is viewed by customers, suppliers and the general public. Techniques commonly used include:

- internet and e-mail
- letters
- the company annual report
- advertisements
- faxes.

KEY CONCEPTS

Communication is the process of exchanging information or ideas between two or more individuals or groups.

External communication is the exchange of information with individuals or groups outside the business.

Internal communication is the exchange of information with other people or groups within the same business.

STOP & THINK

What benefits might a business gain from good communication with other businesses?

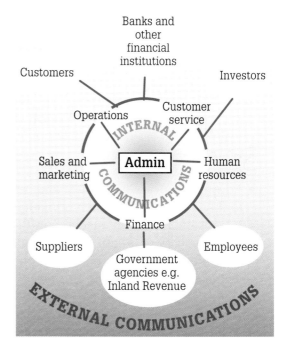

A Internal and external communication

Choosing a method of communication

Good communication is important in helping businesses to achieve their objectives. The correct method of communication will depend on the circumstances. It is not possible to say that any one method will always be the best.

- To inform large numbers of customers about a new product, a television advertisement would be suitable.
- To send the same brief message to large numbers of people in an organisation, a memo might be used.
- To discuss new products in detail with the sales force, a meeting might be the best choice.
- To contact a customer in another country to confirm details of an order, an e-mail might be the answer.
- To advise colleagues in a small factory about a social event, the notice board would be effective.

STOP & THINK

How many internal communication methods might Ford (a multinational business with factories and offices in over thirty countries) use? Would these differ from those used by Morgan – a sports car manufacturer with a single factory in Worcestershire?

STOP & THINK

Look at the five scenarios described under 'Choosing a method of communication'. For each one, select a second method of communication that would also be suitable.

Building an Airbus

C A S E   S T U D Y

Communications at British Aerospace

British Aerospace manufactures aircraft and military equipment. It has 46,000 employees. Communication between the different business functions within British Aerospace takes place freely and in ways that work best for those involved. Team meetings are scheduled a year ahead of the date of the meeting.

Other internal communication tools and methods include:
- electronic methods for urgent news
- the 'Value Plan', outlining the annual business plan and distributed to all employees
- senior managers' walkabouts and events such as lunches hosted by them
- notice boards – and themed posters for special campaigns – in the manufacturing areas
- the bi-monthly company journal, *Arrow*, which covers broad-based, company-wide information, and local house magazines
- a twice-yearly magazine-style video programme, reporting on progress and performance, shown to all employees.

Tasks

British Aerospace is one of four European aircraft manufacturers building the Airbus. Working on a joint project with other businesses makes good external communication very important.

1 How might British Aerospace communicate with other businesses building the Airbus?

2 Why is good communication so important for the company?

3 Do you think that the methods of internal communication used by British Aerospace are suitable for a large company? Explain your answer.

REVISION 2

The previous 20 pages have extended your knowledge of how businesses work. You should now be able to answer the questions that follow.

10 revision questions

Check your knowledge by tackling these questions.

1 List four functional areas that might exist within a business. (4marks)

2 Describe two tasks carried out by the operations department of a business. (6 marks)

3 Explain two ways in which using IT can help a business to carry out its range of functions. (6 marks)

4 Describe two marketing and sales activities that may help a business to meet the needs of its customers. (6 marks)

5 Explain what is meant by the term 'research and development'? (3 marks)

6 Give two reasons why businesses might invest money into research and development. (6 marks)

7 List three ways in which businesses might use IT to communicate with customers. (3 marks)

8 Describe three methods of written communication that a business might use. (9 marks)

9 Explain what is meant by the term "graphical communication". (3 marks)

10 Give two reasons why it is important for businesses to communicate with other businesses. (4 marks)

Total = 50 marks

Continuing your investigation

You should have completed the first part of your portfolio evidence by now. This will have looked at the activities, aims and objectives, location and ownership of your two chosen businesses.

The second part of the portfolio evidence will cover many of the topics you have studied recently. You will need to have the following information about each of the two businesses you are studying:

- how the business is organised and the areas (or functions) that make up the business
- the methods of communication used inside and outside the business.

Once again, you will need to check which Awarding Body (AQA, Edexcel or OCR) you are using. When you know this, you can choose the correct column from the table below. This will guide you in writing the second part of your portfolio evidence.

CASE STUDY

AstraZeneca

AstraZeneca is one of the world's leading pharmaceutical companies, producing a variety of medicines for patients throughout the world. AstraZeneca contains all the business functions looked at earlier. Which of these functions do you think might be particularly important to the company? You can find out more about AstraZeneca at www.astrazeneca.com/About Us/Key facts.

AWARDING BODY			
What you have to do	**AQA**	**Edexcel**	**OCR**
Describe	• the types of work done in each of the functional areas of each of the businesses (except human resources and customer services) • the different methods of oral and written communication used by each of the businesses, with examples of when they would be used (this should be a presentation)	• the purpose of three or more of the functional areas within the two businesses • the communication techniques used in each of the functional areas described • how communication techniques help functional areas to work effectively	• the types of work carried out by at least three functional areas in one of the chosen businesses • the methods of oral and written communication used by one of the businesses and how IT is used in communication

Explain	• how the functional areas of the businesses help them to achieve their aims
	
	• how the functional areas of the businesses support each other
	
	• why the methods of internal and external communication used by the businesses are right for the circumstances
		• what the businesses' functional areas do and why they are needed
		
		• the main techniques of internal and external communication used by functional areas within each of the businesses
			• how at least three functional areas of one of the chosen businesses work together to achieve the business's aims and objectives
			
			• the effectiveness of communication methods used
			  ▪ inside functional areas
			  ▪ between functional areas
			  ▪ outside the business.

Evaluate (this may mean making judgements or offering and justifying suggestions)	• how effectively the functional areas of the businesses work together to achieve the businesses' aims
	
	• how IT might be used more effectively in the future
	
	• how the businesses may communicate more effectively with customers
		• the effectiveness of the functional areas of the businesses in helping the businesses to achieve their aims and objectives
		
		• the importance of communications in supporting the work of the functional areas and in helping the businesses to achieve their aims
			• how well at least three of the functional areas of one of the businesses work together to achieve the aims and objectives of that business
			
			• Suggest and justify alternative or improved communication methods:
			  ▪ within functions
			  ▪ between functions
			  ▪ outside the business

Making products competitive

Businesses can decide on their type of ownership, their aims and objectives and the products they will supply. They can control the functions, such as marketing, that make up the business. However, a series of external factors are beyond their control. These factors include:

- the activities of competitors
- changes in the business world, for example rising prices of raw materials
- new laws controlling the pollution caused by businesses.

What is a competitive business?

Nearly all businesses face competition from other firms. A competitive business is one that can equal or better the performance of its rivals. A business is competitive if it can:

- retain its existing customers
- win new customers
- consistently achieve its objectives (such as making profits).

A business can make its products competitive with those of other firms by concentrating on three factors.

1 **Making sure its products are price competitive.** This means that the business should aim to:
   - have prices that are lower than those of competitors
   - charge higher prices only for clearly understood reasons, such as the product being of higher quality or more technologically sophisticated.
2 **Supplying high-quality products.** A quality product is one that satisfies customers as fully as possible. This can be achieved in a number of ways:
   - the product lasting longer or looking better than competitors' products
   - customers receiving advice and support from the business, for example after-sales service
   - researching customers' opinions to ensure products meet their needs as fully as possible.
3 **Making the products available to as many customers as possible.** The best products sold at the cheapest prices will not make a firm competitive if consumers cannot buy them. Products should be available to the largest possible number of people. This may involve selling in shops, on the internet and through mail order.

STOP & THINK

Businesses selling fast food compete heavily in terms of price. Write down four other products for which being price competitive is important.

STOP & THINK

How important do you think customer services departments are in making a supermarket competitive? Which functions are important in making a car manufacturer competitive?

Targeting the customers

Very few products are bought by everybody. Most businesses aim their products at certain groups of people. Dividing up markets in this way is called segmentation.

Consumers in the UK can be classified according to the following factors:

- **Age.** Popular music is bought mainly by young people. Music companies such as EMI target this age group by, for example, advertising their products in magazines read by young people. Coach holidays are most popular with older people, and so would be promoted to this age group.
- **Gender**. Women are important customers for mail order businesses, so companies such as Freeman's design their catalogues to attract women. However, men purchase the majority of do-it-yourself (DIY) equipment, so DIY stores advertise price reductions to catch the attention of men.
- **Income.** Expensive products, such as Rolex watches, are aimed at the higher-income groups, while supermarkets such as Netto and Aldi target people with modest incomes.
- **Lifestyle.** Young, single men are a popular target for businesses selling alcohol, whereas ready-made meals may be aimed at professional people who lead busy lives.
- **Where they live.** The location of consumers is important to businesses. For example, petrol retailers such as Esso and Shell will not open forecourts in small villages with small populations.

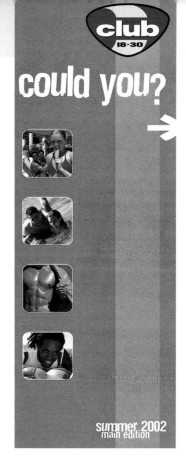

club 18-30

could you?

summer 2002
main edition

STOP & THINK

Club 18–30 sells more holidays to young people than any other holiday firm. What benefits might Club 18–30 gain from targeting its products at young people?

OVER TO YOU

Choose two products with which you are familiar and collect a number of advertisements for them from newspapers and magazines. Examine the advertisements closely and, for each of the products, answer the following questions.

- Is the product aimed at a particular age group? If so, which one? What evidence was there for reaching this conclusion?
- Is the product aimed at men or women or both? The magazine or newspaper in which the advertisement appeared should give you a clue!
- Do you think that the product is aimed at those with low or high incomes? Why do think so?

- Looking at the advertisements for one of your products, how do you think targeting a particular consumer group helps to make that product more competitive?

Local, national and international competitors

All businesses face competition. Competitors can be local, national or international.

1 **Local competitors**. These are rival firms within a few kilometres' radius, offering an opportunity for customers to switch from one business to another. Local competitors are common in the following types of businesses:
   - small retail businesses, such as grocery shops and post offices
   - leisure organisations, such as pubs and restaurants, selling mainly to local people
   - businesses supplying certain services who often compete with other small businesses within a certain geographical area, for example plumbers, hairdressers and window cleaners.

Local competition occurs when businesses are small and easy to establish and people regularly buy their products.

2 **National competitors**. A business has national competitors if firms in other parts of the UK are competing for the same customers. Both small and large businesses can face national competitors.
   - Professionals, such as accountants, face national competitors. Price Waterhouse Coopers offers accountancy services throughout the UK, competing both with other large accountancy businesses and with small, local firms of accountants.
   - Banks compete with each other at a national level. For example, both Lloyds TSB and Barclays have hundreds of UK branches in a bid to get customers.
   - Manufacturing firms often face competition at a national level. For example, firms supplying building materials for new houses compete in the national market.

3 **International competition**. An increasing number of products are supplied by multinational companies. We often buy from firms that are foreign or from UK companies facing international competition.
   - Most fast food restaurants are American. This means that British restaurants face international competition – a fairly recent change.
   - Costly manufactured goods, or goods or services that are easily transported, are frequently sold in international markets. For example, firms selling cars or computer software compete internationally.

KEY CONCEPTS

Multinationals are businesses that produce goods and services in more than one country.

Industry	Share of sales of largest five firms
Betting shops	70.0%
Newspapers	53.9%
Brewers	53.3%
Hotels	49.8%

A Some industries where businesses face national competitors

STOP & THINK

Use the internet or your local library to find the major brewing companies in the UK. Can you think of reasons why some brewing businesses compete nationally while others compete internationally?

• Products, such as steel, that need to be produced on a very large scale and require high sales to be profitable will most probably be sold in many countries, leading to international competition.

Changes in competition

The use of technology has made it possible for even small businesses to compete in much larger markets than before.

■ **Telephone sales.** Selling products on the telephone allows businesses to trade for long hours. It is also a relatively cheap method of selling, as there is no need for shops. Many services such as insurance and holidays are frequently sold over the telephone.

■ **The internet.** Selling on the internet is taking over in many cases from telephone sales. The advantage of the internet selling method is that customers can see the products they are intending to buy. Popular purchases on the internet include air travel and CDs.

A steel foundry in Indonesia

OVER TO YOU

Use the internet to search for firms selling one of the following products: pottery; hand-knitted woollens; website design; garden products (plants and gardening equipment).

Search for a small company that sells its products nationally.

■ In what ways does your chosen business use information technology to sell its products?

■ Does it compete in:
  • price
  • quality
  • product availability?

■ Could your chosen business compete nationally without the internet?
Explain your answer.

STOP & THINK

Why do you think that competition in the steel industry comes from international businesses? What other goods and services are produced by firms that compete internationally?

Changes in the economy

Even a very well managed business can experience problems because of changes in the economy as a whole. Changes in interest rates, the rate at which prices are rising (called inflation), or the value of the pound can have significant effects on all businesses.

Interest rates

Interest rates represent both the cost of borrowing money, and the reward for saving it. They are expressed as a percentage of the sum of money in question. An interest rate of 6 per cent would mean that a business borrowing £1,000 would be charged £60 each year in interest by the lender of the money. Each month, the Bank of England sets the rate of interest, known as the base rate. The base rate affects the rates set by all the other UK banks.

Raising or lowering the interest rate can help control the economy, by making it dearer or cheaper for businesses to borrow money. Using this control contributes to creating a stable economic environment, which in the long run benefits both businesses and consumers.

Rising interest rates	Falling interest rates
The effects of rising interest rates:	The effects of a falling interest rates:
• Businesses may experience falling sales as consumers increase savings	• Sales are likely to increase, especially for products bought on credit
• Sales products purchased on credit (e.g. cars) may fall	• Production is likely to be stimulated, increasing employment
• Businesses may reduce production to match sales	• Businesses may invest in new resources (for example, factories) to increase production
• Businesses may postpone expansion plans – building new factories, for example	• Businesses may need to employ extra employees to increase production.

Price increases

Price increases in products have a number of possible causes.

- Employees may negotiate higher wages.
- Raw materials or components may increase in price.

A Effects of changes in interest rates on businesses

STOP & THINK

How might the following businesses be affected by a rise in interest rates? Do you think that they would all be equally affected?
- Vodafone
- Dairy Crest (milk and other dairy products)
- Comet
- Persimmon Homes (house builders)
- Aldi supermarkets

- Higher interest rates may mean businesses have to pay more for their borrowing. (As a result, businesses may increase their prices, thereby causing more inflation.)

Inflation can have two main consequences for businesses.

- Businesses may suffer falling sales in a period of inflation. At such times, consumers save more and spend less.
- It can be difficult to be competitive (especially internationally) during periods of inflation. Rising costs may force firms to raise prices or to accept lower profits.

In some industries, for example car manufacturing, it is vital to be able match competitors' prices. Inflation can make it difficult to compete with international rivals who have lower rates of inflation in their countries.

Exchange rates

The price of one currency expressed in terms of another currency is called the exchange rate. Exchange rates are very important to businesses that:

- sell their products in foreign countries
- purchase raw materials from other countries.

Exchange rate of the pound	Example	Price of UK exports in local currency	Prices of products imported into UK (£)
Increases	£1 originally worth US $1.50, increases in value to be worth $1.25	Rise	Fall
Decreases	£1 originally worth US $1.50, decreases in value to be worth $1.75	Fall	Rise

B The effects of changes in the value of the UK£

Changes in exchange rates affect the price at which imports and exports are sold.

An increase in the exchange rate can assist a business that imports raw materials or components, as these become cheaper. However, an exporter would suffer, as the prices of their products in overseas markets would rise. Conversely, a decrease in the exchange rate would make imported goods dearer but exports cheaper.

STOP & THINK

Rover cars has found it difficult to compete with rivals in terms of price. In what other ways might the company compete with foreign producers?

STOP & THINK

Rank Hovis McDougall manufactures a range of food products. The company imports raw materials from overseas and sells some products abroad. How might the company be affected by a fall in the exchange rate?

OVER TO YOU

Research the exchange rate of the pound against the following currencies one year ago and today:

- the euro
- the United States dollar.

In each case, explain how these changes might affect Jaguar cars, which sell their models both in Europe and the United States. Could Jaguar do or have done anything to lessen the effects of the changes in exchange rates?

Management of the economy

The government and the Bank of England have used fiscal (taxation and spending) policy and monetary, policy (interest rates) with three main aims:

- **Price stability**. This means controlling the rate of inflation. In the 1980s the UK suffered high rates of inflation, but these have declined steadily since then. Since 2000 inflation has been around 2.5–3 per cent. Having an inflation rate below that of other countries helps the competitiveness of the UK's businesses.
- **Steady and sustained growth in the economy**. Economic growth means increased production and an overall increase in prosperity and improvement in living standards. Economic growth offers businesses the opportunity of more sales and greater profits.
- **A low rate of unemployment**. It is impossible for everyone in the economy to be employed. Unemployment in 2001 hovered around the one million mark, a relatively low figure compared with over 3 million unemployed in the 1980s.

If a government can achieve these aims, then it is able to provide stable economic conditions for businesses. Most businesses do not like sudden and dramatic changes in the economy.

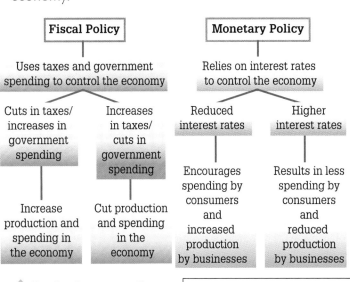

A Fiscal and monetary policy

Bank of England website
Source: www.bankofengland.co.uk

KEY CONCEPTS

Fiscal policy is the use of rates of taxation and levels of government spending to control the economy.

Inflation is the rate at which prices are increasing. This is usually measured as a percentage increase on the previous year.

Monetary policy is the use of interest rates to manage the economy.

STOP & THINK

In 1997 the government gave the Bank of England control over the setting of interest rates for the UK to help the government achieve its economic aims.

Find out when the Bank of England last changed interest rates. Did they rise or fall? How might a business selling fitted bathrooms be affected by the latest change in interest rates?

Stable economic conditions

Two important factors that indicate how well the government has managed the economy are shown in  B .

- the rate of inflation in the UK since January 1996
- the level of interest rates in operation since the beginning of 1996.

If the government achieves its aims of providing stable economic conditions, this means that:

- inflation will be low
- interest rates are stable
- the exchange rate between the pound and other currencies is stable
- firms and the economy are growing steadily.

Year	Inflation (%)	Interest rates (%) at 31 December
1996	2.4	5.95
1997	3.1	7.25
1998	3.4	6.25
1999	1.5	5.50
2000	3.0	6.00
2001	1.8	4.00

B Inflation and interest rates in the UK 1996–2001

Business can benefit in a number of ways from stable economic conditions.

- Businesses can plan more confidently for the future. This is because they can:
  - forecast their sales with some accuracy
  - employ the right number of workers
  - take decisions on whether to build new factories and offices.
- Businesses can also set competitive prices (because they are not paying high interest rates for loans, or suffering from high rates of inflation or large changes in the exchange rate).
- Customers will spend more confidently if inflation rates are low. In times of high inflation, people often save more because they are unsure about the future. For example, they might fear that they would lose their jobs if UK firms were not competitive.
- Low interest rates will encourage consumers to spend more money, as it is cheaper to borrow money. This can lead to greatly increased sales for businesses selling expensive products such as houses, cars and exotic foreign holidays.

STOP & THINK

Compare the levels of interest rates and inflation for 1996 and 2001 shown in B . Do you think that it was easier for UK firms to be competitive in 2001 than in 1996? Explain your answer.

C A S E   S T U D Y

Nissan worried by exchange rate

Nissan, one of the world's largest manufacturers of cars, has a major factory in Sunderland.

However, the chairman of Nissan, Carlos Ghosn, has stated that the exchange rate of the pound is too high, making it difficult for the company to make profits in this country. Despite the profitability of the Sunderland factory, Nissan might seek to expand in other countries in future.

Tasks

1 Explain why the pound's high exchange rate makes it difficult for Nissan to sell cars produced at its Sunderland factory.

2 What other factors determine Nissan's competitiveness, apart from the price at which it sells its cars?

Controlling pollution

Businesses can pollute the environment in a number of ways:

- **Air pollution.** Many businesses release acid substances and hydrocarbons into the atmosphere. These contaminate the air and later cause acid rain. Acid rain damages trees and animals as well as buildings. Lorries and vans are also responsible for polluting the air by creating carbon monoxide. The release of CFCs (commonly found in refrigerators and air-conditioning systems) damages the ozone layer above the earth. Scientists believe this contributes to global warming.

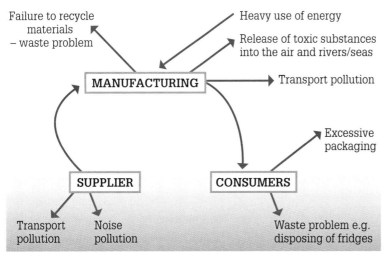

A Business and pollution

KEY CONCEPTS

CFCs stands for chlorofluorocarbons. These are gases used in some products, for example refrigerators, which when released into the atmosphere damage the ozone layer, contributing to global warming.

Global warming is a steady increase in world temperatures, which can cause flooding and other problems around the world.

Pollution is damage done to the natural environment by the activities of businesses.

An **environmental audit** is an assessment of the effects on the environment of the activities of a business.

- **Noise pollution.** Businesses can create noise in a number of ways. Transport causes a great deal of noise pollution. Airlines cause large amounts of noise pollution around airports, and road traffic causes noise problems throughout the UK.
- **Water pollution.** The UK's rivers and seas are cleaner in 2001 than they have been for many years. However, businesses still create much water pollution. The chemical industry and agriculture produce large amounts of waste, some of which is toxic and finds its way into the water system. For example, nitrates used by farmers in East Anglia as a form of fertiliser have been discovered in local rivers, causing damage to wildlife and plants.
- **Wasteful use of resources.** The UK's businesses are criticised for being wasteful in the way they use resources. Businesses make little use of recycling, often preferring to dump materials rather than reuse them. This causes a waste disposal problem and it means that more resources are needed to continue production. UK businesses create over 500 million tonnes of waste each year.

STOP & THINK

What can the national government or local councils do to reduce the amount of waste produced by businesses and households? Make two proposals and consider the advantages and disadvantages of each one.

Laws against pollution

In November 2001, the government appealed to people not to buy new refrigerators or freezers, as new European laws made it impossible to dispose of the old ones. From 1 January 2002, all materials causing the release of CFCs had to be removed from disused fridges and freezers to prevent further damage to the ozone layer. At the time, the UK had no facilities for removing and recycling the parts that leaked CFCs.

New refrigerators on sale

Some of the most important laws passed by the government and the European Union to limit the amount of pollution caused by businesses are:

- **Clean Air Act, 1956**, which called for reductions in the amount of smoke emitted from chimneys in the UK. Later Acts required that only smokeless fuels be used. The 1993 Clean Air Act controlled the lead content in petrol.
- **Environmental Protection Act, 1991**, which introduced Integrated Pollution Control, recognising that it is important to control all causes of pollution at the same time. The Act strengthened environmental controls on industry and set higher standards for emissions of pollutants and for waste disposal.
- **Pollution Prevention and Control Act, 2000**, which requires industries to:
  - use the best available techniques for preventing pollution
  - use energy efficiently
  - return land to its natural state once businesses cease using it
  - minimise waste produced by businesses
  - place strict controls on noise and polluting emissions.

Some businesses have taken environmental protection a step further, publishing an annual environmental audit. This is an assessment of the effects of the activities of a business on the environment. An independent person or organisation normally carries out the audit. Businesses accused of pollution, for example oil companies – such as Shell and BP Amoco – have been the first to publish environmental audits. An environmental audit can help to improve the public's view of a business and perhaps thereby help the company to gain an advantage over the competition.

OVER TO YOU

Use the internet to investigate a company in the oil or chemical industries. You might choose Shell, BP Amoco or ICI, for example. Research the environmental audits produced by one of these companies. Use this information to answer these questions.

1 What aspects of the company's activities does the audit refer to?

2 How does this change the way in which the company carries out its business?

3 In view of this audit do you think that laws to control pollution are not needed?

REVISION 3

In the last 10 pages we considered factors that make businesses competitive locally, nationally and internationally. You should now be able to answer the questions that follow.

10 revision questions

Check your knowledge by tackling these questions.

1 State **three** external influences that might affect businesses. (3 marks)

2 Explain **three** ways in which a business may make its products more competitive. (9 marks)

3 What is meant by the term 'segmentation'? (3 marks)

4 Explain **three** ways in which a business might segment its market. (6 marks)

5 What is the difference between local competitors and national competitors? (4 marks)

6 How has technology made it easier for small firms to compete internationally? (5 marks)

7 Marks & Spencer sell clothing and food in shops throughout Britain. Explain **two** possible effects on the company that a rise in interest rates might have. (6 marks)

8 If the exchange rate of the pound falls against the euro, state what will happen to the price of:
   • British goods exported to France
   • goods imported from Italy. (2 marks)

9 Describe **two** goals the government tries to meet in managing the economy. (6 marks)

10 Explain **two** ways in which businesses might pollute the environment. (6 marks)

Total = 50 marks

Completing your investigation

By this stage of Unit 1, you should be writing the final part of your portfolio evidence. This will cover many of the topics you have been taught recently. Your report should look at the external influences of the business including:

■ competitors
■ economic factors such as interest and exchange rates
■ environmental constraints.

Some awarding bodies (AQA and OCR) also include the location of the business in this final section.

Again, you will need to check which Awarding Body (AQA, Edexcel or OCR) you are using. Once you know this, you can choose the correct column from the following table. This will guide you in writing the final section of your portfolio evidence.

CASE STUDY

Allied Domecq

Allied Domecq produces and sells wines and spirits in many countries. Which external factors do you think, apart from exchange rates, might affect the company's competitiveness?

AWARDING BODY			
What you have to do	**AQA**	**Edexcel**	**OCR**
Describe	▪ the location of each of the businesses ▪ the major customers and the main competitors of each of the businesses	▪ the main external influences on the two selected organisations: ▪ competition between the major firms ▪ economic conditions such as booms and slumps ▪ environmental pressures	▪ the main external influences including ▪ competitors ▪ location ▪ environmental constraints on each of the two businesses
Explain	▪ the marketing activities of each business ▪ how successful you think that the marketing activities of each business are	▪ the impact of each of the external influences on each of the businesses ▪ the effects of changes in the external influences (e.g. new competitors entering the market) on each of the businesses	▪ the impact on each of the businesses of changes in external influences including: ▪ competitors ▪ location ▪ environmental constraints
Evaluate (this may mean making judgements or offering and justifying suggestions)	▪ Using one example from each of the external influences: ▪ competition ▪ economic conditions ▪ environmental law, compare ▪ how they have, or might have, affected each business.	▪ the importance of particular external influences to each of the businesses ▪ the extent to which each business might be affected by the external influences ▪ the strengths and weaknesses of each business in relation to the external influences	▪ Suggest and justify ways in which the two chosen businesses could respond to the changes in their external influences.

Unit 1 contains a number of important themes. These are highlighted in the following figures.

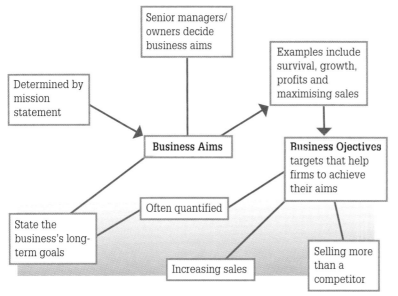

A Business aims and objectives

STOP & THINK

What might be the aims of Oxfam, one of the UK's most famous charities? How do you think these may differ from the aims of British Airways?

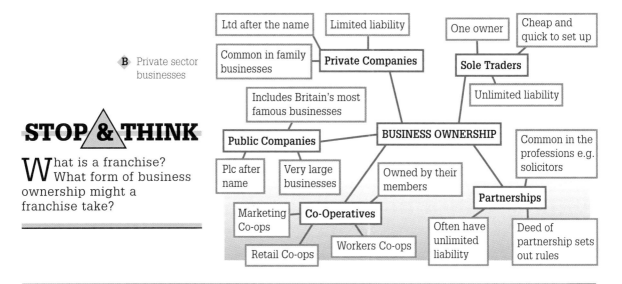

B Private sector businesses

STOP & THINK

What is a franchise? What form of business ownership might a franchise take?

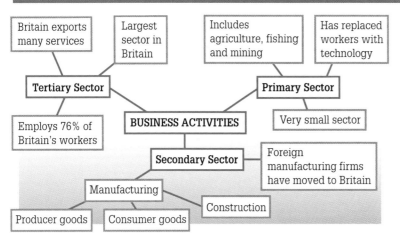

C UK business activities

STOP & THINK

Which well-known UK businesses operate in more than one of the three business sectors? How might the production of a cup of tea involve all three sectors?

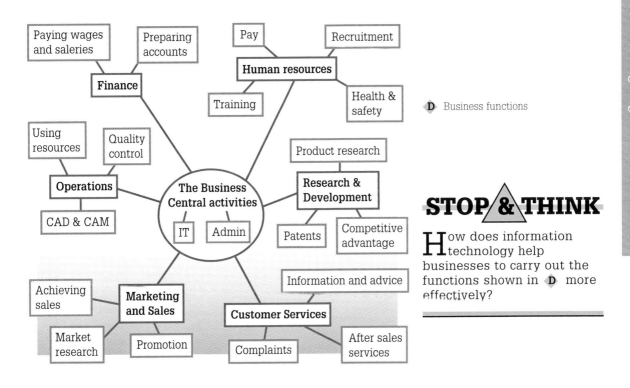

D Business functions

STOP & THINK

How does information technology help businesses to carry out the functions shown in D more effectively?

E External factors and businesses

STOP & THINK

Are small businesses more affected by changes in interest rates and exchange rates than large businesses?

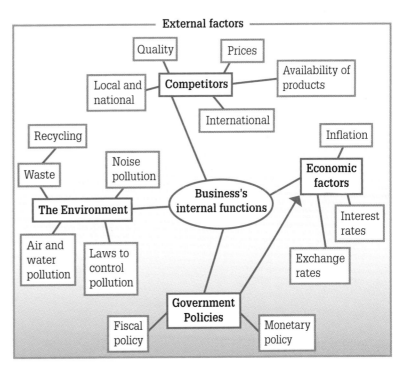

People and business

Unit 2 looks at the roles that people play in businesses, and introduces you to all the interested parties. It explains how different groups and individuals have different interests in the operation of businesses. It stresses that people are one of the most valuable resources that any business can have; and helps to prepare you for joining the workforce of a business. Customers are important to all businesses. This unit also examines the relationship between businesses and their customers.

You will learn about:

- how businesses organise themselves to be as efficient as possible
- what is expected of employees
- the different roles that employees play within a business
- the rights and responsibilities of an employee
- the typical working arrangements experienced by employees
- how businesses communicate with their customers
- the role of a customer services department
- how businesses try to ensure that customers are satisfied
- the laws that businesses must obey when dealing with customers.

A feature of this unit is looking at people within businesses from the viewpoints both of employers and of employees. Importantly, this unit offers practical guidance on applying for a first job. It explains the process by which businesses choose employees, and the training that you might receive as a new employee.

Unit 2 of this book covers Unit 2, People and business, of the GCSE Applied Business award.

People and business

Businesses rely on people. Without them, businesses wouldn't be able to produce and sell goods or provide services. Employees are needed to make or supply the products, and customers are needed to buy them. But for businesses to be successful, they also need many other people. Take the example of Capital Radio.

Better music. More of it.

KEY CONCEPTS

A **business** is any organisation that produces or supplies goods or services.

A **stakeholder** is any individual or group with an interest in a business.

A **human resources department** within a business is the department responsible for making the best use of that business's workforce.

A **product** is a general term that includes both goods and services.

Customers are individuals or organisations that buy products from businesses.

CASE STUDY

Capital Radio

The Capital Radio Group operates 19 radio stations broadcasting to over half of the UK's adult population. It is the UK's largest commercial radio group in terms of revenue and profit. The company's ambition is to add new stations to its group and build digital radio and internet businesses. In 2000, Capital Radio bought Beat 106, adding a further four stations to the group. The company is developing a digital radio network and working hard to establish its websites as the premier music sites in the UK.

Task

Which other people or groups of people might help Capital Radio achieve its ambitions of increasing the number of its radio stations, developing digital radio services and creating top-quality websites?

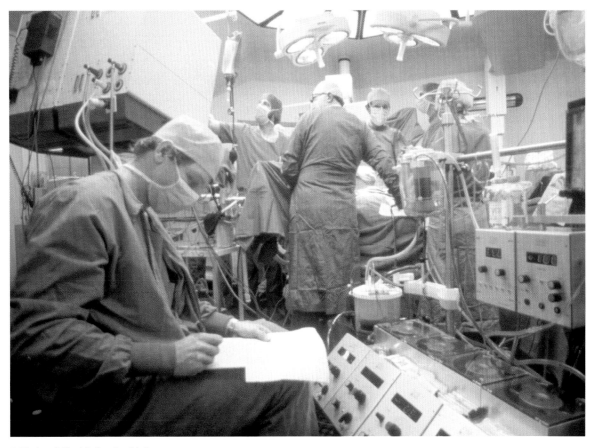

A National Health Service high-technology operating theatre

The National Health Service is one of the UK's largest employers. What, do you think, are the advantages and disadvantages of working in a very large organisation such as the NHS?

Visit a local branch of a bank or building society and take a look around. Make a note of all the ways that the business tries to help its customers and keep them happy. Look at things such as:

■ queuing systems designed to save time

■ information leaflets and brochures

■ help desks.

Compare your results with those of others in your group. Which bank or building society was the most customer-friendly? Why do you think this aspect of the business is important to banks and building societies?

Types of stakeholders

Any person or group of people having an interest in a business is called a stakeholder.

There are two main types of stakeholders:

- **internal and connected** (for example, employees, including managers, and shareholders)
- **external** (the local community and the government).

Internal and connected stakeholders

Internal stakeholders include ordinary employees and managers of a business. Shareholders, customers and other groups or individuals having close ties with a business are called connected stakeholders. All of these are very important to businesses, so the managers do their best to ensure that they are satisfied with the actions of the business.

1 **Employees.** All employees whether part-time or full-time are important stakeholders for businesses. Because they are closely involved with the business, they are likely to have a strong influence on how it is run. Employees' expectations are likely to include the following:
   - a clean and safe working environment
   - job security
   - competitive pay rates and benefits such as discounts on company products
   - interesting and rewarding work
   - opportunities for promotion and a career structure.

2 **Managers.** All managers as well as the directors of a company are stakeholders. Managers will have a bigger say than more-junior employees in how a business is run. Managers' expectations from the business will be similar to those of employees, but will also include:
   - developing a local or national reputation as a successful manager
   - working in a business that is growing
   - having a greater role in decision-making.

STOP & THINK

Using **A**, classify each of the following either as an internal/connected stakeholder or as an external stakeholder:

- a trade union
- a local council
- the Inland Revenue
- a local water company
- a rival business.

EXTERNAL STAKEHOLDERS
· Society
CONNECTED STAKEHOLDERS
· Pressure Groups
· Suppliers
INTERNAL STAKEHOLDERS
· Employees
· Managers
· Bankers
· Shareholders
· Customers
· Government agencies
· Local communities
· Trade unions

A Types of stakeholders

3 **Shareholders.** This group of stakeholders will probably have a financial interest in the business.
- Shareholders want to receive a large and increasing proportion of the company's profits (such payments to shareholders are called dividends).
- Shareholders hope that, in the longer term, the company's share price will rise.
- Some shareholders have interests other than just making money. For example, shareholders in companies such as Body Shop International often invest in them because they trade fairly and try to avoid environmental damage.

4 **Customers.** Many businesses in the UK are customer-focused. This means that they place great importance on fulfilling customers' needs and expectations. These include:
- good-quality products delivered on time
- fair prices
- after-sales service and support, especially for high-technology products.

Some customers are very powerful. For instance, Tesco, the UK's largest retailer, buys enormous amounts of products from suppliers and so has great influence.

5 **Suppliers.** They expect to be paid on time and to receive regular orders from their customers. They will be interested in any developments that might affect the number and size of the orders placed.

6 **Bankers.** Banks and other financial organisations lend money to businesses and will be concerned that their money is safe. They will want the business to run successfully and to earn profits, but not to take risks. They will also want information on the business's financial position.

CASE STUDY

Who are the stakeholders?

Another Kettle of Fish is a small shop in a Norfolk village selling health foods and fresh fish. The business is a partnership and is owned and managed by Caroline and Billy. It is very popular with locals and with tourists.

Who are the main stakeholders of this business? What do you think they want from it? How might the stakeholders of Another Kettle of Fish differ from those of a large company such as Shell?

STOP & THINK

What actions do you think firms can take to meet the expectations of:
- employees
- managers
- customers
- shareholders?

Kwik-Fit is well known as a company supplying batteries, tyres and other services to motorists. In the 1990s Tom Farmer, the Chair and founder of Kwik-Fit, switched his company's policy from one of aiming for 'customer satisfaction' to one of aiming to achieve 'customer delight'.

Visit Kwik-Fit's website (www.kwikfit.com) and find out how the company tries to delight its customers. Why do you think that Tom Farmer introduced this policy?

External stakeholders

Some people, groups and organisations may have an interest in a business without having a close relationship with it. They are called external stakeholders. A business is likely to have a number of external stakeholders.

1 **Government agencies.** The government has a variety of reasons to be interested in businesses:

- The Inland Revenue collects income tax and corporation tax from businesses. This government agency is particularly interested in the financial affairs of businesses.
- Customs and Excise is another government agency with a duty to collect taxes. It collects Value Added Tax (VAT) and keeps a close eye on the financial affairs of all but the smallest businesses.
- The government's regional offices collect a wide range of information on businesses on behalf of the government.

Businesses have to respond to the government's request for information and are legally obliged to pay taxes to the Inland Revenue and Customs and Excise.

2 **Pressure groups.** These are organisations that exist to promote causes. For example, Greenpeace and Friends of the Earth seek to protect the environment; Compassion in World Farming (CiWF) campaigns against the export of live animals. Pressure groups attempt to influence businesses by:

- campaigning (for example, organising protest marches) against firms that behave in 'undesirable' ways, to attract publicity to their cause
- taking direct action against some firms. Pressure groups have destroyed fields of genetically engineered (GE) crops as part of a campaign against large companies, such as Monsanto, that promote GE products.

Businesses respond to pressure groups because they want to have a good public image. They may, for instance, produce 'green' or environmentally friendly goods and not sell products that have been tested on animals. Body Shop International has received much positive publicity for its environmentally friendly policies. This approach has given the company an advantage in a competitive market.

3 **Local communities and society.** Businesses are an important part of society. A large business such as Cadbury's in Birmingham is an important part of the community.

KEY CONCEPTS

An **external stakeholder** is any individual or organisation that has an interest in a business but does not have a close relationship with that business.

A **pressure group** is any group of people who combine to promote a particular view or cause.

STOP & THINK

What might happen to firms such as Monsanto, which produce genetically engineered products, if they ignore the protests of pressure groups?

STOP & THINK

Barclays Mortgages, a division of the high-street bank, has pioneered an 'hour-for-hour' voluntary work scheme. For each hour of leisure time an employee gives up to work in the community, the bank grants a matching hour off work. More than 40 per cent of the company's employees have taken part in the scheme.

This scheme is very costly for Barclays to operate. Why do you think they have chosen to do this?

Local communities expect Cadbury's to:

- provide stable employment for people in Birmingham and other parts of the country
- offer work to many other businesses, such as the haulage firms that transport the company's products across the world
- avoid causing environmental pollution, noise or other problems that might offend the local community.

Businesses such as Cadbury's try to maintain good relations with local communities. They avoid cutting any jobs if they can, they offer financial support for local charities and they seek to be respected members of the local community.

C A S E   S T U D Y

Shell's business principles

Shell is one of the UK's leading producers of oil and gas, supplying energy from oil wells and from beneath the North Sea to homes, factories and petrol stations. Shell produces 20 per cent of the UK's crude oil, 17 per cent of its gas and 15 per cent of its petrochemicals.

Source: www.shell.com

Shell is one of the first companies in the UK to produce a statement of its business principles. The company recognises five areas of responsibility:

- **shareholders** – to protect shareholders' investment and provide an acceptable return to shareholders

- **customers** – to win and maintain customers by developing and providing products and services that offer value in terms of price, quality, safety and environmental impact

- **employees** – to respect the human rights of employees, to provide them with safe conditions of service, to promote the development and best use of employees and to offer equal opportunities

- **suppliers and contractors** – to seek mutually beneficial relationships with all those with whom the company does business

- **society** – to conduct business as responsible corporate members of society, to observe the laws of those countries where the company operates, to express support for human rights and to give proper regard to health, safety and the environment.

Source: Adapted from Shell Statement of General Business Principles

Tasks

1 List three other stakeholders with an interest in Shell.

2 Explain why Shell might find it difficult to meet the needs of employees and shareholders at the same time.

3 Why might Shell find it difficult to meet the expectations of society?

Relations with employees

Businesses are more likely to be successful if employers have good working relationships with their employees. A number of factors can help achieve this.

- Employees should have a clear understanding of what is expected of them and what their duties are.
- Employers and employees should communicate clearly and regularly with each other and avoid misunderstandings.
- Everybody should know his or her rights and responsibilities within the business – that is, what he or she is entitled to and what is expected of him or her.

A Rights and responsibilities of employers and employees

OVER TO YOU

Ask a relative or friend to show you their contract of employment. They may not want you to see the section relating to pay, so just ask to look at the main areas of the contract. Alternatively, ask one of the businesses that you base your study on to let you have a blank contract of employment. List the subjects covered by the contract. Are there others you expected to see but didn't?

KEY CONCEPTS

A **contract of employment** is a legal document stating the hours, rates of pay, duties and other conditions under which a person is employed.

An **employer** is a person or an organisation that hires people to work for the business.

Health and safety is that part of business's activities intended to provide all employees with a secure and risk-free working environment.

A **right** is something to which an employer is entitled, for example the right to expect employees to arrive on time for work.

A **responsibility** is something an employer is expected to do, for example, the responsibility to provide a safe working environment for employees.

What employers expect of employees

Employers have a numbers of rights, many of which form part of the laws relating to employment. These rights become responsibilities for employees.

1 **The right to expect employers to meet the terms of their contract of employment.** Thus they can expect employees to:
   - attend work for the hours stated in the contract
   - carry out the duties expected of them, for example, in the case of a footballer, to attend training sessions and play in matches
   - take the holidays only as set out in the contract.

2 **The right to expect employees to co-operate in achieving the business's objectives.** Such objectives might include:

- survival
- making a profit
- maximising sales
- improving the quality of the product.

If a business is to be successful, all employees should accept responsibility for working towards the same objectives.

The full range of objectives that a business might pursue is set out on pages 14–15 of Unit 1. Have a look at this and think about how employees might assist businesses in achieving their objectives.

3 **The right to expect employees to follow health and safety regulations.** All businesses have health and safety regulations. Their purpose is to:

- prevent workplace accidents
- make sure employees do not become ill as a result of their work
- identify possible hazards in the workplace that might cause an accident or injury.

Businesses display prominent health and safety notices, for example advising employees of the need to wear safety clothing. However, regulations and notices are of little use if employees ignore them.

The main law covering health and safety in the workplace is the Health and Safety Act of 1974. Employees are legally obliged to follow any safety rules drawn up by a business. Anyone who fails to do so may be prosecuted.

STOP & THINK

According to a report by the Health and Safety Executive (a government body responsible for looking after heath and safety in the workplace), farming is one of the most dangerous industries in the UK. In 2001, 128 employees were killed on farms. How might employers and employees work together to make farms safer?

A British farm – a dangerous working environment

Visit a local firm and ask about its health and safety policies. In particular, see if you can find:

- safety notices on walls

- a written health and safety policy

- safety equipment for the use of employees.

Employers' responsibilities

As in the case of employers, who have a number of rights that become the responsibilities of employees, so too, employees have rights that are the responsibilities of their employers.

1 **The right to be paid according to the contract of employment.** An employee's contract of employment will state:
   - how much he or she will be paid
   - how frequently payment will be made (weekly or monthly, for example)
   - when the payment will be made (for example, the last Friday on the month)
   - how the payment will be made (often transferred directly to an employee's bank account).

Any employee who is not paid on time is likely to be very dissatisfied. In some cases, employees might take legal action against employers who fail to pay on time.

2 **The right to be provided with a safe working environment.** The Health and Safety Act, 1974, requires employers to:
   - provide a safe working environment for employees
   - provide safety equipment and safety clothing free of charge
   - display a written safety policy (if there are more than five employees)
   - allow unions to appoint safety representatives.

Firms that do not meet the requirements of the Health and Safety Act are liable to heavy fines and may receive bad publicity.

KEY CONCEPTS

An **employee** is a person who works for another person or for a business.

A **staff association** is a body of employees in one particular business whose representatives discuss issues such as pay or working conditions with the employers.

A **trade union** is an organisation of workers from many businesses that represents its members in negotiations with employers on a range of issues from pay to job security.

STOP & THINK

Working with someone else in your group, identify three advantages and three disadvantages to a business of meeting its health and safety responsibilities.

3 **The right to be appropriately trained.** Different employees at different times may need different types of training:
   - induction training, when newly employed, to help familiarise them with the business
   - training to prepare them for new duties, for example when promoted to a more senior job
   - training to use new equipment, such as the latest information technology
   - training in health and safety issues. For example, workers on oil rigs must undergo survival training, in case of an accident in which the helicopter taking them to or from the rig crashes into the sea.

STOP & THINK

What disadvantages might a firm suffer if it decided not to train its employees? Can you think how a firm might reduce the amount of training it offers to employees?

Training can help to make employees more efficient at their jobs, and this in turn can help to make a business more competitive.

4 **The right to join a trade union.** Employees join a trade union for a variety of reasons:

- to have experts negotiating their wages and working conditions with employers
- to have support in case of a dispute with an employer
- to have free legal advice.

For many years, the number of employees belonging to trade unions was falling. However, since 1999 the figure for trade union membership has begun to rise.

5 **The right to see confidential computer records.** Most businesses keep records about their employees. Often these are simply personal details such as addresses and employment history. But a firm may also hold on computer:

- copies of references written for an employee when he or she applied for a new job
- details of any dispute between the employee and the firm.

The law requires that employees be allowed to read any such records about them held by the company.

STOP & THINK

Many people consider Marks & Spencer to be one of the UK's best employers. How might a business earn a reputation as a 'good' employer?

OVER TO YOU

Some of the UK's largest and best-known trade unions are:

- Unison
- Transport and General Workers' Union (T&G)
- Communication Workers Union (CWU)
- Union of Shop, Distributive and Allied Workers (USDAW)
- Manufacturing Science Finance Union (MSF).

Select one of these unions and find out the following:

- in which industries the trade union represents employees
- what benefits employees get from union membership
- how many members the union has
- how much it costs to belong to the union.

Most unions operate websites, but if you want to write for information, all these unions' addresses can be found on the website of the Trades Union Congress – www.tuc.org.

What benefits might an employer gain from having employees represented by a trade union?

The first 10 pages of Unit 2 have introduced you to some important business ideas. You should now be able to answer the questions that follow.

10 revision questions

Check your knowledge of the first part of Unit 2 by tackling these questions.

1 Explain the meaning of the term 'stakeholders'. (2 marks)

2 Distinguish between internal and external stakeholders. (4 marks)

3 State whether each of the following are internal or external stakeholders:
- customers
- the Inland Revenue
- employees
- managers
- pressure groups
- the local community. (6 marks)

4 Explain why a large public limited company, such as Shell or Marks & Spencer, should be concerned about the views of their employees. (6 marks)

5 Outline **two** problems a business might face if it ignored the opinions of pressure groups. (6 marks)

6 Explain **two** benefits that a new, small business might gain from meeting the needs of its customers as fully as possible. (6 marks)

7 List **three** rights that employers may have. (3 marks)

8 Explain, with the aid of examples, **two** responsibilities for employees that may be included in a contract of employment. (6 marks)

9 The Health and Safety at Work Act gives employees a number of rights. Outline **two** of these rights. (6 marks)

10 Explain the different types of training an employee might expect to receive as a right. (5 marks)

Total = 50 marks

An ICI factory on Teeside

Imperial Chemical Industries (ICI) manufactures chemicals that are included in foods, beauty products and electronic materials. The company also makes some of the world's top paint and decorative product brands. Altogether it manufactures over 50,000 different products and employs more than 45,000 people worldwide.

OVER TO YOU

Identify **five** of ICI's stakeholders. In each case explain:

- what the stakeholders might expect from the company

- how ICI might meet the needs of its stakeholders.

PUTTING IT INTO PRACTICE

Deciding on your business

Even at this early stage in studying Unit 2 of your GCSE in Applied Business, you should be thinking about your assignment. Look for a medium-sized to large business and collect the following information on your chosen business:

- the roles and importance of the business's stakeholders
- job roles and working arrangements in the business
- employer/employee rights, including procedures to deal with disputes and health and safety issues
- employee recruitment and training
- customer service and consumer protection.

Looking at a company's website will be helpful in finding this information, but you might also need to write to the business. If you still cannot find out all you need to know, choose another business.

You can select and research a business with one or more students in your group, but each of you must write a separate piece of evidence for your portfolios.

Starting to write your portfolio evidence

So far in Unit 2 you will only have learnt about stakeholders. However, you should be able to write the first part of your evidence for your portfolio looking at their roles and importance. Make sure you know which Awarding Body (AQA, Edexcel or OCR) you are following. Once you know this, choose the correct column from the chart to guide you in writing the first part of your portfolio evidence.

AWARDING BODY			
What you have to do	**AQA**	**Edexcel**	**OCR**
Describe or identify	<ul><li>Identify the stakeholders of the business.</li><li>Describe how the business affects the various stakeholders.</li></ul>	<ul><li>Describe the roles of the business's major stakeholders.</li><li>Describe the importance of the business's major stakeholders.</li></ul>	<ul><li>Identify the stakeholders in the business and the roles they perform.</li></ul>
Explain or analyse	<ul><li>Explain the influence of stakeholders on the business.</li><li>Explain the different interests that stakeholders might have and how these may cause conflict.</li></ul>	<ul><li>Explain the role of **all** of the business's stakeholders.</li><li>Explain the relative importance of **all** of the major stakeholders (saying which are the most important and why).</li></ul>	<ul><li>Explain the interest that each stakeholder has in the business.</li></ul>
Evaluate (this may mean making judgements or offering and justifying suggestions)	<ul><li>Suggest how businesses might meet the needs of all their stakeholders.</li></ul>	<ul><li>Suggest why certain stakeholders are more influential than others.</li></ul>	<ul><li>Evaluate the extent to which each stakeholder is able to influence the business and the way in which the business operates.</li></ul>

Key employees and their responsibilities

All businesses have a number of key job roles that must be carried out effectively if the business is to succeed. Some of these key roles and how they fit into the structure of the organisation are shown in **A**.

1 **Managers.** Managers play a vital role in businesses.
   ■ They have responsibility for an aspect of the business's work under the guidance of a director. For example, a manager might take responsibility for employee training, under guidance from the director of human resources.
   ■ Managers plan activities, look after teams of employees, manage finances and attempt to meet targets set by the directors of the business.
   ■ Managers' jobs are normally secure, as they usually have permanent full-time contracts.
   ■ Central to the manager's job are taking decisions (for example, whether to increase production levels) and solving problems (such as finding extra employees for a night shift).

   Managers often have a professional qualification in an area such as accountancy or marketing. They need to be good communicators, able to use IT, use time effectively and control finances. Managers' pay varies according to the seniority of the position, but it can be over £100,000 a year. Other benefits that are common are company cars and private health insurance.

2 **Supervisors.** In some businesses supervisors are also called team leaders. Supervisors provide a link between operatives and managers. They:
   ■ monitor the work of junior employees (operatives)
   ■ ensure that production and quality targets set by managers are met whenever possible
   ■ advise managers of problems or difficulties in the work of the business.

A Key roles in the business

KEY CONCEPTS

Managers draw up plans, look after human and non-human resources and attempt to meet the business's targets.

Operatives carry out the basic functions of the business, for example working on a production line.

Supervisors have a day-to-day responsibility for operatives, ensuring that they work effectively and dealing with problems as and when they arise.

Support staff provide essential services to allow a business to function. For instance, they might help in information technology by giving training in the use of new software.

STOP & THINK

Why is a manager paid much more than an operative?

CHIEF EXECUTIVE, MANAGING DIRECTOR AND OTHER DIRECTORS

BOARD OF DIRECTORS
Responsible for establishing business's objectives and providing a broad sense of direction

MANAGERS
Have responsibility for achieving short- and medium-term targets.

MIDDLE MANAGERS
Usually have responsibility for a function, e.g. sales

SUPERVISORS/TEAM LEADERS
Given authority for certain tasks on a day-to-day basis (e.g. monitoring product quality)

Workers at this level have recently been given increased authority in many businesses.

OPERATIVES/SHOP FLOOR WORKERS
These are individuals and groups of workers carrying out basic tasks within the business, e.g. working on a production line or serving customers.

In some businesses, supervisors have been given responsibility for some of the roles previously carried out by managers. For instance, they may recruit new employees or lead training sessions. The pay of supervisors depends on how much authority they have, but they are normally paid more than operatives.

Operatives learning about a new piece of machinery

3 **Operatives.** The most junior employees in the business are the operatives. In a factory, they would work on the production line; in a shop they would be the sales assistants. Their role in a business is as follows.

■ They are normally only responsible for their own work.
■ They usually carry out routine tasks, though some employers do provide more varied and interesting work.
■ They often have little job security. Many are employed on temporary contracts, and when the contract runs out they many find themselves unemployed. Others find they are no longer needed because their jobs have been replaced by machinery.
■ In a minority of businesses, they are allowed to take decisions such as stopping the production line to remove poor-quality products.

Many operatives are relatively unskilled. Sales assistants may have some training and qualifications in customer service, but some factory workers on production lines have no qualifications. Because of this, pay rates for operatives are normally low.

4 **Support staff.** Specialist skills in businesses are provided by the support staff. They may offer expertise in the areas of security or information technology or provide secretarial skills. Support staff can operate at various levels in the organisation.

■ They offer advice and assistance in their specialist areas to other employees. Thus, IT staff may recommend new software or hardware, provide training and sort out computer problems.
■ Some support staff are managers looking after teams of people and are in charge of finances; others carry out routine tasks.
■ Senior support staff take important decisions, such as spending on computer systems.

STOP & THINK

Many firms are making greater use of technology in production. How do you think this might affect the jobs of supervisors and operatives?

OVER TO YOU

Imagine you are the manager of your local McDonald's restaurant. Write down what would be your tasks and responsibilities in this job. How might supervisors help you to manage the restaurant?

Organisation charts

The plan that shows how the work within a business is divided up among the employees, and who reports to whom, is often in the form of an organisation chart.

The business represented by the organisation chart in **A** has five levels of hierarchy, or layers of authority.

- Operatives are responsible to and report to supervisors (their 'bosses').
- Supervisors report to managers, each manager being responsible for a group of supervisors (in this case, three).
- Managers report to individual directors, who in turn report to the chief executive or managing director.
- The chief executive or managing director has ultimate authority in the business.

Each director, manager and supervisor on the chart is directly responsible for three employees – a span of control of three. As can be seen in more detail in **B** , each of the three supervisors has a span of control of three. But so too does the manager, since only the three supervisors (not the operatives) are directly responsible to him or her.

Organisation charts help employees to see how they fit into the business. They show who is an employee's immediate superior, or line manager. They also show the other people in the organisation and give some idea of their roles in the business.

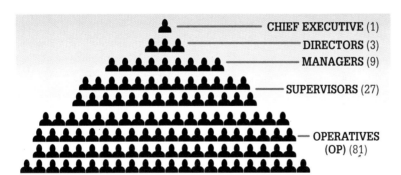

CHIEF EXECUTIVE (1)
DIRECTORS (3)
MANAGERS (9)
SUPERVISORS (27)
OPERATIVES (OP) (81)

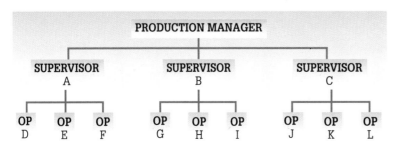

B A detailed section of the organisational chart in **A**

KEY CONCEPTS

A **job description** is a document setting out the duties and tasks associated with a particular position.

Levels of hierarchy are the layers of authority within an organisation.

An **organisation chart** is a plan showing how the roles within a particular business are arranged to enable the business to meet its objectives.

A **span of control** is the number of workers directly supervised by a more senior employee.

A **line manager** is an employee's immediate boss (this may be a supervisor), who gives instructions and advice and answers questions.

Authority is the power that senior employees have to take decisions and control the actions of other employees.

A A simplified organisation chart showing that this business has five levels of hierarchy

STOP & THINK

The organisation chart in **A** and **B** is for a small to medium-sized business. How might it differ from the organisation chart of a very large business?

OVER TO YOU

Talk to a friend or relative who works in a medium-sized or large business. Find out who is his or her boss (the person your friend reports to). Ask how that person helps your friend or relative to carry out his or her job.

STOP & THINK

Imagine you have just started your first day at work in a large business. How might your line manager or boss help you at this time?

In what ways might an organisation chart be helpful when you start a new job?

Job descriptions

Whereas an organisation chart shows how employees fit into the business, a job description gives details about what is expected of the individual employee. Job applicants normally receive a job description when they apply for a position with a business. A job description usually contains the following information:

- the title of the job (for example, sales manager)
- the tasks to be completed as part of the job (for example, having to write monthly sales reports, in the case of a sales manager)
- the responsibilities of the job (for example, a sales manager might be responsible for managing a team of sales representatives)
- information on working conditions linked to the job, such as rates of pay, hours to be worked and holidays
- a description of how the job fits into the organisational structure.

Many businesses also issue person specifications. These state the qualities and qualifications that they are looking for in applicants for the job. Thus, a business wanting to appoint a sales manager might expect applicants to have five or more years' experience in a sales job and some qualifications in sales.

To help you understand the part played by job descriptions, obtain a copy of a job description for a position suitable for a school-leaver in a medium- or large-scale business. You can acquire a job description in a number of ways.

- Friends or relatives may be able to get you one from the business in which they work.

- You could write to a large, local business and ask for one, explaining that looking at job descriptions is part of your GCSE course.

- You could look on the internet, as many large businesses advertise jobs and include job descriptions on their websites.

OVER TO YOU

Once you have a job description, decide how useful it would be in telling you about the job. Is there any extra information you would want? How does your job description compare with those acquired by others in your group? Is it better or worse?

What is in a contract of employment?

Employers are required by law to provide employees with a written contract of employment within eight weeks of the employee starting work. The contract sets out clearly the terms and conditions under which the person is employed. Having it all in writing can help to avoid possible future misunderstandings or disputes.

The areas covered by employment contracts are shown in **A**.

1   **Type of work.** Workers can be employed in a number of ways.
   - A permanent contract of employment means that the employee has a job for an unlimited time. There is no date stating when employment will cease.
   - Temporary contracts of employment last for only a certain period of time, normally up to one year. They are becoming increasingly common.

2   **Hours of work.** The contract of employment should clearly state the number of hours an employee has to work each week. It should say whether the employee is full-time or part-time and set out the terms of any other arrangement such as the following:
   - **Flexitime.** Some employees are allowed to work hours to suit them, although they have to work 'core' hours. For instance, an employee might be required to work 35 hours each week and be at work between 10 am and 12 pm and 2 pm and 4 pm each day (the core hours). The other 15 hours can be fitted in to suit the employee.
   - **Shift work.** Some contracts of employment require employees to work shifts. Shift work is continuous, with different groups of employees working a set number of hours at different times (shifts). Nurses, for example, might work morning, afternoon or night

KEY CONCEPTS

A **contract of employment** is a legal document stating the hours, rate of pay, duties and other conditions under which a person is employed.

Flexitime is a system that allows employees to carry out their agreed hours of work at times that suit them.

Teleworking is working from home, and away from the office, using computers and other high-technology communications equipment. Teleworkers include accountants and newspaper journalists.

Temporary employment is when an employee is offered work for only a fixed period of time. Holiday representatives are often employed on temporary contracts.

STOP & THINK

In what ways might a contract of employment be helpful to a new employee just starting his or her first job?

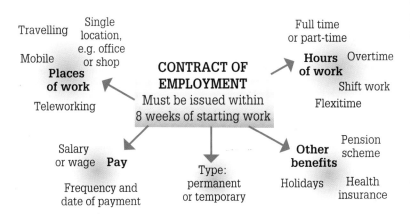

A What a contract of employment contains

shifts. Shift work is used in businesses where employees are required to work long hours (sometimes as much as 24 hours) each day.

- **Overtime.** The contract should state which hours would be overtime – that is, time worked beyond the normal working hours. It should state the rate of pay offered for working overtime.

3 **Place of work.** Some employees always work at the same place. Workers often live within a short distance of their place of employment, and people on their way to the office or factory every morning is a familiar sight. However, a contract of employment may include some other arrangements.
   - Over a million people work at home, using computers to communicate with other people in the business. They are called teleworkers.
   - Some employees are mobile. Hairdressers and car maintenance workers often travel to customers' homes.
   - Some employees are expected to travel regularly as a part of their job. Sales representatives are an obvious example.

4 **Pay.** A contract of employment must state:
   - how much the employee is to be paid
   - the intervals at which the employee will be paid (weekly or monthly, for example).

5 **Other benefits.** The contract of employment should also state other benefits received by the employee, including:
   - how much holiday the employee is entitled to
   - how much pay the employee should receive if he or she falls ill (sick pay)
   - pensions arrangements.

STOP & THINK

Businesses are working increasingly long hours. For example, many supermarkets are open 24 hours a day. What problems might managers face when organising employees into shifts?

STOP & THINK

When you start work, would you prefer to be paid weekly or monthly? Explain your answer. Many employers choose to pay their employees monthly. Why do they choose to do this?

OVER TO YOU

Tasks

1 Using the table to calculate the percentage of UK employees who were temporary in 1992, 1995 and 2000.

2 Research the latest figures for the number of people employed in the UK on temporary contracts.

3 Why do many businesses prefer to hire people on temporary contracts?

Source: Office for National Statistics

Trends in employment in the UK 1992–2000			
	Total employment (millions)	Full-time employees (millions)	Temporary employees (millions)
1992	25.17	16.45	1.49
1995	26.25	16.95	1.86
2000	27.98	18.40	1.96

Flexible employment

UK businesses have employed increasing numbers of part-time and temporary employees.

They have also used self-employed workers, who hire out their skills to firms but are their own bosses. At the same time, businesses have made use of more flexible contracts of employment, in some cases with annualised hours (hours worked in a year) included instead of hours per week. High proportions of these types of employees in businesses are called flexible workforces.

Changing patterns of employment

In recent years, a number of trends have emerged in the UK's workforce.

- **More temporary workers.** The number of workers on temporary contracts has risen since the early 1980s, although in the last few years it has levelled out. In 2000, nearly two million workers were on temporary contracts.
- **Use of annualised hours.** Many businesses face an uneven pattern of work over the year. For example, farms are very busy in the summer months harvesting crops, but are quiet in the winter. Without annualised hours, farmers might pay overtime in the summer and not have enough work to keep employees busy during the winter months.
- **More part-time working.** The number of employees within the UK who work part-time has increased each year. By 2000, more than one-quarter of all employees – nearly seven million people – were part-time workers.
- **Self-employment.** The number of self-employed has fallen recently, but 2.5 million people still work for themselves.
- **Hiring consultants.** Many businesses have replaced full-time employees with consultants, who work for a business for a short time. Consultants are usually very highly skilled, for example IT experts.
- **Use of contractors** Many businesses employ other firms to carry out particular duties. The exact arrangements are set out in a contract between the businesses involved. It is common, for example, to hire contract staff for cleaning, rather than use permanent full-time employees.

STOP & THINK

It is common for businesses to use self-employed people in a number of roles. What benefits might businesses gain from hiring self-employed people?

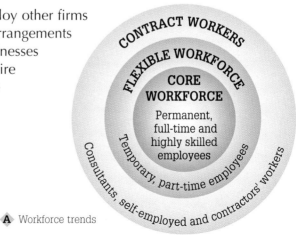

A Workforce trends

Increase in flexible workforces 1992–2000

Source: Office for
National Statistics
www.statistics.gov.uk

	Total employment (millions)	Full-time employees (% of total)	Part-time employees (% of total)	Temporary employees (% of total)	Self-employed (% of total)
1992	25.17	65.37	21.94	5.6	10.26
1995	26.25	64.56	24.43	7.1	10.38
2000	27.98	65.75	25.05	7.0	8.8

■ **Fewer full-time, permanent employees.** Firms use fewer full-time employees than in the past. Full-time employees are expensive, because the business has to pay for their training and contribute to pension schemes on their behalf. Full-time employees normally have to be highly skilled and carry out important roles within a business.

Advantages of flexible workforces to firms

Using flexible workforces offers a number of benefits to businesses.

■ Flexible employees are cheaper. Businesses do not have to pay many of the costs of full-time employment, such as paying workers who are sick. Wages are also generally lower, which helps to keep costs down and to make the business more competitive.

■ Flexible workforces assist businesses in coping with sudden changes in sales. Calling on part-time or self-employed workers at a busy time helps to keep customers satisfied. For example, the Post Office uses large numbers of temporary workers at Christmas.

■ Firms can reduce training costs by employing other businesses to do a particular job, or by hiring self-employed workers who already have the necessary, up-to-date skills.

The UK has 2.5 million self-employed people, about 9 per cent of the workforce. Carry out some research to discover the advantages and disadvantages of being self-employed. Possible sources of information include the following:

■ talking to people who are self-employed and learning from their experiences (this is probably the best source of information)

■ the guides to self-employment that are produced by many banks (these include sections on

OVER TO YOU

its advantages and disadvantages, and you should be able to get a copy from a local branch)

■ websites on self-employment on the internet.

Flexibility, productivity and competition

Flexible working arrangements help businesses to reduce costs by increasing productivity. Productivity is a measurement of how much an employee produces in a fixed time. Higher productivity can enable businesses to step up the competition with other businesses.

1 **Productivity.** If employees increase their output of goods or services each week or month, the business can benefit in several ways.
   - Increased productivity lowers the costs of a business. For example, it takes fewer worker-hours (hours per worker) to produce each car.
   - A business will be able to sell its products at lower prices because they are cheaper to produce. This should mean the business wins more customers.
   - A business may choose to leave its prices unchanged. Because its products have been produced more cheaply, profits on each sale will be greater.

2 **Greater competitiveness.** If a business is more competitive than other firms are, it will be able to:
   - make its products more cheaply
   - supply higher-quality goods
   - have better-designed or more technologically advanced goods
   - provide better advice and support to customers
   - supply goods more quickly.

KEY CONCEPTS

Multi-skilled employees are workers who can carry out a number of jobs within a business.

Productivity is the amount of goods or services produced by an employee over a time period such as a year

Quality is the extent to which a good or service satisfies a consumer. A high-quality product will completely satisfy the customer.

Teamworking is a group of employees working together to complete a task or tasks.

How does UK productivity shown in **A** compare with productivity in countries such as the USA, Germany and Japan? Use the internet and other sources to find out the productivity figures for other countries over the last 10–15 years.

A Productivity figures for UK manufacturing industry, 1984–2001.

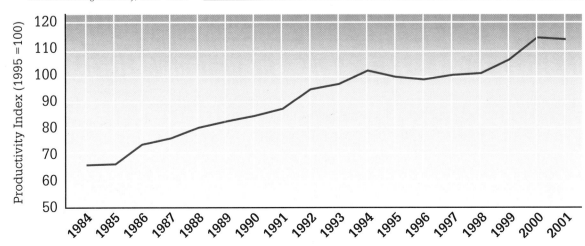

STOP & THINK

Tesco has a large number of supermarkets open for 24 hours a day from Monday to Saturday. What do you think might be the advantages and disadvantages of working in a supermarket with these opening hours?

3 **Improved quality of products.** Nowadays, it is more important for businesses to produce high-quality products. Today's customers are not prepared to accept goods or services that fail to measure up to their expectations. For example, many shops are expected to stay open longer, which means that employees need to be more flexible. They may have to work longer hours, perhaps on a shift system, or be available on a temporary basis to deal with sudden, large orders. Specialist workers may also be employed on temporary contracts to help design new and better products.

4 **New technology.** Introducing new technology has helped businesses to become more competitive. But technology often requires changes in working arrangements.

- Employers will usually want to run expensive machinery 24 hours a day. As a result, employees may be asked to work shifts.
- Machinery may replace full-time jobs. Employees may be offered only temporary or part-time jobs as a result.
- New technology may mean that some employees become teleworkers, such as newspaper journalists who work from home, sending articles to their editors by e-mail.

5 **Teamworking and multi-skilled employees.** Many UK businesses have formed their employees into teams. Each team consists of between five and twenty workers. Teamworking allows employees to use flexitime or shifts so that some staff members are always on duty. Workers in teams should also be multi-skilled so that they can switch easily between jobs.

CASE STUDY

Productivity in the British car industry

The levels of productivity achieved by three British-based Japanese car manufacturers in 2000 are shown below.

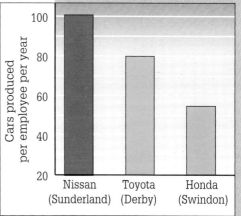

Tasks

1 What is productivity?

2 What advantages might Nissan gain as a result of having the highest level of productivity in the UK (in fact the highest in Europe)?

3 Explain the types of working arrangements that Nissan may have used to achieve high levels of productivity

Benefits and drawbacks

The benefits to employers of more flexible workforces were discussed on pages 94–7. These are summarised in **A** alongside the possible drawbacks. Equally, the effects of changes in working arrangements can have good and bad effects on employees.

Good effects on employees

- Some employees, such as those with responsibilities for looking after young children, want only part-time or temporary work. They would be happy to be part of a flexible workforce.
- Working as part of a team can be a good experience. Employees may enjoy working with other people and learning from more experienced workers. Research shows that working in teams can raise morale.
- Some employees may prefer to be employed as teleworkers, working from home. Teleworkers do not have the cost and the bother of travelling to work every day. They can live where they wish and need not be close to the business that employs them.

A Advantages and disadvantages to businesses of employing flexible workforces

KEY CONCEPTS

Communication is the exchange of information between two or more parties, by talking, writing or other means.

Labour turnover is the number of employees that leave a business each year, expressed as a percentage of the whole workforce. Thus, if 16 employees out of 200 leave during the year, the labour turnover is 8 per cent (16/200 x 100% = 8%).

STOP & THINK

What types of businesses do you think are suited to using flexible workforces?

Advantages to employers	Disadvantages to employers
• Lower costs. Flexible workforces can reduce employment costs, helping a business to compete more effectively with other businesses. For example, using teleworkers means that employers do not have to provide accommodation or heating.	• Communication problems. Employers find it more difficult to communicate with employees who work part-time or with consultants or contractors who may only be available at certain times of the week. Employees also find it more difficult to communicate with one another.
• Experts. Using consultants and self-employed people brings expertise into the business. Businesses need only employ these expensive workers for a short time.	• High labour turnover. People on temporary or part-time contracts might leave if a permanent full-time job becomes available. Businesses with flexible workforces might need to employ new workers frequently. This can be costly.
• Businesses can cope with sudden and unexpected changes in sales. If there is a sudden increase, part-time workers may work longer hours. This means that customers are not kept waiting.	• Businesses that suffer from high levels of labour turnover might have a poor reputation as employers. Even if they offer permanent, full-time jobs, employers with a flexible workforce might find it difficult to attract high-quality workers.
• Training costs. The use of consultants and self-employed people means that businesses do not have to pay to train them. This can save large sums of money.	

- Some employees may like to travel regularly, and do not mind working from different offices or spending time visiting customers. They enjoy the changes and would not like to work in the same office all the time.

Bad effects on employees

- Some workers may be very dissatisfied with temporary contracts. They might want the security of a permanent job and not feel committed to the business. They may feel unsettled, and want to look for other work.
- Workers may find it difficult to form friendships at work if they are always working with different people or moving around between different factories and offices. Teleworking can be very lonely, as there is little contact with other people.
- Many employees do not like working shifts, especially if they change regularly from day to night shifts. Sleeping patterns may be upset, affecting their health, and it can be difficult to have a social life.

CASE STUDY

Honda

Honda is one of the biggest car manufacturers in Britain. It has a large factory in Swindon.

The basic approach to work at Honda is through teamwork. Each employee is a team member, who needs to understand the team goals as well as what his or her individual role is. Every team member has the opportunity to contribute equally to the team.

Source: www.mfg.honda.co.uk

Task

How might working in teams help a new employee starting work with Honda?

OVER TO YOU

Teleworking is becoming more popular in the UK. Try to find out the answers to the following questions about teleworkers:

1 What is it like to be a teleworker?

2 What benefits do businesses gain from employing teleworkers?

The internet is an ideal place to start your research. Some useful websites are:

www.teleworking.co.uk

www.teleworking-survey.co.uk

www.teleworker.nildram.co.uk

The previous 12 pages have given you some idea of what it is like to work in a business. You should now be able to answer the questions that follow.

10 revision questions

Check your knowledge by tackling these questions.

1 Describe **three** tasks carried out by managers within a business. (6 marks)

2 Explain the difference between a supervisor and an operative. (4 marks)

3 Outline **two** activities that support staff may carry out in a business. (6 marks)

4 List **four** things that an organisation chart might tell you about a business. (4 marks)

5 Explain **two** items that might be included in the contract of employment of a teacher. (6 marks)

6 What is meant by the term 'productivity'? (3 marks)

7 Explain **two** benefits that increasing levels of productivity might offer to a business. (6 marks)

8 What is meant by the term 'flexible workforce'? (3 marks)

9 Explain **one** advantage and **one** disadvantage to a business that might result from employing a flexible workforce. (6 marks)

10 Explain **one** advantage and **one** disadvantage to an employee that might result from being part of a flexible workforce. (6 marks)

Total = 50 marks

C A S E   S T U D Y

Lastminute.com

Lastminute.com is an internet-based company that supplies theatre tickets, holidays, travel arrangements, restaurant bookings and other personal services, often at short notice. The company does not have any shops. All orders are taken over the internet and customers pay using credit cards.

Lastminute.com regularly advertises jobs on its website. In what ways might working for this company be different from working in a high street shop, such as Debenhams?

Martha Lane Fox and Brent Hoberman, the founders of lastminute.com Source: www.guardian.co.uk/galleryguide

PUTTING IT INTO PRACTICE

By now, you should have completed the first part of your portfolio evidence, looking at the roles and importance of stakeholders for your chosen business.

The second part will cover many of the topics you have studied recently. You will need to consider:

- the way in which your business is organised, including major job roles
- the working arrangements that exist within the business.

Again, you will need to check which Awarding Body (AQA, Edexcel or OCR) you are using. Once you know this, you can choose the correct column from the following table. This will guide you in writing the second part of your portfolio evidence.

	AWARDING BODY		
What you have to do	**AQA**	**Edexcel**	**OCR**
Describe or identify	• Describe, using notes and a chart, how the business is organised. • Identify the roles of three different people in the same functional area of the business (for example, marketing or administration).	• Describe three important job roles carried out within your chosen business. • Describe the working arrangements for these three employees noting similarities and differences.	• Describe the roles of three employees who have different roles and responsibilities within the business.
Explain or analyse	• Explain how the roles of the three people described earlier in your portfolio evidence are different. • Explain the working arrangements and rewards (pay and holidays, for example) for your three chosen employees showing similarities and differences.	• Analyse how the job roles carried out help the business to operate effectively. • Analyse the working arrangements in place in the business based on detailed research.	• Explain the contract of employment for one of the three people described in the previous part of your portfolio evidence. This should include terms and conditions of employment and working arrangements.
Evaluate (this may mean making judgements or offering and justifying suggestions)	• Suggest ways in which the business might make use of flexible working arrangements in the future.	• Suggest how job roles and working arrangements might be altered to improve the performance of the business.	• Evaluate, using examples, how well the contract of employment explained earlier in your portfolio evidence meets the needs of the employees and the business. • Based on this, recommend and justify some suitable changes to the contract of employment.

OVER TO YOU

Recent advances in information technology have had a huge impact on businesses. IT has:

■ changed the working arrangements for many employees

■ altered the ways in which people carry out their jobs.

Work with someone else in your teaching group, and each of you try to arrange to talk to two people working in business. If possible, the two people you talk to should be in different jobs with different businesses. Ask them:

■ how they use IT in their jobs

■ how IT has changed the ways in which they work.

Then prepare a report on your findings to present to the rest of the group.

Fairness in employment law

The law is a framework of rules controlling the way that society is run. These rules apply to businesses and to individuals. Employment law attempts to strike a balance in the workplace between the rights of employers and the rights of employees. It tries to allow employers to use labour flexibly, but prevent them from treating employees unfairly.

Unfair treatment includes unfair discrimination – that is, treating employees differently for reasons of their gender, their race or any disability that they may have.

On pages 82–4 we looked at the rights of employers and employees. Reread those pages and then see how employment law tries to protect these rights.

Laws on the rights of individual employees

Laws protecting the rights of individual employees have increased greatly over the last thirty years or so. The most important laws are the following:

1 **National Minimum Wage Act, 1998.** This highly publicised Act came into force on 1 April 1999. The key features of the new legislation were:
   - a general minimum wage of £3.60 per hour;
   - a minimum level of £3.00 an hour for 18–21 year olds;
   - employees on piece-work (work paid for by the amount produced) must receive at least the minimum wage;
   - all part-time and temporary workers must be paid the minimum wage.

In 2002 the general minimum wage was set at £4.20 per hour, and the 18–21 year olds' minimum wage at £3.60 per hour.

2 **Equal Pay Act, 1970.** This Act says that businesses must treat employees of both sexes equally. Therefore a woman doing the same job as a man must receive the same pay and have similar working conditions.

STOP & THINK

If you felt your employer had discriminated against you, to whom might you turn for advice and support?

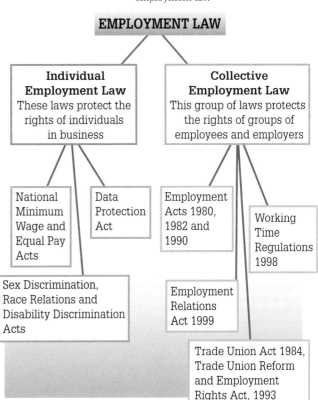

A Individual and collective employment law

EMPLOYMENT LAW

Individual Employment Law
These laws protect the rights of individuals in business

- National Minimum Wage and Equal Pay Acts
- Data Protection Act
- Sex Discrimination, Race Relations and Disability Discrimination Acts

Collective Employment Law
This group of laws protects the rights of groups of employees and employers

- Employment Acts 1980, 1982 and 1990
- Working Time Regulations 1998
- Employment Relations Act 1999
- Trade Union Act 1984, Trade Union Reform and Employment Rights Act, 1993

3 **Sex Discrimination Acts, 1975 and 1986.** These Acts outlaw discrimination on grounds of sex or marital status in employment and education. Thus, businesses cannot advertise jobs for only men (or only women) and must not treat men and women differently when choosing employees for promotion. It is also illegal to discriminate against someone because he or she is married, or because that person is unmarried.

4 **Race Relations Act, 1976.** This Act makes it unlawful to discriminate, in employment, against men or women on the grounds of race, colour or ethnic background. For example, it would be illegal for businesses to refuse to employ workers because they were black or because they were Asian.

5 **Disability Discrimination Act, 1995.** This Act makes it illegal for an employer to treat a disabled person less favourably than other staff. It further requires employers to make 'reasonable adjustments' to the working environment so that disabled people can be employed. Employers might be expected to build ramps to allow wheelchair access and to adapt equipment so that disabled people can use it.

6 **Data Protection Act, 1998.** This Act protects employees who have information about them held on computer. Businesses holding information in this way must keep the data secure and ensure that it is accurate. Under the Act, employees have the right to see their personal files, and personal details cannot be passed on to other businesses without their agreement.

You have more options at school than ever before. Don't limit yourself. Because if you think differently, you will go further.
For more information contact Education.Training@eoc.org.uk
Telephone: 0161 838 8331 www.eoc.org.uk
Women. Men. Different. Equal.
Equal Opportunities Commission

STOP & THINK

In spite of the Equal Pay Act of 1970, women still generally earn less than men do. Why do you think that this happens?

Industrial tribunals

If an employee makes a claim against an employer for discrimination or other unfair treatment, the case will be heard at an industrial tribunal. These are informal courts, set up to hear employees' complaints about their employers. Each tribunal consists of three people: a chairperson, who has legal training, and two others, one of whom represents the employer's interests, and the other the interests of the employee. If a tribunal decides in favour of the employee, he or she may receive compensation.

OVER TO YOU

The Equal Opportunities Commission supports employees who have been discriminated against. Find out more about their work and the types of cases they get involved in.

You can write to them, phone them, fax them, e-mail them or look at their website.

Equal Opportunities Commission, 36 Broadway, London, SW1H 0BH.

Tel: 020 7222 0004; Fax: 020 7222 2810
E-mail: media@eoc.org.uk

Website: www.eoc.org.uk.

Employment laws

Since 1980, many laws have been passed covering the relationship between employers and employees, the activities of trade unions and health and safety. Laws passed since 1997, under a Labour government, have generally been more favourable to the interests of employees and trade unions than the laws introduced earlier by the Conservative government.

The major laws passed include:

1 **Employment Acts, 1980 and 1982.** These Acts reduced the power of trade unions in the workplace.
   - They allowed employers to refuse to negotiate with unions.
   - Striking employees were allowed to picket only their own place of work.

2 **The Trade Union Act, 1984.** This Act required trade unions to allow its members at a workplace to vote by secret ballot before the union could take industrial action such as strike action.

3 **Employment Act, 1990.** Closed shops (workplaces where employees had to belong to a trade union) were made illegal under this law. Also, employers were allowed to sack employees who took strike action without first conducting a secret ballot.

4 **Trade Union Reform and Employment Rights Act, 1993.** This Act required unions to give employers a week's notice of industrial action. The idea was to provide a 'cooling off' period, which was intended to make industrial action less likely.

5 **Employment Relations Act, 1999.** This Act gave up to three months' parental leave to both mothers and fathers, and increased the compensation paid to employees who had been unfairly treated. The Act also required an employer to recognise a trade union that is supported by over 50 per cent of the employees in a business. Being recognised gives the union the legal right to negotiate with the employer on pay and working conditions.

6 **Working-time Regulations, 1998.** This law was passed by the European Union. The regulations make it illegal for an employer to force employees to work more than an average of 48 hours a week. It also limits hours that can be worked during shifts.

KEY CONCEPTS

Health and safety is the part of a business's activities that is devoted to providing all employees with a secure and risk-free working environment.

A **trade union** is an organisation of workers from many businesses that represents its members in negotiations with employers and seeks to protect their interests.

Industrial action is any action taken against an employer by employees, usually trade union members, during a dispute. Examples include strikes and 'go-slows' (when employees work more slowly than usual).

STOP & THINK

Under closed shop agreements, you had to be a member of a particular trade union before you could work in a particular business; or you had to join a particular trade union once you were employed in a particular business. How did closed shops affect the rights of employees and employers?

Health and safety laws

Health and safety laws prevent businesses putting employees in danger, and protect the workforce. The laws try to stop accidents happening in the workplace.

The main act in the UK is the Health and Safety Act of 1974. Under this law, employers are required to 'ensure that they safeguard all their employees' health, safety and welfare at work'. The Act covers many business activities:

■ installing and maintaining safety equipment, and supplying safety clothing
■ maintaining workplace temperatures
■ giving employees sufficient breaks during the working day
■ providing protection against dangerous substances
■ fitting guards on dangerous machinery
■ writing and displaying a safety policy.

The Act also requires employees to follow all health and safety procedures and to take care of their own and others' safety. The Health and Safety Executive (HSE) oversees the operation of the Act, carries out inspections of business premises and conducts investigations after any serious accident in the workplace.

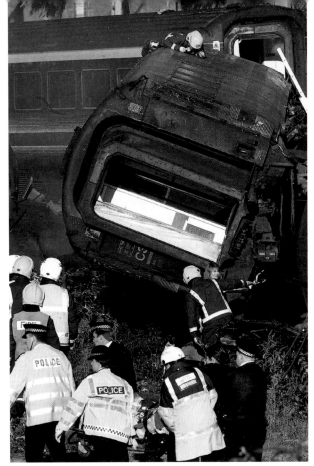

Paddington rail crash 1999

STOP & THINK

Health and safety laws are regularly updated. The rail crash at Paddington in October 1999 led to new laws on health and safety for rail companies. The introduction of new technology can also bring about the need for new health and safety laws.

In what ways might using computers for long hours cause a health risk for employees?

OVER TO YOU

This activity requires you to write to a trade union for information. Choose a trade union that might operate in the business that you plan to use for your Unit 2 assignment. If you do not know the address of your chosen trade union, you will find it listed on the TUC's website (www.tuc.org.uk). Ask the trade union for information on:

■ employees' rights in the workplace

■ employers' rights in the workplace

■ the role of trade unions within businesses.

This information will help you to complete your assignment.

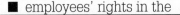

STOP & THINK

In what ways can employees help to make the workplace safer?

Disagreements and disputes

Disputes at the workplace can occur for a variety of reasons. Disagreement over pay or the threat of unemployment is often the cause. Sometimes employees' jobs are threatened because the employer no longer needs those jobs to be done, or wants to change the working arrangements. Job losses in these circumstances are called redundancies.

Disputes can arise when, for example:

- employers and employees cannot reach an agreement over pay rates or working conditions
- employers want to make some employees redundant and the employees affected are not prepared to lose their jobs
- employees believe that they have been unfairly dismissed
- employees have a major disagreement with another employee or a manager.

Using internal methods to settle disagreements

Businesses can attempt to settle disagreements or grievances (charges of unfair treatment by employees) internally. They can talk to the other parties involved, such as the employees concerned or the trade union representing them.

1 **Using business grievance procedures.** A grievance procedure is a set of rules stating the methods to be used to settle a grievance. Grievances can occur when an employee appears to treat a work colleague unfairly.
   - The number of stages in the grievance procedure will depend on the size of the business. Small businesses may only have a single stage.

KEY CONCEPTS

A **grievance** is a complaint by an employee about his or her treatment at work.

Redundancy is a situation affecting one or more employees in which employment is ended because their job or jobs no longer exist.

Unfair dismissal is the ending of a worker's contract of employment without good reason.

STOP & THINK

Why do most businesses seek to settle a grievance at the informal stage – as close to the start of the complaint as possible?

A A typical grievance procedure

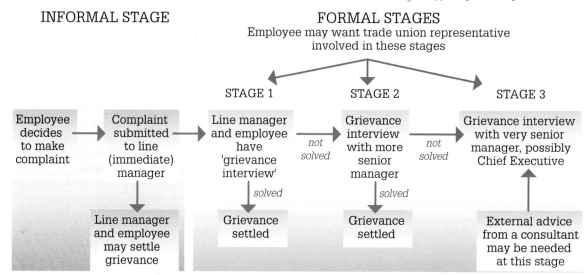

INFORMAL STAGE

FORMAL STAGES
Employee may want trade union representative involved in these stages

STAGE 1   STAGE 2   STAGE 3

Employee decides to make complaint → Complaint submitted to line (immediate) manager → Line manager and employee have 'grievance interview' — *not solved* → Grievance interview with more senior manager — *not solved* → Grievance interview with very senior manager, possibly Chief Executive

Line manager and employee may settle grievance

solved → Grievance settled

solved → Grievance settled

External advice from a consultant may be needed at this stage

STOP & THINK

What advantages might employees gain from working for a business that has a grievance procedure?

CASE STUDY

Union negotiations end dispute

Train drivers working for Britain's biggest railway company, Connex, have reached an agreement over the length of the working week. The agreement came after lengthy negotiations between the company and the train drivers' union, ASLEF.

The drivers had wanted an immediate reduction in working time to 35 hours a week. An agreement was reached giving a 36-hour week immediately, with a further one-hour reduction in a year's time. It is thought that this will result in the company needing an extra 80 train drivers.

Source: Adapted from BBC news on www.bbc.co.uk, 28 January 2000

Tasks

1 Suggest two actions that the trade union might have taken in support of its claim.

2 What factors might have helped the train driver's union (ASLEF) to reach a settlement in the negotiations?

3 Do you think that disputes are more easily settled when trade unions are involved in negotiations?

- Managers should respond quickly to a grievance interview and give a decision within about ten days.
- Employees have the legal right to have a trade union official or a friend sit in on every stage of the grievance procedure.
- All medium-size and large businesses are required by law to have a formal grievance procedure.
- A copy of the grievance procedure is often given to new employees with their contract of employment.

2 **Negotiations with trade unions or other employee organisations.** Trade unions or other groups representing employees may play a role in settling some disagreements. Trade unions are likely to become involved in disputes about pay and working conditions as well as claims of unfair dismissal. Trade unions may help to settle disagreements in a number of ways.

- Trade union members who are employees of the business may talk to managers on behalf of other employees and attempt to settle the dispute.
- The trade union may call in its full-time officials (employees of the union who are usually skilled negotiators and experts in employment issues) to help to settle the dispute.
- The trade union can place the management under pressure by threatening to take industrial action. The threat of a strike may persuade the employer to reach a settlement.

If a dispute remains unsettled, a number of outside organisations can be called on to help resolve the issue. We will look at these organisations on pages 108–9.

Using external organisations

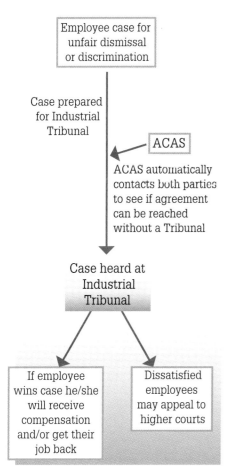

```
┌─────────────────┐
│ Employee case for│
│ unfair dismissal │
│ or discrimination│
└─────────────────┘
        │
        ▼
Case prepared
for Industrial        ┌──────┐
Tribunal              │ ACAS │
                      └──────┘
        ACAS automatically
        contacts both parties
        to see if agreement
        can be reached
        without a Tribunal
        │
        ▼
┌─────────────────┐
│   Case heard at │
│   Industrial    │
│   Tribunal      │
└─────────────────┘
     │         │
     ▼         ▼
┌──────────┐ ┌──────────┐
│If employee│ │Dissatisfied│
│wins case  │ │employees  │
│he/she     │ │may appeal │
│will receive│ │to higher  │
│compensation│ │courts     │
│and/or get  │ └──────────┘
│their      │
│job back   │
└──────────┘
```

A ACAS and industrial tribunal procedures

Industrial tribunals

Also known as 'employment tribunals', industrial tribunals are used to settle most disputes about discrimination and unfair dismissal.

- Industrial tribunals are, in reality, informal courts where employees can put their own cases.
- Employees can take their case to an industrial tribunal at no charge.
- Tribunals are made up of three members: a lawyer as a chairperson, an employer representative and an employee representative.
- Industrial tribunals are found throughout the country, so there is one close to most businesses.

Advisory, Conciliation and Arbitration Service (ACAS)

ACAS was set up in 1975 with the aim of preventing or settling industrial disputes. ACAS works on behalf of both employers and employees and offers a number of services to both.

It can act as a mediator – a go-between – in a dispute, talking to each of the parties involved.

It can also, with the agreement of the parties in a dispute, impose a settlement.

1 **Arbitration.** This is a method of settling a dispute where the arbitrator – a neutral person (or persons) – is appointed. The arbitrator listens to the arguments of both sides and then makes a decision. There are three main types of arbitration:

KEY CONCEPTS

Arbitration is an attempt to settle a dispute through the use of a neutral third party.

Conciliation is negotiation with the intention of reaching an agreement in a dispute.

An **industrial dispute** is a major disagreement between an employer and employees (or trade union) over matters such as pay and working conditions.

Mediation is acting as a go-between by talking to both sides in a dispute.

STOP & THINK

Why might an employee be nervous about taking an employer to an industrial tribunal?

Enter the ACAS website (www.acas.org,uk) and select the questions and answers page.
Find out the minimum holiday entitlement for all employees.

- non-binding arbitration, in which the arbitrator makes a decision that the employer and employees do not have to accept
- binding arbitration, in which employers and employees must accept the decision of the arbitrator
- pendulum arbitration, a special form of binding arbitration in which the arbitrator has to decide to accept completely the case of one side or the other and may not offer a compromise.

2 **Conciliation.** This is a method of settling individual or collective disputes where a neutral third party, called a conciliator, encourages both sides to keep talking. The conciliator hopes to avoid industrial action by employees, by encouraging both sides to reach a settlement. The conciliator's role does not involve making any decisions.

The main roles of ACAS are:

- preventing and settling industrial disputes through the use of arbitration, mediation and conciliation
- settling disputes over employment rights, including cases of discrimination and unfair dismissal, before they reach an industrial tribunal
- providing information and advice on employment matters, such as negotiation methods, grievance procedures and contracts of employment
- encouraging people to work together effectively to help avoid disagreements.

ACAS has seen a 21 per cent rise in discrimination cases in the last year. In 2000/1 there were 17,657 complaints about sex, race or disability discrimination, compared to 14,543 in 1999/2000. The overall number of complaints referred to ACAS for 2000/1 was 105,304.

The European Court of Justice

The Justice Court, based in Luxembourg, has judges from all the countries of the European Union. It is a final court of appeal for employees who feel that they have not been treated fairly at an industrial tribunal.

The Court rules on issues that relate to laws passed by the European Union. For example, in 2001 it ruled that those on short-term temporary contracts had the right to paid holidays. British courts had decided that employees could not receive holiday pay until they had worked for an employer for at least 13 weeks. The European Court of Justice overruled that decision.

CASE STUDY

ACAS settles prison officers' dispute

ACAS played an important part in settling a dispute over working conditions in Scotland's prisons. ACAS was asked to help, after prison officers went on strike last month. Negotiations had been going on for three years. The disagreement was caused by the employers (Scottish Prisons Service) asking prison officers to move to shift working. The Scottish Prison Service argued that these changes would save money.

ACAS persuaded Scotland's 4,500 prison officers to end their strike action in return for the Scottish Prisons Service's agreeing to binding arbitration.

Source: www.bbc.co.uk/news 29 May 2001

Tasks

1 What is binding arbitration?

2 Why might the prison officers have agreed to call off their strike action in return for binding arbitration?

3 Why do you think the prison officers felt so strongly as to take strike action?

STOP & THINK

Why might pendulum arbitration stop disagreements arising in the first place?

In the previous eight pages you were introduced to the laws that protect employees and employers within businesses and saw how disputes can be settled. You should now be able to answer the questions that follow.

10 revision questions

Check your knowledge by tackling these questions.

1 Name **four** laws that protect individual employees in Britain. (4 marks)

2 What are industrial tribunals? Describe how they can help employees. (5 marks)

3 Outline **two** Acts of Parliament that may affect trade unions. (6 marks)

4 List **four** aspects of the working of businesses that are covered by the Health and Safety at Work Act, 1974. (4 marks)

5 Explain **two** factors that might cause a dispute or disagreement at work. (6 marks)

6 Explain what the term 'grievance procedure' means. (3 marks)

7 Describe **three** duties carried out by the Advisory, Conciliation and Arbitration Service (ACAS). (6 marks)

8 Distinguish between arbitration and conciliation. (4 marks)

9 Explain **three** different types of arbitration. (6 marks)

10 Explain **two** ways in which trade unions might help to settle disputes at work. (6 marks)

Total = 50 marks

The government has confirmed that employment laws banning discrimination on the grounds of age are on the way. The laws on age discrimination will be introduced by 2006 and will be similar to existing race and sex discrimination laws. The new law will cover all workers including young, old, temporary employees and self-employed. Employees found to be suffering from age discrimination will receive compensation.

The new laws will mean that employees can work for as long as they like. There will not be a compulsory retirement age for employees. What might be the **disadvantages** of this for:

■ employers
■ employees?

PUTTING IT INTO PRACTICE

By this stage, your portfolio evidence should be well under way. You should already have written about stakeholders, job roles and working arrangements. The third part of your evidence will cover:

- how a business settles disputes at work
- employment law, which you studied recently, as well as employee and employer rights, which you studied earlier.

Once again, you will need to check which Awarding Body (AQA, Edexcel or OCR) you are using. Then, you can choose the correct column from the following table. This will guide you in writing the third part of your portfolio evidence.

AWARDING BODY			
What you have to do	AQA	Edexcel	OCR
Describe or identify	▪ Describe the main laws that protect employees at work. ▪ Identify possible health and safety risks at work for the three different people identified earlier in your portfolio evidence. ▪ Identify the groups that employees may join to help create good working relationships.	▪ Describe employer and employee rights within your chosen business. ▪ Describe procedures to deal with disputes and health and safety issues within the business. ▪ Describe the main laws relating to employer and employee rights.	▪ Describe the rights of employers and employees, using examples from your chosen business.
Explain or analyse	▪ Explain what the business does to stop accidents occurring at work. ▪ Explain how the business deals with disputes at work.	▪ Explain how employment law protects the rights of employees and employers within your chosen business. ▪ Explain how procedures have been used in the selected business during a dispute.	▪ Explain how the business settles disagreements with its employees over employment rights and working conditions. You should use examples from your chosen business.
Evaluate (this may mean making judgements or offering and justifying suggestions)	▪ Evaluate how successful one of the employee groups has been in implementing a recent change in the business. Such changes might include a change in the law or a new pay system.	▪ Evaluate the effectiveness of the procedures in the business for settling disputes and dealing with health and safety issues. You must support your arguments with evidence from your chosen business.	▪ Evaluate the extent to which your chosen business makes sure that it has good working relationships with its employees.

Recruitment and training

If a business is to succeed, it is important that the employees have the right skills and attitudes. This can be achieved through recruitment and training, as shown in . The human resources department has responsibility for recruiting and training employees.

We looked at the work of the human resources department in Unit 1 (pages 38–9). Recruitment and training are just two of the many responsibilities of this department.

Internal recruitment

Firms may recruit internally by promoting or retraining existing employees. This can offer a number of benefits.

- Candidates will have experience of the business and will be familiar with the firm's procedures.
- Internal candidates will know many of the people they will be working with.
- Internal recruitment provides employees with the chance of promotion, which may help to motivate them.
- Internal recruitment is cheaper, as it avoids the need for expensive advertising.
- Choosing the right candidate may be easier, as more is known about the applicants.

However, internal candidates are drawn from a limited number of applicants, and the skills and experience of this group of people may not meet the needs of the business. Internal recruitment is unlikely to be used to appoint senior managers.

External recruitment

Employers may be keen to have a wider choice of candidates and seek to recruit externally. Appointing from outside the business can have certain advantages.

- It can attract applications from higher-quality candidates, especially if the job is advertised nationally.

STOP & THINK

Why might employees need to have training regularly throughout their working lives?

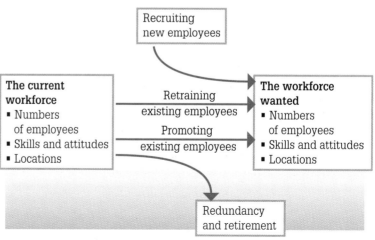

A Getting the right workforce

STOP & THINK

Do you think an organisation with a low level of labour turnover should try to recruit internally? Explain your answer.

OVER TO YOU

Look at the job advertisements in your local newspaper (Many local newspapers have a jobs' supplement on one day each week.) Are there any jobs advertised there that you think you could apply for? Are there any that you would like to apply for? Do you have the right skills for the jobs that attract you?

- External candidates can bring new ideas and fresh enthusiasm into the business.
- External recruitment can bring in new employees with the necessary skills, without the need for retraining, which can take time.

But although external recruitment offers the benefits of a greater number of candidates, it is likely to be expensive. External recruitment is also more risky because candidates are not well known to the employer.

Firms recruiting externally use a range of methods.

- **Headhunting.** Firms try to attract high-quality employees (usually senior managers) working for other organisations to come and work for them instead. This is called headhunting. For example, the television sports presenter Des Lynam was headhunted by ITV from the BBC. He was given a four-year contract of employment, estimated to be worth £1.25 million, to present 'The Premiership', a football programme.
- **Advertising.** Businesses advertise in newspapers and magazines, or on the web, and invite interested people to apply by a certain date. Advertising is a common method of filling job vacancies.
- **Job centres.** The Department for Education and Skills (DES) runs job centres, which can put businesses in touch with suitably qualified, unemployed workers.
- **Employment agencies.** The private-sector equivalent of job centres are employment agencies. These provide employers with details of suitable applicants for posts that they may have vacant.

CASE STUDY

Debenhams

The high-street department store Debenhams has said that it is to open two new shops, one in Bradford and one in Londonderry, in Northern Ireland. The company says that this will create 500 new jobs in areas with high unemployment.

Debenhams is continuing with its objective of growth, and will have 106 stores in the UK by the end of 2006. The company also announced that its annual profits had risen by nearly 13 per cent over the previous year to £146 million.

Source: Text adapted from www.bbc.co.uk/news 23 October, 2001

Tasks

1 How might Debenhams recruit the employees for its new stores?

2 What, do you think, would be the advantages and disadvantages of working for a large business like Debenhams?

Attracting the right applicants

Every business tries to develop a body of employees that will enable it to attain its objectives. This process is called workforce planning. Getting the right person to fill a job vacancy is very important. If someone is chosen who turns out to be unsuitable, a business may suffer.

- The person appointed will not do the job effectively.
- The business will have the expense of recruiting someone else.

Some businesses employ specialist staff to look after recruitment for the whole organisation. In other businesses, managers and team leaders have responsibility for recruitment.

Filling job vacancies

Information for applicants to fill job vacancies is provided by business in several ways.

1 **Job descriptions.** A job description gives detailed information about the position to be filled. It also explains what is expected of the person appointed to the job.

We examined job descriptions in detail on pages 90–1. It may be worth looking at these pages again before reading further.

2 **Person specifications.**
Sometimes these are called job specifications. They set out the qualifications and skills required in an employee, which might include the following:
- certain educational and vocational qualifications
- special skills, for example, excellent communication skills
- the ability to work as part of a team
- any necessary experience.

Some qualities and qualifications may be listed as 'essential', others as 'desirable'. Person specifications are very important to businesses. They serve as a measure against which applications can be judged. Someone whose qualities and qualifications closely match the person specification may prove to be very suitable for the post.

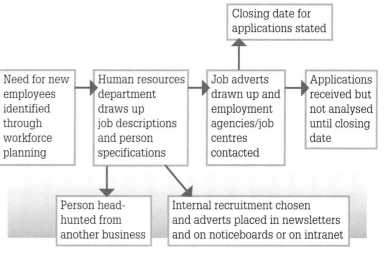

| Need for new employees identified through workforce planning | Human resources department draws up job descriptions and person specifications | Job adverts drawn up and employment agencies/job centres contacted | Applications received but not analysed until closing date |

Closing date for applications stated

Person head-hunted from another business

Internal recruitment chosen and adverts placed in newsletters and on noticeboards or on intranet

A The stages in the recruitment process

If you were interested in a job and the business had sent you an application form, what other information would you expect to receive from them at the same time?

STOP & THINK

Imagine you have decided to apply for a job and have received information about the position. What use do you think you could make of the person specification?

3 Job advertisements. These will contain information such as:

- the name of the business advertising the job
- information about the business
- the job title
- some description of the duties of the advertised post
- an outline of the qualities and qualifications expected in applicants
- where the job is located
- possible salary and working hours.

Highly skilled and professional positions might require advertising nationally, or even internationally. Some businesses use employment agencies to draw up their job descriptions and person specifications and place their job advertisements.

Stages in the application process

Businesses that get the application procedure right will simplify the selection process by reducing the number of candidates.

The business should advertise the job and send job descriptions and person specifications to all candidates expressing an interest. Some candidates will take their application no further because they see that they are unsuitable for the position. Those who are left, who do pursue their application, are likely to be

- genuinely interested in the position
- better qualified for it.

STOP & THINK

Why might a business decide to use an employment agency to advertise its jobs?

B An extract from an advertisement for a job at a primary school

We can offer you:

- A vibrant culturally and socially diverse community in which to work
- Committed and hardworking staff who help children to reach their full potential
- The opportunity to build your own senior management team
- Supportive and committed Governors
- Opportunities for the school to benefit from the new Sports Centre development

Can you offer us?

- Substantial teaching experience and the ability to lead by example
- School management experience as a team leader or deputy in the primary range
- The drive to continue to improve all aspects of the school
- The ability to inspire and motivate all who work in and with the school
- Awareness of and commitment to working in a multicultural school

OVER TO YOU

Imagine you are a human resources manager for Next plc – the fashion clothing shop. You want to appoint a manager for a new shop you are opening in Warwick. Use ICT to design a job advert, giving relevant information. Use the list under '3 Job advertisements' and **B** as a guide on what to include. You can make up details such as addresses, working conditions and pay.

Choosing the right person

Once an employer has drawn up a 'shortlist' of applicants – a list of those who, from their written applications, would seem to be the best candidates for the job – various techniques are used to make the final choice.

```
┌─────────────────────────┐
│ Consider applications   │
│ (match against person   │
│ specification)          │
└─────────────────────────┘
            │
            ▼
┌─────────────────────────┐
│ Draw up shortlist of    │
│ applicants (6–12 people)│
└─────────────────────────┘
            │
            ▼
┌─────────────────────────┐
│ Shortlisted applicants  │
│ attend selection        │
│ procedures              │
│    • interviews         │
│    • psychometric tests │
│    • aptitude tests     │
│    • assessment centres │
│ • references from       │
│   previous employers    │
└─────────────────────────┘
            │
            ▼
┌─────────────────────────┐
│ Select best applicant   │
│ on basis of application │
│ and performance in      │
│ selection procedures    │
└─────────────────────────┘
            │
            ▼
┌─────────────────────────┐
│ Send applicant letter   │
│ of appointment          │
└─────────────────────────┘
```

A The selection procedure

STOP & THINK

Do you think that businesses should tell unsuccessful candidates why they haven't got the job? Explain your answer.

KEY CONCEPTS

Selection is the process of assessing applicants for a job in order to pick the most suitable one (or ones).

Ethical behaviour is doing what you know is right, and not being swayed by other considerations.

1 **Interviews.** A face-to-face interview with the candidate has been, and still is, the commonest method of selection.
   - An interview may be conducted by one or two interviewers or even by a panel of up to twelve people.
   - Interviews are relatively cheap and allow a two-way exchange of information.
   - But they are not entirely reliable as a method of selection, as some people naturally come across better at an interview than others.
   - Applicants that interview well will not always perform well if appointed.

2 **Psychometric tests.** Special tests, called psychometric tests, are designed to reveal a candidate's personality. They are used to assess whether a person is suitable for recruitment or promotion. Often the tests include multiple-choice questions intended to show an applicant's commitment or ability to work as part of a team.

3 **Assessment centres.** Because businesses are aware of the high costs of selecting the wrong applicant, they are making more use of assessment centres. There, the shortlisted applicants go through a range of selection techniques, which can take from two to four days. The selection procedures might include some or all of the following:
   - simulations of circumstances that might occur within the job
   - various interviews
   - role-plays involving a number of the candidates and assessment centre staff
   - psychometric tests.

The use of assessment centres allows applicants to be compared in situations that they might face in the job and

Face-to-face interviews are not always a reliable way of choosing the best applicant!

under the same pressures. To increase the efficiency of this process, some centres bring in staff that will be working with the person selected.

Evidence suggests that assessment centres are effective in selecting employees for managerial positions. However, using them is much more expensive than traditional interviews, so they are less likely to be used to recruit more-junior staff.

4 **Aptitude tests.** Tests designed to provide an insight into a candidate's current ability and his or her potential are called aptitude tests. These can also be used to assess intelligence and job-related skills.

5 **References.** Most businesses ask applicants to provide references from previous employers or from people who know them well. These referees, as they are called, are normally asked to comment on the applicant's suitability for the job. Firms usually ask for two references.

The law in recruitment and selection

Businesses must obey employment laws when recruiting and selecting new employees (see pages 102–3). Discriminating against applicants in the recruitment and selection process on the grounds of their race, sex or disability is illegal.

- When a new position is advertised, existing employees who may want to apply must be given the same opportunities as outside candidates.
- To refuse to employ someone because that person is, or because he or she is not, a member of a trade union is illegal.
- Applicants who believe that they have been refused a job unfairly may take their case to an industrial tribunal. If they win, they will receive compensation.
- It is a criminal offence to recruit someone to work in the UK who has no immigration authorisation.

Ethical recruitment

Even if employers do not break the law in their recruitment methods, they should still behave ethically – that is, properly and impartially. It is easy for managers to allow their personal feelings to influence the recruitment and selection process. For example, they might put someone on the shortlist because they think that person is attractive, or because they know the applicant personally. No one who favours any of the candidates for reasons other than trying to find the best person to fill the post should be conducting job interviews.

STOP & THINK

People applying for their first job are normally interviewed. What do you think an employer can find out from interviewing someone who is applying for his or her first job? What might the employer not find out?

Working in pairs, prepare questions for an interview for the position of manager of the Warwick branch of Next. You drew up the job advert in 'Over to You' on page 115. Once your questions are complete, interview one another with your teacher watching, to give advice and help.

Writing a job application

A written application for a job will require you to prepare two important documents:

- a curriculum vitae (CV) – a summary of your education and work experience – or a completed application form (rarely both)
- a letter of application.

CURRICULUM VITAE

Personal details:	*Name, address, telephone number, date of birth*
Education:	*Dates (years), names of schools and colleges*
Qualifications:	*Dates (year only), examinations, subjects and grades*
Work experience:	*Start with your most recent or present job. Give the dates (year or month and year) of employment, name of firm and address, if relevant. Include details of holiday jobs and any temporary or voluntary work.*
Achievements:	*Information about specific achievements. These might be work-related; personal, such as getting awards for voluntary work or winning prizes; or non-academic qualifications, such as in first aid or sport.*
Interests and hobbies:	*Give examples, and especially ones that demonstrate interests or skills relevant to your application.*
Additional information:	*Provide any other information that you think will support your application, such as specialist knowledge or an ability to speak another language.*
References:	*Referees are usually teachers and/or employers. You can use ministers of religion, youth leaders or someone who knows you well. (You must ask referees' permission before you include them on your CV).*

A The structure and contents of a CV

Curriculum vitae (CV)

CVs are often requested in job advertisements. Your CV is a personal marketing tool. It gives you the chance to sell yourself to potential employers. Use your CV to emphasise your strong points.

- Employers use CVs (along with a letter of application) to decide which candidates to interview.
- If a CV is requested in the job advert, do as is asked and send in your CV.
- When you send in your CV, always enclose a covering letter.
- A general, all-purpose CV is one that can be copied and sent for every job application.
- Keep your CV up to date by amending it regularly.

Composing a CV

Decide on the headings that best present your positive points. You might, for instance, decide to start with your skills, abilities and achievements that have been gained through hobbies, sport or similar activities. This could be useful for young applicants who have little or no employment or work experience to offer.

Completing application forms

If you are sent an application form, do not rush in filling it out. To avoid making mistakes, you might find it worthwhile to take a photocopy of the form and complete that first.

- Do not answer questions on the form unless you are sure of their meaning.
- Make sure that you answer all the questions that you are supposed to answer.

Letters of application

Letters of application are usually written in support of a CV or completed application form.

- The letter should explain why you are applying for the job and how your experience, skills and qualifications make you a suitable applicant.
- You should be positive and emphasise your strengths.
- Address your letter to a named person, if possible. If you don't have a name, telephone the business and ask.
- Put your own address and telephone number at the top right of the letter and the date and the name and address of the organisation at the top left.
- Preferably, use a computer to write the letter, as a first draft can then easily be amended. Ask a teacher or relative to check your letter before sending it.
- Your letter should sound enthusiastic about the job being advertised.
- Say where you saw the vacancy, or where you heard about the company.
- If there is a closing date for applications, make sure you send yours off to arrive in good time.

STOP & THINK

How might the job description and person specification help you to write a letter of application for a job?

OVER TO YOU

Now that you have read the advice on how to do it, prepare a CV for yourself. Using a computer, type and print a draft copy following the format shown in **A**. When you have done this, show it to your teacher for comment. Once your CV is complete, be sure to keep it on computer file, so that is available for when you apply for a job. By then, it might need updating.

The interview

Getting invited to an interview means that your CV (or application form) and letter of application must have impressed the business enough for them to want to meet you. However, your application on paper must be followed up by thorough preparation for the interview. You need to discover as much as you can about the business and to plan carefully for the big day.

Find out about the employer and the job. In particular, try to discover the answers to the following questions:

- What type of business organisation is it?
- What products does the firm sell?
- Does the firm sell to other businesses or to certain types of customers?
- Precisely what tasks would you have to carry out if you were to work for this business?
- How might you prepare yourself for a job with this firm?

To find out information on a company you could:

- ask if the business has an information pack
- talk to people that you know who are, or have been, employed by the business
- look up the business in a directory such as UK Kompass Register at your local or school library.

KEY CONCEPTS

A **psychometric test** is a method designed to assess someone's intelligence and personality by asking questions.

Preparing for the interview

You need to think ahead to the day of the interview about practical matters such as where you have to go and what to wear.

- Dressing well makes a good first impression. Ensure you have smart (and appropriate) clothes available. Many psychologists believe that employers make a decision about an applicant within a few minutes of meeting them.
- Find out if you will have to take a test, such as a psychometric test (one that is intended to assess your personality and intelligence). Ask the business for examples of the kind of things you'll do in the test.
- Be clear about where the interview is to be held. Plan your travel arrangements so you can be sure to get there in plenty of time. You must not be late!

Preparing thoroughly will help you to perform well during an interview. You should think about the questions you might be asked and how you would answer them. To help you, here are some examples of such questions along with ideas for possible answers.

Q: *Why do you want to work here?*

A: The business has a reputation as a good employer.
   The business offers employees training.
   (Explain that you are very interested in the work of the firm.)

Q: *Aren't you too young for this type of job?*

A: (Explain that you may be young but are enthusiastic and hardworking.)
(Describe the skills you have that may prove useful in the job.)

Q: *What makes a good member of a team?*

A: Someone who
- is a good communicator
- is flexible and adaptable and can carry out different roles
- is willing to co-operate with other team members
- has a sense of humour.

Q: *Do you have any questions?*

It would be sensible to prepare for this question as it is almost always asked at an interview. You could ask, for example:

- Why is the job vacant?
- What training would I receive?
- How would I be paid?
- How soon will I hear about the result of my application?

Some interview tips

- Try to relax, breathe deeply and sit comfortably in the chair (without slouching).
- Speak clearly and avoid speaking too fast.
- Remember to say 'Hello' at the start of your interview and try to remember the interviewer's name.
- Don't just answer 'Yes' or 'No' to questions. Expand your answers and give details.
- Sell yourself by giving details of your experience, your achievements and your hobbies.
- Do ask for a question to be repeated or explained if you don't understand it.
- Smile and make eye contact with the person or people who are interviewing you.
- Don't chew gum or fidget.
- Remember, you can ask questions too. For example, you might want to know about training or holidays – don't just

STOP & THINK

What type of job are you planning to apply for when you have finished studying? What sort of questions might you be asked in an interview for this type of job?

OVER TO YOU

Very probably, in the future some of your applications will be online. Part of the interview process may also be conducted electronically too. Some employers already operate online application forms. Applicants who clear this first hurdle are then sent a CD-ROM containing a psychometric test for completion. Only candidates who get beyond this stage are invited for an interview.

Conduct a search on the internet for online application forms to see what is involved and any possible follow up. Alternatively, go to www. gf-partnership.co.uk/recruit/jobsonline to see an online application form.

Benefits of training

Improving the performance of employees to make them more effective is called staff development. There are a number of ways of developing staff skills and knowledge, of which training is perhaps the best known. Normally, the human resources department of a business is responsible for staff development and training. Providing proper training has benefits for both the individual and the business.

- New employees get induction training to help them familiarise themselves with the business.
- Training can help to reduce expensive mistakes.
- Employees may be more likely to stay with a business if they believe they will receive regular training.
- Training helps to improve the performance of employees, making businesses more competitive.
- Training can help to make employees feel wanted and so improve morale.

Appraisal and training

Over 80 per cent of businesses in the UK have an appraisal system. Appraisals are designed to evaluate an employee's performance over a fixed time. These schemes normally cover part-time and full-time employees. Employees are usually interviewed once or twice a year as part of the appraisal process. Appraisal develops employees by setting targets and by identifying future training needs. Bonuses may be linked to whether an employee reaches agreed targets or gets new qualifications.

KEY CONCEPTS

Appraisal is an assessment of an employee's performance at work over a period of time.

Investors in People (IIP) is an organisation set up by the government to help businesses improve the performance of their employees.

Induction training is the training given to an employee when he or she is new.

National Training Awards are awards made to businesses and individual employees that have achieved success through training.

Staff development is a general term describing ways that a business might try to improve the performance of its employees, including training.

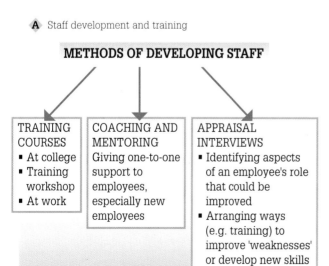

A Staff development and training

METHODS OF DEVELOPING STAFF

TRAINING COURSES	COACHING AND MENTORING	APPRAISAL INTERVIEWS
• At college • Training workshop • At work	Giving one-to-one support to employees, especially new employees	• Identifying aspects of an employee's role that could be improved • Arranging ways (e.g. training) to improve 'weaknesses' or develop new skills

B The appraisal process

APPRAISAL INTERVIEW

- Identify skills needed to do job more effectively
- Discuss performance targets (e.g. sales targets or production targets) set in previous appraisal interview
- Arrange training to develop skills
- Set new targets
- Improve employee performance

NEXT APPRAISAL INTERVIEW

Most employees receive some induction training when they start a new job. The new employee will be introduced to:

- the basic duties of the job
- people with whom he or she with be working
- the layout of the factory or office
- health and safety and security procedures
- holiday entitlement and grievance systems.

After induction training, employees may be required to undergo other forms of training.

- Off-the-job training is given outside the workplace, at a college or university or at the employee's home. It might involve attending regular classes or studying at home.
- On-the-job training happens at the workplace. Learning is by watching and talking with more experienced workers. The trainee will perhaps also work through instruction manuals and have a mentor to help him or her learn the job.

Well-managed businesses offer regular training for their employees. That way, workers can acquire the latest skills, helping the business to remain competitive. Up-to-date knowledge can also allow firms to introduce new methods of production and new products. At the same time, regular training helps to maintain high morale among employees.

Government schemes

The government believes that a highly trained workforce is very important if UK businesses are to compete internationally. The government encourages training in many ways, including the New Deal programme, which was introduced to help unemployed people gain the training necessary to find jobs. Two other government schemes are also designed to encourage and further training.

1 **Investors in People (IIP).** Firms that meet the national standard for the training and development of employees to help those firms attain their business objectives receive the IIP award. These businesses can use a logo identifying them as having reached the IIP standard.

2 **National Training Awards.** Businesses and individual employees that have achieved success through training may receive National Training Awards. The awards are made to businesses that have run effective training schemes, and to employees who have benefited from them. Businesses ranging from hospices (which look after patients who are dying) to BP Amoco have received National Training Awards.

STOP & THINK

A modern production line in operation is shown in **C**. Why might this business have to spend heavily on training? Why might it choose to do so?

C Workers on a food production line

Find out what the logo used by firms that have received the Investors in People Award looks like. Use the internet (www.iipuk.co.uk) or talk to a manager at a business that has the IIP award and ask:

- What did your business do to get an IIP award?
- Do you think that your business benefits from the having the award, and if so, how?

In the previous 12 pages we looked at how businesses encourage people to apply to work for them. We also considered how businesses decide which applicants to employ, and gave advice on how to apply for jobs. You should now be able to answer the questions that follow.

10 revision questions

Check your knowledge by tackling these questions.

1 Distinguish between internal and external recruitment. (4 marks)

2 Explain **one** advantage and **one** disadvantage of using external recruitment. (6 marks)

3 Explain **two** methods that businesses can use to convert their existing workforce into the workforce that they would like. (6 marks)

4 List **four** items you might expect to be included in a job description. (4 marks)

5 Why do businesses use person specifications? (5 marks)

6 Outline **one** advantage and **one** disadvantage of using assessment centres to select employees. (6 marks)

7 List **five** pieces of information that you should include in your CV. (5 marks)

8 State **four** pieces of information that you might attempt to find out about a business before attending an interview. (4 marks)

9 Explain **two** benefits that a business might gain from training its staff. (6 marks)

10 Distinguish between off-the-job and on-the-job training. (4 marks)

Total = 50 marks

PUTTING IT INTO PRACTICE

Your investigation into the human resources department of the business should have gathered information on the following:

- how to write a CV and complete an application form
- how the business recruits and selects its employees
- how the business uses information technology to assist with its recruitment
- what training is offered by the business
- how training employees helps the business to reach its objectives.

This information will help you make judgements about the effectiveness of the recruitment, selection and training within your chosen business.

Again, you will need to check which Awarding Body (AQA, Edexcel or OCR) you are using. Once you know this, you can choose the correct column from the following table. This will guide you in writing the second part of your portfolio evidence.

STOP & THINK

List three advantages and three disadvantages of a business spending large sums of money on training. Can businesses be competitive without training their employees regularly?

IT-based training

AWARDING BODY			
What you have to do	**AQA**	**Edexcel**	**OCR**
Describe or identify	• Draw up a CV and complete an application form for a job of your own choice advertised by your chosen business. • Identity the training that you might receive if you were appointed.	• Describe the recruitment process within your chosen business and identify each of the stages involved. • Describe the main ways in which businesses can train and develop staff. Where possible, you should support your work by using documents such as job descriptions from your chosen business.	• Describe the recruitment and selection process used by your chosen business. • Describe the business's procedures for: ▪ staff training ▪ appraisal ▪ retraining for new ▪ technology or new ▪ working practices ▪ any national ▪ training initiatives ▪ health and safety ▪ training.
Explain or analyse	• Explain how your application relates to the job description for the post. • Explain the process the business may undertake before deciding whether or not to select you. • Analyse the effective ness of the training that the business offers.	• Analyse the process of recruitment and training within your chosen business and show their importance for the efficient operation of the business. • Analyse potential problems that might exist within the recruitment process and the problems associated with training.	• Explain why your chosen business uses its particular procedures for recruitment and selection to meet its staffing needs. • Analyse how the business's procedures for training and appraisal help employees to: ▪ carry out their jobs efficiently ▪ maintain a safe and secure workplace.
Evaluate (this may mean making judgements or offering and justifying suggestions)	• Suggest other training that the business might offer in the future. You should justify your suggestion(s).	• Evaluate how recruitment and training procedures might be used to assist the business in improving its performance. • Evaluate the effectiveness of recruitment and selection procedures.	• Suggest and justify improvements to documentation and procedures. • Suggest and justify additional procedures that might improve: ▪ employee performance ▪ the safety of the workplace.

Types of customer

Businesses have two types of customers, internal and external. An example is shown in  **A**.

- **Internal customers.** Many businesses have departments or sections that serve as internal customers. Their job is to check products as they pass from one section or department to another. Internal customers help the business to supply high-quality products to their outside customers.

- **External customers.** Customers who buy goods and services for their own use are the external customers. They are the final consumers. The people you see buying groceries in a supermarket, for example, are final consumers.

We looked at the ways that businesses provide customers with high-quality service in Unit 1. You may find it worthwhile rereading pages 48–9 as an introduction to the topic, before continuing.

Multiyork's workshop in Norfolk

STOP & THINK

Multiyork is a manufacturer and retailer of furniture. Its workshop in Norfolk supplies all the company's shops with sofas and other furniture. Multiyork's shops are the workshop's internal customers, who need to be satisfied with the products they get before they sell them. How does this help the company to satisfy its customers?

KEY CONCEPTS

Consumerism is a movement that makes consumers more knowledgeable about products, and businesses more aware of the interests of consumers.

Customer service describes the extent to which businesses satisfy their customers.

Co-operative's farms supplying meat, vegetables and other foodstuffs

Co-operative shops are INTERNAL customers of the farms as they are all part of the same business

CO-OPERATIVE FOOD STORE

Shoppers are all EXTERNAL customers

People shopping at Co-operative shops throughout Britain

A Internal and external customers

STOP & THINK

Providing good customer services can be expensive. Businesses need to pay the wages of customer services staff and may have to give refunds or compensate dissatisfied customers. Would a business make more profit, do you think, if it didn't have a customer service department?

CASE STUDY

Tesco – the UK's largest retailer

The UK's biggest supermarket chain Tesco spends a lot of money on customer services. Visit www.tesco.com/customerservices/custservhome/ and then try the tasks below.

Tasks

1 State two tasks that are normally carried out by customer services staff.

2 What skills and knowledge do you think an employee working in customer services should have?

3 Why do you think customer services are so important to Tesco?

What do customers expect?

Customers have a number of expectations of a business.

1 **Good-value products.** Value for money is very important. Businesses that do not offer good-value products will lose customers. That is why supermarkets such as Tesco like to keep a close watch on prices charged by rivals – to make sure that their own prices are competitive.

2 **Clear and honest information.** Customers like to know the prices that they are expected to pay. Clear labelling can help. They also want to know about any extra costs. Having hidden charges is not good customer service.

3 **Information about products.** Businesses can win new customers by offering specialist advice about their products. Computer manufacturers, for example, offer advice and after-sales support, and may design and build a computer to meet an individual customer's needs. This aspect of customer service has been encouraged by consumerism – a movement towards a greater understanding of consumer needs.

4 **Having efficient ordering systems.** Good-quality customer service means that customers receive products soon after ordering them. Many businesses have order tracking systems on their websites. These can tell customers when the products that they have ordered will be despatched.

5 **After-sales services.** Products such as refrigerators, televisions and computers can break down. After-sales services include repairs and the replacement of faulty products or parts. Customers expect such repairs to be carried out quickly and efficiently, and faulty products to be replaced without delay.

6 **Dealing quickly with inquiries.** Businesses should always reply promptly to complaints about poor service or low-quality goods. Customers expect to be given telephone numbers and addresses where they can contact customer services when necessary. Supermarkets usually have a customer service desk in their stores.

7 **Help with specific issues.** Modern products can be bought in a number of ways. Customer service departments can help customers in the purchase of goods and services by answering their questions. They can offer advice on arranging a loan, and many businesses will themselves provide customers with loans (known as credit).

8 **Personal attention.** Customers feel more satisfied if they can speak to a member of staff in person to help sort out any problems. Many businesses have 'help areas' where staff are on hand for this purpose.

Benefits of good customer service

Good customer service means keeping customers happy. Businesses with good customer service may offer competitive prices, have helpful and friendly staff and respond quickly to customer complaints.

Offering good customer service also helps businesses to be competitive. Terry Leahy, the chief executive of Tesco, has said that good customer service helps Tesco to compete successfully with other supermarkets. High-quality customer service offers businesses a number of advantages, as shown in 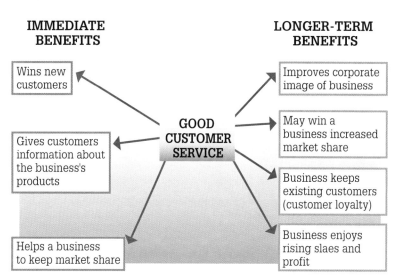 .

IMMEDIATE BENEFITS

Wins new customers

Gives customers information about the business's products

Helps a business to keep market share

GOOD CUSTOMER SERVICE

LONGER-TERM BENEFITS

Improves corporate image of business

May win a business increased market share

Business keeps existing customers (customer loyalty)

Business enjoys rising slaes and profit

A The benefits of providing good customer service

KEY CONCEPTS

Corporate image is the general public's view of a business – for example, Marks & Spencer is seen as a good-quality shop.

Customer loyalty is when customers come back regularly to purchase a business's products.

Market share is the proportion of sales achieved by a firm in a particular market. For example, Nokia has 30.6 per cent share of the UK market for mobile phones.

Sales revenue is the money received by a firm from the sale of its goods and services.

STOP & THINK

Can you think of an instance when you, or someone in your family, received good customer service from a business? How did you (or they) feel about this? How might the business have benefited from it?

1 **Winning new customers.** Some businesses provide similar products to other businesses and charge similar prices. Improving the quality of customer service can help a business to be more competitive. For example, petrol retailers sell a similar product to each other at prices that do not vary by much. But they compete through customer service by opening for long hours and by having mini-supermarkets, with a range of goods for sale, on their forecourts.

2 **Achieving customer satisfaction and loyalty.** Satisfying customers will help to make them loyal to the business and less tempted to buy from competitors. Contented, regular customers provide businesses with regular sales revenue (income from products sold).

3 **Improving a business's corporate image.** Satisfied customers spread good news about a business and influence the views of others. A business with a good corporate image is more likely to win new customers. It may also be able to charge higher prices.

One of Marks & Spencer's oldest shops at Marble Arch, London

4 Getting useful feedback. Good customer service means that businesses listen to their customers. They can find out what customers think about their products. This feedback can be helpful in suggesting ways to improve both the products and the quality of customer service.

5 Helping to keep the market share. Customers who remain loyal to the business, and new customers won over by high-quality services, can help the business retain its share of the market. In other words, the proportion of sales that the business achieves compared to its competitors will not fall. Even in an expanding market, such as the market for mobile phones, good customer service can help a business to keep its market share.

6 Increasing sales revenue and profits. Satisfied customers who buy again from businesses can encourage others to buy too. Getting new customers can increase a business's sales revenue and, because of the business's growing reputation, may allow it to charge higher prices. This can, in turn, increase the business's profits – perhaps the most important reason for providing good customer service.

STOP & THINK

Marks & Spencer have suffered a loss of customer loyalty in recent years, and sales have fallen. To try to recover lost ground, the company launched a customer loyalty card in 2002 along the lines of Tesco's Club Card.

How might this help to improve customer loyalty? What else could Marks & Spencer do to make customers more loyal?

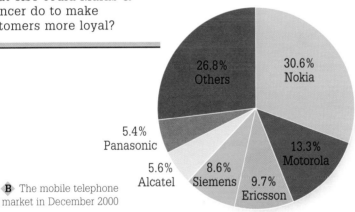

B The mobile telephone market in December 2000

30.6% Nokia

26.8% Others

13.3% Motorola

9.7% Ericsson

8.6% Siemens

5.6% Alcatel

5.4% Panasonic

STOP & THINK

The market shares of different companies for mobile telephones in December 2000 are shown in **B**. Nokia's share has remained steady. How might customer service have helped it to achieve this?

OVER TO YOU

Visit a local hotel and ask for a copy of its customer satisfaction form. (If you cannot get a customer satisfaction form from a local hotel, you can find one on-line at www.weston manor.co.uk/confsatis.htm). Look at the questions listed on the form.

■ Which aspects of the service provided by the hotel are included in the questions?

■ Are you asked for suggestions on how to improve the experience of staying at the hotel?

■ Are there any questions about customer service?

■ Are customers who may wish to complain given a contact name or telephone number?

How might this customer satisfaction form help the hotel to attract customers and keep them?

Measuring customer satisfaction

Businesses need to be able to measure how satisfied their customers are. Otherwise, they will not know whether:

- customers' expectations are being met
- customer service is improving or getting worse.

Measuring customer satisfaction allows businesses to improve the quality of their goods or services. The methods used for measuring customer satisfaction are shown in **A** . These are:

- analysing the sales performance
- looking at customer services figures
- comparing customer satisfaction levels with those of competitors.

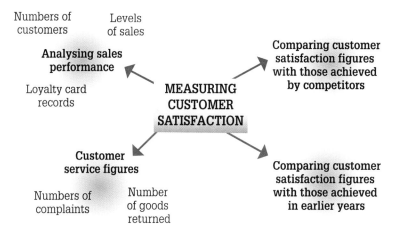

A Methods of measuring customer satisfaction

STOP & THINK

How can customer services staff help in the measuring of customer satisfaction?

STOP & THINK

EMI's sales revenues from recorded music have risen between 1999 and 2001, as shown in **B** . Does this mean that the company's profits must also have increased?

Analysing sales performance

There are three main ways that a business can analyse its sales performance.

1 **Checking sales levels.** A simple measure of customer satisfaction is to look at the level of sales achieved by the business. Sales are usually measured by value. The sales of tape cassettes, CDs and minidiscs achieved by EMI in 2001 are shown in **B** . The sales figures for previous years are also shown. Comparing with earlier years helps the company to judge whether customer satisfaction is improving.

B EMI's sales of recorded music products 1999–2001 (in millions).

1999	2000	2001
2057.0	2032.5	2282.0

Year	1991	1992	1993	1994	1995	1996	1997	1998	1999	2000
Average attendance	43 218	44 984	35 132	44 244	43 682	41 681	55 080	55 164	55 188	58 017

Source: www.m-u-f-c.co.uk/history/attendences

C Average number of spectators at Manchester United's home games 1991–2000

STOP & THINK

Loyalty cards allow supermarkets and other retailers to collect information about customers. What other benefits do you think loyalty cards offer to businesses?

OVER TO YOU

Ask for the customer complaints procedure of the business you are investigating for your assignment. Most medium-size to large businesses have written procedures. Ask the business's employees how the business responds to customer complaints. Does the company collect statistics on customer complaints?

2 **Measuring the number of customers.** For some businesses, the number of customers is a better measure of customer satisfaction than the level of sales. For example, football clubs might measure their customers' satisfaction with the team's performance and the amenities at the football ground by looking at attendance figures (see **C**).

3 **Using information from loyalty card records.** Over three-quarters of all adults in the UK have a loyalty card. The information from these cards tells shops such as Tesco and Sainsbury's what customers like and what they dislike. Knowing this, helps companies to plan the layout of their stores and to decide what products to sell and which of them to put on special offer.

Looking at complaints and returns

By recording and keeping watch on customer services figures, businesses can monitor any signs of dissatisfaction and take appropriate action. There are two areas that need looking at.

1 **The number of complaints.** A rise in the number of complaints probably means that customers are becoming less satisfied with a business's goods or services. Businesses usually analyse the causes of complaints and try to put things right.

2 **The numbers of returned goods.** If customers are returning increasing numbers of goods, very likely they are dissatisfied with the quality of the products. A well-managed business would be sure to identify the reason for customer dissatisfaction.

Making comparisons with competitors

A good measure of a business's customer satisfaction is to compare its own data on customer satisfaction with its competitors' data. Achieving higher levels of customer satisfaction than competitors would please the managers of a business, while unfavourable comparisons could highlight areas in need of improvement.

Finding out customers' views

To remain competitive, businesses need to collect and analyse information about their markets. This is called market research. They need find out:

- which goods and services customers want
- what customers think about the business's current products
- what are the strengths and weaknesses of competitors
- what are the expected future sales of products.

There are a number of ways of finding out more about the views of the customers, which are summarised in **A**.

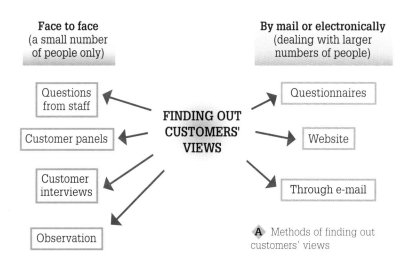

A Methods of finding out customers' views

1 **Questions from staff.** Employees can ask customers questions to find out their views about the business and its products. Usually, people in sales and marketing carry out the market research. For example, a business's sales representatives have regular contact with customers and are ideal people to question them.

2 **Observation.** Businesses sometimes just watch the behaviour of customers, or would-be customers. For example, supermarkets watch (and sometimes videotape) customers' reactions to a new in-store display. If this attracts attention, it may be used in other stores.

3 **Questionnaires.** A very common way of trying to find out what customers think is to get them to complete a questionnaire. These are cheap to produce but only between 2 and 5 per cent of people receiving questionnaires through the post bother to fill them out. Completing a questionnaire with the customer present, as part of an interview, can be effective, but is costly.

STOP & THINK

Methods of market research such as customer panels or customer interviews are expensive, and only a small number of customers are questioned. Why might businesses prefer these types of market research?

STOP & THINK

A supermarket has set up a large, new display of organic foodstuffs. Why might observing how customers respond to the display be better than asking them questions?

STOP & THINK

The supermarket giant Tesco is the UK's largest retailer. The company holds regular meetings with customer panels to discover what its shoppers do and don't like.

In what other ways might Tesco find out about the views of its customers?

4 **Customer panels.** Some businesses use small groups of consumers to report back to them regularly on the experiences of using their products. These customer panels, as they are called, also give their views on the business's advertising, and may suggest ideas for new products and special offers. Customer panels provide businesses with useful, detailed information.

5 **Business websites.** Most businesses, even small ones, have a website. Websites can be used to advertise products and to find out customers' views. A page from the Woolwich Bank's website is shown. The Woolwich is planning to offer more banking services on the internet and is asking customers' opinions before deciding on which services to offer.

6 **E-mail.** Almost every business website has a 'contact us' section with an e-mail link to customer services. In this way, customers are given the chance to offer their views on the business and its products. Customers can also use e-mail links to complain about unsatisfactory products.

STOP & THINK

What are the advantages to the Woolwich Bank of using the internet (see above) to find out customers' views?

OVER TO YOU

Find out more about how businesses use their websites to collect information on customers' views. You might look at the website of the business that you are investigating as part of your assignment for this unit.

Alternatively, you can go to: www.bized.ac.uk/listserv/companies/comlist.htm. This web page provides links to the top 100 UK companies. Once you have found a suitable website, see if the business is using this to collect customers' opinions on a particular

issue. Does the business offer customers the opportunity to contact them and give their views? Do you think the business really wants to receive e-mails from customers?

Good customer service

The exact form that customer service takes will vary from one business to another. However, good customer service should include some of the following features, which are summarised in **A** .

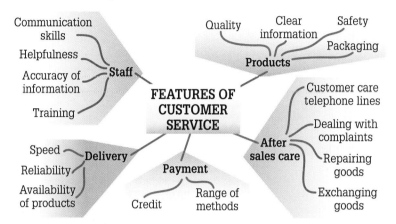

A Features of customer service

1 **Products.** The business must supply products that meet customers' needs.
- Goods should be of good quality. For example, customers expect televisions to be built using the latest technology and to provide many years of reliable service.
- Customers may need to be assured about safety when buying some products. For instance, airlines have to take great care to protect passengers who fly with them.
- The packaging of goods should help customers. They want packaging that is easy to open. For example, businesses now use ring pulls on cans so that customers can open the cans quickly and easily without using a can opener.
- Some customers expect clear information, such as nutritional information on food labels, to help them maintain a balanced diet.

2 **Staff.** Employees need the right skills and attitudes.
- Employees should receive training to make sure that they know about the business and its products, and can easily answer customers' questions.
- Training in communication skills will help employees to give polite and clear answers. This is very important in telephone conversations, when customers cannot see the employee.
- In responding in person to customers' inquiries, employees should reply quickly but be helpful and friendly.
- Wearing a uniform makes it easier for customers to recognise employees.

3 **After-sales care.** A high-quality after-sales service will:
 ■ deal quickly and fairly with complaints
 ■ exchange goods that are faulty or do not meet customers' needs
 ■ repair goods (free of charge if under guarantee)
 ■ offer customers advice and support from the time that they buy the products.

4 **Premises.** Hotels, shops and restaurants must maintain their premises well to keep customers happy.
 ■ Premises should be clean, especially where food is cooked and eaten.
 ■ Customers should be able to find their way around. For example, clear signposting in hospitals is very important.
 ■ Disabled customers should be able to use a business's products. Some airlines, for example, have received bad publicity for not allowing passengers in wheelchairs to travel on their aircraft.
 ■ Customers expect good facilities, for instance changing rooms in high-street shops for mothers with babies.

5 **Delivery.** Customers expect businesses to deliver products without delay. Speed is especially important in the case of perishable goods, such as fresh foods. Businesses must also make sure that products ordered by customers are available.

6 **Payment.** Businesses should give customers a choice of ways of paying. They should accept cheques and credit cards and offer credit terms in the case of costly items.

Using technology

Modern technology has helped businesses to improve their customer services in several ways.

 ■ Websites can offer customers up-to-date information about products and businesses and answer frequently asked questions.
 ■ Many products can be bought on the internet, allowing customers to shop at any time.
 ■ Customers who have any problems or complaints can contact the business directly by e-mail.

STOP & THINK

Many businesses trade in such a way that customers do not visit their premises. Can you think of some examples of this type of business? Do you think this will become more common in the future?

STOP & THINK

What do you think are the most important features of customer service for a Burger King restaurant?

OVER TO YOU

Investigate the features and the quality of customer service provided by the business you are studying. (You will need to do this for your assignment for Unit 2.) Award marks out of 10 on a range of 1 (poor) to 10 (excellent) for as many of the features as possible. Then add up all these marks to give a total score for the quality of customer service given by the business.

Also, suggest ways in which the business might improve the quality of its customer service. This might mean improving existing features of customer service or introducing new ones.

Looking after consumers

Consumer protection looks after consumers in a number of ways. It prevents:

- businesses charging very high prices or very high rates of interest
- dishonest practices, such as selling measures other than those stated on the label
- the sale of unsafe products, such as children's toys with sharp edges
- information about consumers being passed to other businesses without the consumers' permission.

We looked at health and safety legislation in detail earlier in this unit. Reread pages 104–5 before continuing.

Health and safety

A number of laws protect the health and safety of consumers.

- **Health and Safety Act, 1974.** This is the main law in the UK. As well as looking after the interests of employees, it protects consumers, for example by regulating the packaging and labelling of dangerous substances.
- **Food and Drugs Act, 1984.** This law states what may and may not be added to food, and makes it illegal to sell food from dirty or unhygienic premises.
- **Food Safety Act, 1990.** Built on earlier Acts, this law says it is illegal to sell consumers food of a poor standard. The law applies to farmers as well as to restaurants and shops.
- **Consumer Protection Act, 1987.** This law covers dangerous products and consumer safety. Businesses are liable for any harm to consumers caused by their products.

The sale of products

Consumer protection laws look after consumers when they are buying goods and services.

- **Sale of Goods Act, 1979.** Products, when they are sold, must be undamaged and in good working order. They should do what is expected of them and perform as described. For example, a lawn mower must be able to cut grass.
- **Consumer Credit Act, 1974.** Many consumers buying products borrow money from businesses. This Act prevents businesses charging very high rates of interest, and gives consumers a chance to change their minds about borrowing the money.

A The BBC television programme 'Watchdog'

How might television programmes such as 'Watchdog' (see **A**) help businesses?

The labelling of products

Consumers get a lot of information about products from reading labels. This is particularly true of food and drinks. Customers are protected by law from being given false information or given short measure.

- **Labelling of Food Regulations, 1970.** By these regulations, prepacked food must contain a list of ingredients on the label. Food sold in the UK having one per cent or more of genetically modified ingredients must be labelled to make this clear.
- **Weights and Measures Act, 1986.** This Act lays down the weights and measures to be used in trading. Weights and measures must be accurate and must be as shown on the labels.
- **Trades Descriptions Act, 1968.** This Act makes it illegal to give a misleading description of products on packaging or in advertising.

The misuse of information

Businesses collect a lot of information on consumers. If they lend customers money, they will ask for details of their employment and income. Laws exist to prevent businesses misusing this information.

- **Computer Misuse Act, 1990.** It is illegal for people without the proper authority to look at or use confidential information (for example, about customers) held on computers.
- **The Data Protection Act, 1998.** This is the major law governing the use of information about consumers. It requires businesses that store personal information to maintain data securely. Individuals have the right to see the data that concerns them and to ask for changes if it is incorrect. Businesses may not pass on to other businesses the personal details of consumers without their agreement.

STOP & THINK

Businesses that treat customers badly will become unpopular. Is it therefore necessary to have consumer protection laws?

Genetically modified crops
Source: www.1000g-et.com

OVER TO YOU

Trading Standards Offices play an important role in protecting consumers. Your local Trading Standards Office has many publications describing the work that it does. You should find out about:

- the information and advice offered to consumers

- any recent changes in trading standards' laws.

You can get the address of your local office from: www.tradingstandards.gov.uk

This site also provides information on the work of Trading Standards officials.

REVISION 5

In the previous 12 pages we looked at the relationship between businesses and their customers. Customers are very important to all businesses. Without them it is impossible for businesses to survive. You should now be able to answer the questions that follow.

10 revision questions

Check your knowledge by tackling these questions.

1 Distinguish between internal and external customers, using examples of each.

(6 marks)

2 Explain **three** things that customers might expect from a business. (9 marks)

3 Outline **two** benefits a business might receive as a result of giving good customer service. (6 marks)

4 What is meant by the term 'customer loyalty'? (2 marks)

5 What is meant by the term 'customer satisfaction'?

(2 marks)

6 Explain **two** ways in which a business might measure the satisfaction of its customers. (6 marks)

7 State **three** reasons why businesses carry out market research. (3 marks)

8 Explain **two** ways in which a business might discover the views of its customers.

(6 marks)

9 Explain **two** ways in which businesses can provide good quality customer service.

(6 marks)

10 State **four** laws that protect consumers. (4 marks)

Total = 50 marks

CASE STUDY

Clare Florist is a company that specialises in supplying flowers, using the internet. Customers can view the company's products online, pay for their flowers and have them sent to any address in Britain. Customer service is very important to the company. Clare Florist uses technology to satisfy customers – for example, by promising secure payment using a credit card.

Task

How can a florist use the internet to help make sure that its customers are satisfied?

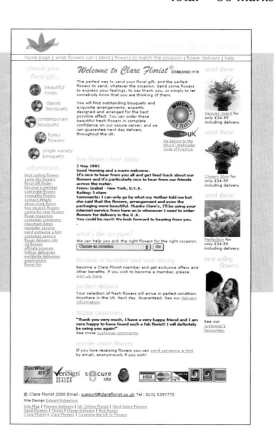

PUTTING IT INTO PRACTICE

By this stage of Unit 2, your assignment should be nearly complete. The final part of your portfolio evidence will need to look at one or both of:

- customer service
- consumer protection.

Once again you will need to check which Awarding Body (AQA, Edexcel or OCR) you are using. When you know this, you can choose the correct column from the following table. This will guide you in writing the final section of your portfolio evidence.

AWARDING BODY			
What you have to do	**AQA**	**Edexcel**	**OCR**
Describe or identify	▪ Describe the customer services provided by your chosen business. This should be in the form of an **oral presentation**.	▪ Describe the arrangements for customer services within your chosen business. ▪ Describe how 'your' business's customers are protected by consumer law.	▪ Describe the rights of customers under consumer law ▪ Identify features within the business you are investigating that help the business to give good quality customer service.

Explain or analyse	▪ Explain how the business finds out about the needs of its customers.	▪ Analyse the strengths and weaknesses of customer service within your chosen business. This may include explaining:
		   ▪ how the business competes by using customer service;
		   ▪ how the business identifies customers' needs;
		   ▪ how it uses employees and technology to improve customer service.
			▪ Analyse how effectively the customer service given by 'your' business meets the needs and expectations of its customers.

Evaluate (this may mean making judgements or offering and justifying suggestions)	▪ Evaluate the success of the customer services of the business. ▪ Suggest possible improvements that could be made, especially through the use of IT.	▪ Evaluate the quality of customer service for the business and its customers. ▪ Suggest ways in which the business could improve its customer service. You should justify your suggestions. ▪ Assess how well the business's customers are protected by consumer law.	▪ Suggest and justify ways in which the quality of customer service given by 'your' business could be improved.

This unit contains a number of important themes, which are highlighted in **A** – **E**.

A A business's stakeholders

STOP & THINK

Looking at **A**, which stakeholders would be the most important to

- Oxfam (a charity)
- British Coal (a mining company)
- Lastminute.com?

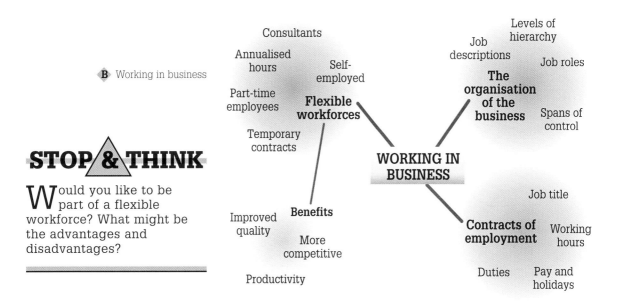

B Working in business

STOP & THINK

Would you like to be part of a flexible workforce? What might be the advantages and disadvantages?

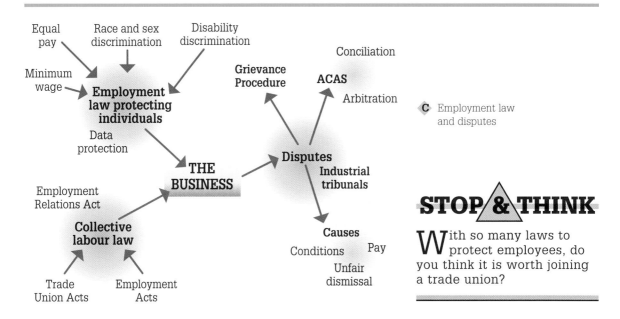

C Employment law and disputes

STOP & THINK

With so many laws to protect employees, do you think it is worth joining a trade union?

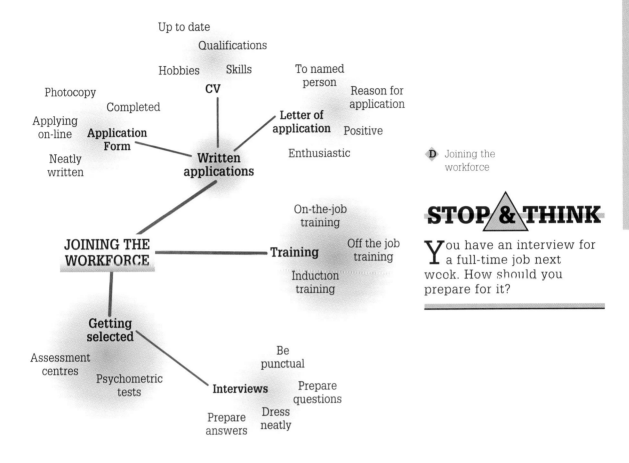

D Joining the workforce

STOP & THINK

You have an interview for a full-time job next week. How should you prepare for it?

E Looking after customers

STOP & THINK

Imagine you are staying in a hotel in London for a weekend. In what ways might the hotel provide you with good customer service?

Business finance

Unit 3 introduces you to business finance. This is a varied and interesting subject that covers a wide area of instruction.

- You will learn out about the variety of documents used by businesses to keep track of their finances. No longer will balance sheets, profit and loss accounts, invoices or credit notes be a mystery!
- All businesses make payments and receive money from customers. This unit will explain how it is done.
- Suppose you were about to set up your own business. You will discover all about the start-up costs and running costs that all businesses have to pay.
- Will I have enough cash to pay my bills? is a common worry for managers. You will learn how to answer that question by finding out about forecast inflows and outflows of cash.
- This unit also covers budgeting, which is another form of financial planning. You will learn how to present this information using a spreadsheet.
- Making a profit is vital to any business – whether it is McDonald's or the corner shop. You will be taught break-even analysis and how to calculate profit and loss.
- All businesses have stakeholders who have an interest in the business. We will examine the reasons for this interest.
- An important theme throughout this unit is how information and communication technology can help businesses to plan and manage their finances.
- Finally, to start up a small business, or to expand a larger one, you need to raise money. We will look at how this is done.

Unit 3 of this book covers Unit 3, Business finance, of the GCSE Applied Business award.

The financial position of a business

Finance is very important to a business. Most groups and individuals involved with businesses will want to ask questions about its financial position. If a business does not keep records of the flows of money into and out of the business, it will not be able to:

- work out whether it is making a profit
- persuade other people and organisations, for example banks, to lend it money
- decide on the prices it should charge customers
- make financial plans for the future.

Customers
What prices are charged?

Shareholders
Is the business profitable?

Managers
Are we doing a good job?

Why is finance important?

Employees
Will we get a pay rise?

Banks
Can the business repay its debts?

Suppliers
When will the business pay our bill?

A **business** is any organisation that produces or supplies goods or services.

Costs are the expenses paid by a business, for example wages.

Debt is money owed by a business to another business or to an individual.

A **product** is a general term that includes both goods and services.

Profit is made when a business earns more than it spends.

A **shareholder** is a person or an organisation that owns shares in a company.

A **stakeholder** is any individual or group with an interest in a business

I magine you were opening a shop selling CDs, minidiscs and other recorded music. What costs might you have to pay at first? What costs would you have to pay each month?

CASE STUDY

Vodafone

Vodafone is a huge company that employs thousands of people. It is one of the largest businesses in Europe.

Task

Why might the government be interested in the financial position of this major UK company?

CASE STUDY

The Humber Bridge

Source: www.northlincs.gov.uk

Plans for a bridge across the Humber river were first drawn up in 1872, but nothing happened for nearly a century. The bridge finally opened to traffic in 1981, having cost £151 million to build. Each year since then, the bridge has made a profit, but interest charges on the loan have swallowed the profit up.

Tasks

1 How might the Humber bridge have earned money since it opened in 1981?

2 Where do you think the money originally came from to build the bridge?

3 Find out about the finances of the Humber Bridge at www.humberbridge.co.uk. You should be able to discover:
   - the amount the bridge earns and its costs
   - when it will be paid for
   - the number of cars and lorries crossing it each year.

4 Which individuals or groups of people might be interested in the finances of the Humber Bridge?

Costs of starting a business

When a new business is being planned, the costs and the revenues (future money from the sale of products) must be worked out carefully. Likewise, when an established business is thinking of selling a new product, it too has to calculate the expected costs and receipts from sales.

The costs that new businesses have to meet before they sell any goods are called start-up costs. Such costs may include payments for market research, for premises, for machinery and for fixtures and fittings in the new premises.

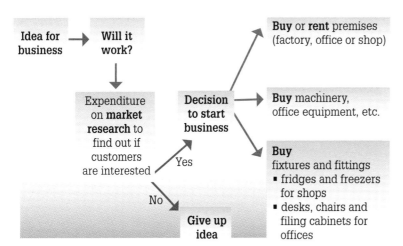

A Start up costs for a new business

JOINED-UP THINKING

We looked at market research in detail in 'Finding out customers' views' in Unit 2. If you are unsure of what is involved, re-read pages 32–3 now.

Market research

Market research helps businesses to find out the answers to several important questions.

- Are customers interested in buying the product?
- What changes do customers want in the product?
- How much might customers be prepared pay?

However, finding out the answers to these important questions can be expensive. There are two ways for a business to carry out market research.

1 **Using a market research agency.** Market research agencies are businesses that are experts in all types of market research. They can be useful to businesses that are inexperienced in market research. However, using a market research agency is likely to be expensive.
2 **Conducting its own research.** Even if a business chooses this course of action, it will still have to meet certain costs.
   - The employees carrying out the market research (by interviewing possible customers or sending out questionnaires) must be paid wages.

- Costs for postage (sending out questionnaires), telephone (interviewing customers) and transport (sending researchers to different areas) must be met.
- Once all the answers have been received, staff will have to be paid to analyse the results to find out customers' views.

Premises

Businesses need premises – somewhere to carry out the business. The type of premises will depend on the type of business.

- Some businesses supplying services, such as accountants or solicitors, need offices.
- Businesses selling goods will need shops or warehouses. Retailers like Next and Body Shop have shops in town and city centres to attract the most customers.
- Manufacturers need factories for making their products. A car producer will require a factory large enough for cars to be made there and with space to store parts.

For any business just starting up, finding premises is usually essential. Businesses can either buy premises, possibly using a loan called a mortgage, or rent premises, paying a monthly fee to the owner for their use.

Machinery

The type of machinery needed by a business varies greatly across businesses. Here are a few examples.

- A car mechanic would need tools to carry out repairs on customers' cars and ramps to lift the cars.
- A newly established dentist would need drills, an X-ray scanner and equipment to polish patients' teeth.
- A lorry manufacturer has to buy expensive production line machinery for turning out the vehicles.

Generally, firms supplying goods need to spend more money buying machinery than do firms supplying services

B A steel mill at work

Fixtures and fittings

Once suitable premises have been found, they have be equipped with the necessary fixtures and fittings. These may include:

- shelving and cupboards for storage
- furniture such as desks and chairs
- display equipment (for example, that used in shops)
- lighting and other electrical equipment.

Imagine you are planning to open a corner shop selling groceries. Make a list of all the things you would need to buy before you could open for business.

Costs of running a business

Start-up costs are paid only when a new business is created, or a new product is launched. Running costs are ongoing expenses that have to be paid by all businesses that provide goods or services. An example is shown in **A**.

Advertising costs

Businesses can advertise their goods or services in many different ways. They may choose to:

- advertise their products on television or radio
- advertise in local newspapers
- deliver letters advertising products to homes or other businesses.

Television advertising is expensive. A 30-second commercial may cost as much as £250,000. First, a film company has to be paid to make the commercial, and then there is the cost of having it broadcast.

Other forms of advertising can be much cheaper. An advert placed in a local newspaper may cost less than £100, while local radio also offers relatively cheap advertising. However, a national radio station, such as Talk FM, would charge much more to carry a commercial. Advertising aimed at a wider group of people is always more expensive than local advertising.

Wages and salaries

Businesses pay their employees weekly wages or monthly salaries for the work that they do. Most businesses need to employ people. But whereas a corner shop might have only one or two employees, Tesco, the UK's largest retailer, has over 190,000. Tesco's employees include:

- managers of their shops
- drivers of the company's delivery lorries
- check-out operators.

KEY CONCEPTS

Advertising is communicating with customers to promote a product, using, for instance, newspapers, radio or television.

Rent is money paid to hire business premises such as factories, offices or shops.

Running costs are day-to-day expenses paid by businesses, for example wages.

Taxes are payments that firms must make to the government.

STOP & THINK

What kind of advertising might be used by the following:

- a fish and chip shop
- Virgin Trains
- a double glazing company?

A Running costs for a Chinese restaurant

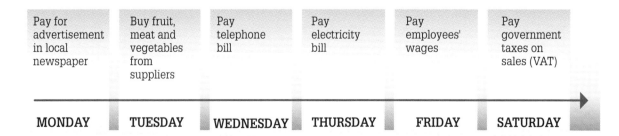

MONDAY	TUESDAY	WEDNESDAY	THURSDAY	FRIDAY	SATURDAY
Pay for advertisement in local newspaper	Buy fruit, meat and vegetables from suppliers	Pay telephone bill	Pay electricity bill	Pay employees' wages	Pay government taxes on sales (VAT)

Raw materials and power

Manufacturing businesses use large amounts of raw materials and these may be their biggest running cost. Raw materials are goods used in the manufacture of other goods. For example, the Jaguar car factory in Coventry uses large amounts of oil and petrol, metal, rubber and leather to manufacture the luxury cars.

Businesses also need to use electricity, gas and other forms of energy and these have to be paid for. For example, hotels need heating, and trains need power to move along the tracks.

B A busy production line

Rent

Businesses that do not own the buildings that they use will pay rent each month to hire the premises. Renting, rather than buying, premises can help a new business by reducing the start-up costs. However, the running costs may be more, because the business will have to pay rent every month. Businesses also have to pay business rates to the local council. Councils use this money to provide services such as street cleaning.

Government taxes

One running cost that all businesses must pay is value added tax (VAT). VAT is paid on goods and services that are bought by businesses, and is normally charged at 17.5 per cent. For example, if a business buys office furniture to the value of £5,000, then VAT amounting to £875 (17.5% x £5,000) will be added to the cost, giving a total of £5,875.

Most businesses pass on the costs of VAT to their customers, by charging extra for the goods or services that they provide. The Customs and Excise department collects on behalf of the government.

STOP & THINK

Study the picture in **B**. What running costs do you think this business would have to pay?

CASE STUDY

Fiona's flower shop

Fiona Marsh has achieved her dream of opening a flower shop in her home town. She used money left to her by an aunt to buy the shop and has given up her job in a supermarket to work for herself. In the first few months of business, Fiona has had to meet various running costs.

She hopes that she will sell enough flowers to be able to meet all these costs. She knows that she must do so, if her business is to be successful.

Tasks

1 Identify **four** running costs that Fiona might have to pay for her flower shop. (4 marks)

2 Fiona has bought her shop. Explain how this might help her to reduce her running costs. (6 marks)

3 Fiona is worried that the costs of her new business are too high. Suggest and justify **two** ways that she might be able to reduce the business's running costs. (10 marks)

Costs and revenues

A business cannot escape incurring start-up costs, when it is first set up, and running costs, once it gets going. Examples of both kinds of costs include:

- wages
- market research costs
- buying premises
- electricity and gas
- government taxes
- buying machinery.

Identify which listed costs are start-up costs and which are running costs.

Why is it important that a business's revenues are greater than its costs?

KEY CONCEPTS

Costs are expenses paid by businesses, for example wages.

Profit is the money left to a firm from its revenue once it has paid all its costs.

Revenues are the earnings or income of businesses.

Costs are money flowing out of a business. Every time a business pays wages or pays an electricity bill, money leaves the business. All revenue is money flowing into the business. Every time a good or service is sold, the business receives money. The costs and revenues for a typical farm are shown in **A** .

Calculating revenue

Revenues can come from many different sources.

- Manufacturing businesses receive revenue from selling goods such as vehicles or furniture.
- Service businesses receive revenue from selling services such as television broadcasting or meals in a restaurant.
- Service businesses can also receive revenue from hiring out facilities such as pleasure boats or hotel rooms.

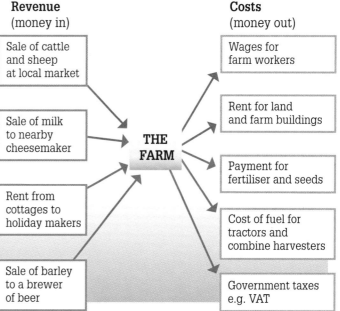

Revenue (money in)

- Sale of cattle and sheep at local market
- Sale of milk to nearby cheesemaker
- Rent from cottages to holiday makers
- Sale of barley to a brewer of beer

THE FARM

Costs (money out)

- Wages for farm workers
- Rent for land and farm buildings
- Payment for fertiliser and seeds
- Cost of fuel for tractors and combine harvesters
- Government taxes e.g. VAT

A Costs and revenues for a farm

A firm can calculate its revenue by using the following formula

Revenue = selling price x number of items sold.

Caledonian Spirit, a whisky manufacturer (or distiller) sells 50,000 bottles of whisky a year. If each bottle sells for £11, Caledonian Spirit's revenue will be £550,000 (50,000 x £11).

Calculating profit

Businesses use their revenues to pay their costs. Any money that is left over, once all the costs have been paid, is the profit that the business has made. Businesses calculate their profits using a simple formula

Profit = revenues – costs.

The managers at Caledonian Spirit add all their costs together and subtract them from the revenue earned by the distillery firm. The resulting figure is the distiller's profits.

If Caledonian Spirit earns revenue of £550,000 in a year and has total costs of £500,000 over the same period, then its profit for that year will be £50,000. A detailed breakdown of these figures is shown in **C** .

Most UK businesses aim to make a profit. Profits are paid to the owners of a business (shareholders or partners, for example) as a reward for:

- investing money into the business
- risking money, as the business might not be successful.

STOP & THINK

How much revenue would a distillers earn if it charged £12 for a bottle of whisky and sold 55,000 bottles a year?

C Caledonian Spirit's revenues, costs and profit

		£
Revenue from selling whisky		**550 000**
Costs of producing whisky	£	
Wages	125 000	
Raw materials (barley, yeast)	90 000	
Rent & rates	75 000	
Fuel	100 000	
Government taxes	80 000	
Advertising	30 000	
Total costs		**500 000**
Profit		**50 000**

C A S E   S T U D Y

Fiona's first year

Fiona has run her flower shop for one year. At the end of the year she has the following figures for her business:

	£
Sales of cut flowers	10 000
Wages	6 500
Materials (buying in flowers)	5 000
Sale of pot plants	7 500
Business Rates	1 500
Electricity and gas	2 000
Advertising	500
Sales of wedding bouquets	2 000

She thinks her business has been successful, but is not sure. She asks a friend to help her decide whether she has made a profit.

Tasks

1 Look at the list Fiona has drawn up. Identify which items are costs and which are revenues. (4 marks)

2 Has Fiona made a profit from her shop over the year? (4 marks)

3 Do you think Fiona would be pleased with her first year of running a business? Justify your answer. (7 marks)

Benefits of information technology

In recent years, information technology has undergone rapid change. No only has IT equipment fallen in price, it has also become more powerful. Technological change has enabled today's businesses to use information in many different ways. The types of information technology available to businesses and how these are used are shown in **A**.

Information technology has changed the way that businesses work. It enables many tasks that were once considered difficult, time-consuming and expensive to be performed quickly and easily. For example, IT can:

- advertise goods and services for sale to customers throughout the world
- design new products
- order raw materials and components from suppliers
- discover customers' opinions on goods and services, new and old
- send messages anywhere in the world instantaneously.

Using IT to cut costs

Information technology can help a business to increase profits by reducing costs in several areas.

1 **Cheaper advertising and marketing.** Using the internet, even a small business can afford to advertise its goods or services throughout the world. The business only has to pay for the design of a website, which can then be seen by customers everywhere. To place advertisements in

KEY
CONCEPTS

Information technology (IT) is the use of electronic equipment for storing and communicating information. It is sometimes called information and communications technology (ICT).

The **internet** is a worldwide communications system of linked computer networks, which is also used for the advertising and selling of products across the world.

Intranets are computer links within a single business, which make it easier for employees to communicate with one another.

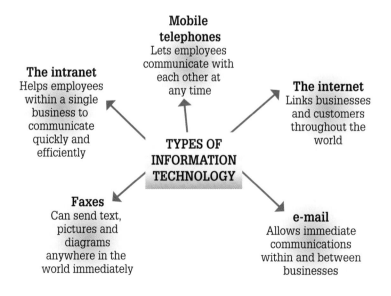

The intranet
Helps employees within a single business to communicate quickly and efficiently

Mobile telephones
Lets employees communicate with each other at any time

The internet
Links businesses and customers throughout the world

TYPES OF INFORMATION TECHNOLOGY

Faxes
Can send text, pictures and diagrams anywhere in the world immediately

e-mail
Allows immediate communications within and between businesses

A Information technology and business

B The Ffolkes Arms – advertising on a website

A Boeing 777 on the production line

STOP & THINK

The aircraft manufacturer Boeing used IT to ensure that the assembly of its 777 aircraft would work in practice. What costs might Boeing have incurred if some of the aircraft's 250,000 parts had not fitted together when they tried to manufacture it?

newspapers in many different countries would be very expensive, but using a website is cheap and considerably reduces advertising costs.

2 **Lower costs of ordering and storing raw materials and finished goods.** Using information technology to record sales and order new, raw materials and parts as required helps to reduce costs. For example, Jaguar uses over 9,000 parts to build each one of its luxury cars at its factory in Coventry. The company holds few components or raw materials on site, but uses IT to order them to arrive just in time for when they are needed. Thus, Jaguar does not need warehouses to store the parts, or need to employ warehouse staff.

3 **Lower design costs.** Designing products using information technology is both cheaper and more effective. The US aircraft manufacturer Boeing used computers and a design program to assemble a virtual Boeing 777. This allowed the company to check that over 250,000 parts would all fit together properly. Any that did not were redesigned. When the first Boeing 777 was finally built, there were few of the normal problems, which saved the company a great deal of money and time.

4 **Easier maintenance of a business's records.** Keeping computer records of the costs and revenues of a business makes it easier to see how the business is performing and to take correct decisions. Holding records on computer may also mean that fewer staff need be employed.

CASE STUDY

Fiona's flowers

'Fiona's Flowers' has had a successful first year. However, Fiona is not satisfied. She would like to attract more customers to her shop and increase her profits.

Fiona's accountant has suggested that she make more use of information technology in running her business. He says that this could help her win more customers cheaply and reduce costs in many ways. Fiona is very interested in these ideas.

Tasks

1 Suggest three ways in which Fiona could use information technology in her business. (3 marks)

2 Choose one of these ways and explain how it might help Fiona to reduce the running costs of 'Fiona's Flowers'. (4 marks)

3 Analyse two problems that Fiona might face if she were to use IT to help her run her new business. (8 marks)

The first 10 pages of Unit 3 introduced you to different types of costs and to revenue. You need to know about:

- the start-up costs of a business
- the different types of running costs that a business has to pay
- how to calculate profit from costs and revenues
- how information technology can help a business to reduce its costs.

EXAMINER'S TIP

Look carefully at the command words (or verbs) in the questions in your Unit 3 examination.

- Words such as 'name', 'state', 'list' or 'identify' require simple answers with no development.

- When questions use the words 'describe', 'outline' or 'explain', some depth is needed in answers.

- The word 'analyse' means that you have to draw conclusions from some figures (for example, whether the business has financial problems) or look at the advantages and/or disadvantages of a particular situation.

- Finally, you will be asked to make supported judgements. This requires you to give your opinions and to justify them. Words such as 'discuss', 'evaluate' and 'suggest and justify' may be used in these circumstances.

Questions asking you to analyse or evaluate will normally carry higher marks. The revision exercises that follow make use of these command words.

KEY WORDS AND PHRASES

Explain the meaning of the following words or phrases:

- costs
- revenue
- information technology
- profit.

(2 marks for each definition)

What is the difference between:

- start-up costs and running costs
- a mortgage and rent
- intranet and the internet?

(4 marks for each distinction)

You should refer back if you are unsure about the meaning of any of these words or phrases.

Revision exercises

Stanley Smith has decided to start business as a plumber.

1 List **four** start up costs that Stanley might have to pay.

(4 marks)

2 Once running his plumbing business, name **four** running costs that he might have to pay.
(4 marks)

3 Mordor Construction is a small building company. Its financial information for the last trading year is shown on the right.
   (a) Which are costs and which are revenues?   (3 marks)
   (b) How much were its running costs for the year?   (5 marks)
   (c) Calculate the amount of profits earned over the year.   (5 marks)

Revenue from building homes	£400 000
Wages	£150 000
Raw materials	£165 000
Advertising	£25 000
Fuel and power	£25 000
Revenue from doing repairs and other small jobs	£50 000

4 List four running costs that have to be paid by each of the following businesses:
   (i)   a business manufacturing computers   (2 marks)
   (ii) a country hotel   (2 marks)
   (iii) a fashion clothing shop.   (2 marks)

5 **Angela's pottery**
   Angela Martin is planning to open 'Loddon Pottery' in Norfolk. Angela is a very talented potter and makes pots and plates that are very popular.
   (a) Give **three** reasons why Angela should spend money on market research.   (3 marks)
   (b) List **four** other costs Angela might have to pay before starting her business.   (4 marks)
   (c) Analyse why it is important for Angela to keep her start-up costs to a minimum.   (6 marks)
   (d) State **four** running costs that Angela might have to pay.   (4 marks)
   (e) (i) Angela thinks that she might sell 500 pots at £25 each in the first six months. How much revenue will she earn? How much would she earn if she sold 600 pots but charged £22 each?   (5 marks)
        (ii) If Angela's running costs for the first six months are £10,000, how much profit will she make?   (5 marks)
   (f) If Angela adds VAT at 17.5 per cent to the £25 that she normally charges for one of her pots, how much will a customer have to pay?   (6 marks)
   (g) Suggest and justify two ways in which using information technology might help Angela to reduce the running costs of the Loddon Pottery.   (8 marks)

Angela Martin loading her pottery into the kiln for firing

   (h) Discuss how Angela might use the internet to help make her new business more successful?   (9 marks)

   Total = 50 marks

Keeping financial records

All businesses keep financial records of the transactions in which they take part. Any transaction involving money will result in several documents being produced. For example, the flow of documents following an order for pasta placed by a supermarket is shown in 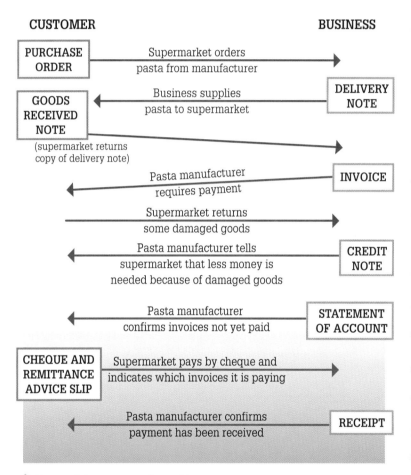 **A**. Both the supermarket and the pasta manufacturer need to keep documents as proof that the transaction has taken place.

A Financial documents exchanged between a supermarket and a pasta manufacturer

STOP & THINK

You have just been to the shops and bought a new pair of jeans. Which financial document will the sales assistant have put in the bag with the jeans?

STOP & THINK

In the exchange of documents between the supermarket and its pasta supplier, shown in **A**, which documents should the supermarket have copies of at the end of the transaction?

KEY CONCEPTS

A **cheque** is a document instructing a bank to pay money from one account into another.

Credit notes are documents that tell customers that they need pay less than they were previously asked to pay, or that a refund is due.

Delivery notes arrive with goods delivered and are signed by the receiver to confirm that the goods are correct and undamaged.

A **goods received note** is a copy of the delivery note left with the customer.

An **invoice** is a request for payment, listing the products supplied and the amount owing, sent by a business to a customer.

Purchase orders are documents requesting businesses to supply goods or services to customers.

A **statement of account** is a document, sent to a customer, listing all previous invoices and stating the amount of money still owed.

A **receipt** is a document sent by a supplier to a customer to confirm that payment has been received.

Remittance advice slips are sent by the customer to confirm which invoices are being paid.

Why keep financial documents?

Businesses keep financial documents for a variety of reasons.

1. **To avoid misunderstandings.** Financial documents help businesses and their customers to have a clear understanding of the transaction that has taken place. The documents confirm each stage of the transaction:
   - the customer's order
   - the prices to be paid
   - the delivery arrangements
   - the amount owed to the supplier
   - when the payment should be made
   - the amount that was paid.

2. **For legal reasons.** The government has passed laws stating which financial records businesses must keep.
   - All businesses must keep accurate financial records so that they pay the correct amounts of tax on profits. The Inland Revenue has the right to inspect business's financial records.
   - All but the smallest businesses keep accurate records to make sure that they pay the right amount of value added tax (VAT) to Customs and Excise.
   - Companies are controlled by the Companies Acts. They have to keep detailed financial records and to present them in a certain way.

3. **To help managers control the business.** Managers need information on the financial position of a business to help them to take the right decisions. The information from financial documents can help managers to:
   - calculate the business's sales
   - see which customers have paid for goods and services
   - advertise the business's products more widely
   - seek new suppliers for raw materials.

Computerised accounting systems

Nowadays, businesses are making more use of computers to record and store information on their financial transactions. Large businesses, such as British Telecom, use computers to send out their customer invoices. Computerised accounting systems are used as follows.

- Customer's details are entered into the computer.
- The accounting system prints out delivery notes, invoices, credit notes, statements of account and receipts.
- The system can provide managers with important information such as how much money is earned by the business.

STOP & THINK

Why might employees insist that a business keeps accurate financial records?

STOP & THINK

The electronic tills found at supermarket checkouts keep accurate records of the sales made by the business. What other benefits might an electronic till offer to a business?

OVER TO YOU

Talk to a friend or relative who runs a small business. Ask him or her the following questions.

- What financial records do you keep about your business?

- Do you use computers to help you keep these records?

- What would happen if you didn't keep accurate financial records?

Purchase orders, deliveries and goods received notes

Delivery notes, goods received notes and purchase orders are all belong to the early stages of the flow of documents in a financial transaction. They come into use from the moment an order is placed to time that the goods are delivered.

Purchase orders

As a first step in buying a good or service, the customer sends a purchase order form, like the one shown in , to the supplier. The form, as in , should include the customer details and the following information:

1   the supplier's name and address
2   the date when the order was placed
3   a reference number and an order number – to help identify an order in case of a problem
4   the quantity of goods or services being ordered, with further details in the description box, if required
5   a clear description of the products ordered – necessary if The County Hotel is to receive the right types of beer
6   the price the customer has agreed to pay, shown as both a price breakdown and a total figure, and normally excluding VAT
7   the address to which the goods should be delivered and the invoice sent – important for a large business, which may have several addresses.
8   the signature of a senior employee authorising the order – important for ensuring that the order is genuine.

Later, when the goods are delivered, the customer will use the purchase order to check that:
- the goods received are correct
- the prices on the supplier's invoice match the prices on purchase order.

KEY CONCEPTS

Delivery notes arrive with the goods and are signed by the receiver to confirm the goods are correct and undamaged.

A **goods received note** is a copy of the delivery note left with the customer.

Purchase orders are documents requesting businesses to supply goods or services to customers.

A **supplier** is any business that sells goods to another business or an individual.

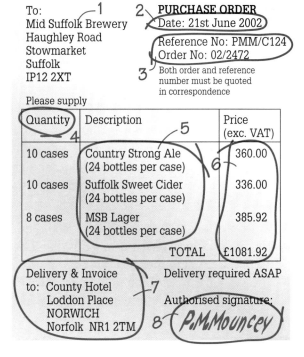

A A purchase order form addressed to Mid-Suffolk Brewery

Delivery notes

Having received an order, the supplier checks that the goods that have been ordered are available and makes arrangements for delivery. When the goods are sent to a customer, a delivery note, such as the one shown in **B**, is sent with them. A delivery note lists the items that are being delivered.

When the goods arrive the customer will:

- check the goods to make sure that they match what is on the delivery note
- make sure the items received are in good condition
- check that the goods match those listed on the purchase order form
- sign the delivery note to confirm that the goods have arrived safely

Signing a delivery note is an important step. After this, the customer is legally bound to pay for them.

Goods received notes

A goods received note is for the customer's use. It contains details of both the supplier and the customer, and of the goods supplied. It is very similar to a delivery note. There are two types of goods received note.

- In some businesses, a copy of the delivery note that accompanies the goods serves as a goods received note.
- Other businesses prepare their own goods received notes for their own, internal use.

By comparing the goods received note with the purchase order form, customers can ensure that their business is paying only for the goods it has received.

Mid Suffolk Brewery
Haughley Road
Stowmarket
Suffolk
IP12 2XT

Telephone 01449 272480
Delivery route 12b

INVOICE to
County Hotel
Loddon Place
Norwich
Norfolk NR1 2TM

DELIVER to
County Hotel
Loddon Place
Norwich
Norfolk NR1 2TM

Ref: CH/0242 **Account:** County Hotel
Date: 24th June 2002

Product	Description	Pack size	Quantity sent	To follow
CSA 24	County Strong Ale	24 bottles	10	0
SSC 24	Suffolk Sweet Cider	24 bottles	10	0
MSBL	MSB Lager	24 bottles	8	0

Received by:

Signature

B A delivery note sent from Mid-Suffolk Brewery sent with the delivery to The County Hotel

STOP & THINK

Suppose a case of County Strong Ale sent by the Mid-Suffolk Brewery to The County Hotel had been damaged in delivery. What should the hotel employee who receives the goods do in this situation?

To help you understand the contents of a purchase order form and a delivery note, you should design your own.

- Make up your own business name, address and other details such as telephone numbers and web site addresses.

- You will need two different businesses: one placing the order and the other delivering it.
- Design a logo for 'your' businesses.
- Complete the two financial documents with suitable details.

OVER TO YOU

Although you can draw up these documents by hand, it is much better to use information technology, if possible.

Invoices and credit notes

Invoices and, if necessary, credit notes are documents that are used in the middle stages of the buying process. They relate to the payment for the goods and services.

Invoices

Once the customer has received the goods or services, the supplier sends an invoice. This document states how much has to be paid for the products supplied, and by what date. An invoice, such as the one shown in **A**, normally contains the following detailed information:

- the address, telephone number and fax number of the supplier
- a description of each item supplied
- the quantity of each type of good supplied

Mid Suffolk Brewery
Haughley Road
Stowmarket
Suffolk
IP12 2XT

Telephone 01449 272480
Fax   01449 272712

3 — VAT reg. no: 121 8221394

Your order no: 02/2472

2

INVOICE to
County Hotel
Loddon Place
Norwich
Norfolk NR1 2TM

1

Invoice No: 2/TCH412   **Account:** County Hotel

Date: 5th July 2002

5   6

Product	Description	Quantity	Price	Net value
CSA 24	County Strong Ale	10	36.00	360.00
SSC 24	Suffolk Sweet Cider	10	33.60	336.00
MSBL	MSB Lager	8	48.24	385.92

4

10   7   Goods value £1081.92
8   VAT £189.34
Payment is due by 4th August 2002   Amount due £1271.26
9

A An invoice sent by Mid-Suffolk Brewery to The County Hotel requesting payment for the order supplied

STOP & THINK

How much VAT would The County Hotel pay on the invoice shown in **A** if the rate were 20 per cent?

Credit notes tell customers that they need pay less than they were previously asked to pay, or that a refund is due.

Invoices are requests for payment sent from the supplier to the customer.

Value added tax (**VAT**) is a tax paid by most businesses on the value of the products that they sell. Businesses can reclaim VAT paid on raw materials and components.

A **VAT registration number** is a unique number given to a business that has to collect VAT from its customers and pay the tax to Customs and Excise.

1 a number that identifies the particular invoice
2 the customer's order number – to show the customer which order the invoice refers to
3 the supplier's VAT registration number
4 the product codes for the goods or services supplied
5 the price per unit of each good supplied – in the example, the price per case of 24 bottles
6 the net value of each item supplied – that is, the value before VAT is added
7 the total net value of goods ordered
8 the amount of VAT due on the order – normally 17.5 per cent of the total value of the goods ordered
9 the total amount of the invoice – the total amount that the customer has to pay
10 the date by which payment is due. Businesses often allow customers a period of 30 or 60 days within which to pay the invoice.

Businesses must ensure that the invoices they send out are accurate.

- If the payments requested on the invoices are less than they should be, the business may not make a profit.
- If the invoices are for more than they should be, customers will be unhappy and may decide to buy from other businesses in the future.

Credit notes

Sometimes customers may be unhappy with the goods they receive. This can happen for a number of reasons.

- The goods may be damaged (for example, some of the bottles of beer ordered by The County Hotel could be broken during delivery).
- The wrong goods may have been sent, or the wrong quantities.
- The goods may be faulty (for instance, electrical products may not work).

In such circumstances, the supplier will send the customer a credit note. A credit note, which looks like a bit like an invoice, reduces the amount owed by the customer. An example is shown in **B** . This credit note was issued because two cases of Country Strong Ale delivered to The County Hotel were damaged.

To avoid confusion with invoices, credit notes are often printed in red. Credit notes are used reduce the sum that the customer has to pay or, if payment has already been made, to show that a refund, in some form, is due.

STOP & THINK

Can you think of any other reasons, apart from those already given, why a business might want to avoid sending out incorrect invoices?

B A credit note issued by Mid-Suffolk Brewery and sent to The County Hotel

CREDIT NOTE

Mid Suffolk Brewery
Haughley Road
Stowmarket
Suffolk
IP12 2XT

Telephone 01449 272480
Fax 01449 272712

VAT reg. no: 121 8221394
Your Order no: 02/2472

CREDIT to
County Hotel
Loddon Place
Norwich
Norfolk NR1 2TM

Credit No: 1/B6725 **Account:** County Hotel
Date: 24th July 2002

Product	Description	Quantity	Price	Net value
CSA 24	County Strong Ale	2	36.00	72.00

Goods value	£72.00
VAT	£12.60
Total Credit	£84.60

STOP & THINK

Look at the invoice and the credit note sent by Mid-Suffolk Brewery to The County Hotel. How much would the hotel end up paying?

OVER TO YOU

Previously you designed a purchase order form and a delivery note. Use the details of the two companies you created there to carry out the following tasks.

- Design an invoice and a credit note.
- Complete the invoice, requesting payment for the goods or services

ordered on the purchase order form that you designed earlier.

- Include a deliberate mistake, so that the company supplying the goods or services has to correct it.

Statements of account and remittance advice

If a supplier sends a customer invoices regularly, it may not always be clear which of those invoices have been paid and which are still unpaid. Statements of account and remittance advice slips help avoid such confusion.

Statements of account

At the end of every month, a supplier normally sends each of its customers a statement of account. This document lists the invoices and credit notes sent to the customer during that month. It also records any payments made by the customer in that time. At the bottom of the statement is the amount owed by the customer on the date that the statement was drawn up. The money owed by a customer to a supplier is known as the 'outstanding balance'.

KEY CONCEPTS

A **statement of account** is a document, sent to a customer, listing all previous invoices and showing the amount of money still owed.

Remittance advice slips are sent by the customer to confirm which invoices are being paid.

Outstanding balance is the amount of money owed by a customer to a business.

Mid Suffolk Brewery Haughley Road Stowmarket Suffolk IP12 2XT	STATEMENT	REMITTANCE ADVICE **Mid Suffolk Brewery** Haughley Road Stowmarket Suffolk IP12 2XT

Account date: 31st July 2002
Account: County Hotel 7/2002

County Hotel
Loddon Place
Norwich
Norfolk NR1 2TM

Account: County Hotel 7/2002

Please show the items you are paying (✔) and return this advice with your payment.

Date	Type	Reference	Value	Outstanding	Reference	Outstanding	✔
5 July 2002	Invoice	2/TCH412	1271.26	1186.66	2/TCH412	1186.66	
24 July 2002	Credit note	1/B6725	84.60				

A A statement of account sent by Mid-Suffolk Brewery to The County Hotel

The statement of account received by The County Hotel from Mid-Suffolk Brewery is shown in **A** . It would be normal for a statement like this to contain details of several invoices. The statement also records any credit notes received by the customer.

Perhaps The County Hotel will wait until it receives a statement of account and then pay all the invoices listed on it. However, before a business pays the amount shown on a statement, a number of checks will be made.

STOP & THINK

What might cause a statement of account to be inaccurate? What might be the consequences of an inaccurate statement of account?

- Were the goods ordered by someone with the authority to do so? Normally, a purchase order form is signed by a senior employee.

STOP & THINK

Why do you think that a senior employee has to sign a purchase order?

- Were the goods received in satisfactory condition?
- Were all the goods delivered?

Checking all the invoices against the purchase orders and goods received notes helps to avoid mistakes, so that customers end up paying the correct amounts to their suppliers.

Remittance advice slips

If everything is in order, the customer will pay the full amount shown on the statement of account. The statement may have a tear-off part called a remittance advice slip, as shown in **A**. Some businesses draw up their own remittance advice slips to send with their payment. This is easily done, using a computer.

Remittance advice slips help both the customer and the supplier.

- They make it clear which customer is paying for goods or services.
- They show which invoices customers are paying, for example by putting ticks next to them.
- They can be enclosed with the payment.

RHM Foodservice Ltd's website, showing a few of the company's products

STOP & THINK

RHM Foodservice Ltd supplies over 700 products to thousands of customers and, to ensure freshness, makes deliveries every day.

1 Why might it be important for RHM to send out remittance advice slips with its statements of account?

2 Suggest **two** things that might happen if RHM Foodservice Ltd were to send out inaccurate statements of account.

You work in the finance department of Mid-Suffolk Brewery. You have been asked to write a statement of account and remittance advice slip for The County Hotel for August 2002.
You have been given the following details of invoices and credit notes sent to the hotel:

- 12 August 2002. Invoice. Reference number 3/TCH578. Value £674.78

- 19 August 2002. Credit Note. Reference number 2/B6845. Value £112.43

- 26 August 2002. Invoice. Reference number 3/TCH579. Value £1,259.98.

Create your own documents, using IT if possible. Use the statement of account and remittance advice slip shown in **A** as a guide. This also gives addresses, telephone numbers and other details.

Cheques and receipts

Cheques and receipts are documents that are used near the end of a transaction. The supplier receives money from the customer and confirms that it has arrived. The business that pays the cheque is called the drawer. The business that is being paid is the 'payee'.

Cheques

A cheque is normally used to pay an invoice or a statement of account. Cheques are printed by banks for use by businesses. They are supplied in books of 50 or 100 and contain the features shown in .

- The name and address of the bank is shown clearly.
- The bank's sort code is shown in the top right-hand corner. Each branch of a bank has its own sort code.
- The name of the business whose account it is and the account number are shown at the bottom of the cheque.

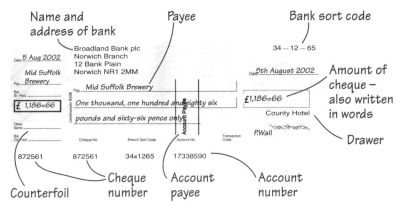

A cheque

H ow else might The County Hotel pay its statement of account other than by cheque?

- The drawer's name is also shown on the cheque.
- The drawer writes the payee's name on the top line of the cheque.
- The value of the cheque is written in words and numbers. (These must be the same!)
- The cheque is dated and signed by the drawer. It is common for business cheques to have two signatures. This helps to prevent cheques being used for the wrong purpose. Only senior employees are allowed to sign cheques.
- Most cheques are marked 'Account Payee', meaning that the cheque can only be used by the person (or business) named as the payee. This prevents theft.
- When a cheque is removed from the chequebook, a counterfoil is left. The counterfoil gives a record of the cheque, including its number, the amount paid and the name of the payee.

STOP & THINK

What are the advantages to The County Hotel of paying by cheque?

A cheque is only valid for six months from the date on which it is written. Businesses should pay cheques into their bank accounts as quickly as possible.

Receipts

A receipt confirms that payment has been made. Every time you spend money in a shop, you are given a receipt. Receipts given to businesses are similar.

A receipt proves that an invoice or statement of account has been paid. It is the last financial document used by businesses to record a transaction. Receipts usually contain the following information:

STOP & THINK

What advantages might a business gain from using an electronic till?

- the name and address of the business receiving the money
- the VAT registration number of the business (if it has a number)
- some details of the product that has been bought
- the date that the receipt was issued
- the amount paid and the amount of VAT charged.

```
              BONDS
        All Saints Green
            Norwich
            NR1 3LX
        TEL: 01603 660021

Speedo Scale
849.20125          1      19.75
Plain Jar m/s
720.29006          1      22.75
China Mug
720.90992          1      12.00
720.90993          1      12.00
Canister
822.62604          1       7.95

               TOTAL      74.45

        ACCOUNT              74.45

Reg Tran Asst Brch
034 4705 3711 035 29/09/01 15:20


Please keep this receipt for reference

       CUSTOMER RECEIPT

   A JOHN LEWIS DEPARTMENT STORE
```

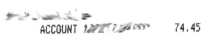

B A receipt produced by an electronic till

OVER TO YOU

We have now looked at the full range of financial documents used by businesses. To confirm your understanding of this topic, complete the following tasks.

1 Draw a flow chart to show the financial documents used by a business. Make sure you draw the documents in the right order.

2 By each of the documents, write a sentence saying what the document does. For example, next to an invoice you might write: 'The invoice is a request for payment sent to the customer.'

3 For each of the documents, say who sends it.

4 Which documents can be used to check that the figures in an invoice are correct?

The previous 10 pages introduced you to the financial documents used by businesses. You need to know:

- all the documents that are used and what details are included in each
- the order in which the documents are used (which document is used first, whether a delivery note is used before a remittance advice slip and so on)
- how the information on one financial document can be used to check another (for example, how a purchase order could be used to check the accuracy of an invoice)
- why it is important that documents are completed accurately.

Later (pages 180–1 and 202–3) we will see how computers can be used to produce financial documents.

EXAMINER'S TIP

It is important that you spend about the right amount of time answering each part of your Unit 3 examination. You can work out how long to spend on each question by finding out:

- the number of marks for the Unit 3 paper as a whole
- how long you have to complete the examination.

Then you should divide the number of marks available by the length of time you have to complete the exam, allowing a little time to read the questions. For example, if your examination is worth 100 marks in total and lasts for two hours (120 minutes), then you could allow 20 minutes to read the examination paper. That leaves 100 minutes to gain 100 marks. So, you should spend 5 minutes on a 5-mark question and 10 minutes on a 10-mark question.

KEY WORDS AND PHRASES

Explain the meaning of the following words or phrases:

- a supplier
- VAT
- a VAT registration number
- an outstanding balance.
(2 marks for each definition)

What is the difference between:

- a cost and a debt
- a credit note and a delivery note
- an invoice and a purchase order
- a statement of account and a receipt?
(4 marks for each distinction)

Refer back if you are unsure about the meaning of any of these words or phrases.

Revision exercises

1 State two reasons explaining why a purchase order is an important document. (2 marks)

2 Fill in the missing words in the following sentences.
.... documents request businesses to supply goods or services to customers. Delivery notes arrive with the .... and are signed by the .... to confirm the goods are correct and undamaged. A goods received note is a copy of the .... left with the customer. Invoices are requests for .... sent from the supplier to the customer. .... notes are documents that tell customers that they need to pay less than they were previously asked to pay, or that a refund is due. Statements of account are sent to the customer and list all the .... sent to the customer and the amount of money still owed. .... advice slips are sent by the customer to confirm which invoices are being paid. Cheques are instructions to a ...... to pay money from one account into another. The supplier sends a .... to the customer as confirmation that payment has been received. (11 marks)

3 Chiltern Pine Ltd

You are employed by Chiltern Pine Ltd. You have sent the invoice shown below to a local hotel, The George. They have returned it because it has errors.

(a) Identify each error in the invoice by drawing a circle around it. (4 marks)

(b) Explain two possible consequences of these errors. (6 marks)

(c) List three things that have been excluded from the invoice. (3 marks)

(d) Analyse the advantages to a business of producing accurate financial documents. (7 marks)

Total = 20 marks

4 Ludlow Fashions

You have just received a message from your boss, the manager of Ludlow Fashions. She has sent you a note, asking you to write out an order.

Will you please order the goods listed below from Baker & Sons, Armani Avenue, Shrewsbury, Shropshire SW2 3HP?

- 12 velvet jackets (blue) at £75 each
- 3 red evening dresses (scarleti style) at £84 each
- 8 silk scarves (white) at £50 each

Delivery is required with one week. The order number is BS/1234. You can sign the order.
Thanks
Sally

Complete this form to place the order for Sally, your boss. (10 marks)

I N V O I C E

Chiltern Pine Ltd
12 Swan Lane
Wendover
Bucks
HP12 9PM

Fax 01202 756398

Your order number: 65/2309

Invoice to:
George Hotel
High Street
Buckingham
HP19 6DT

Invoice number: 12/TG598   Account: The George Hotel

Product	Description	Quantiy	Price	Value
PBS12	Pine bar stools	20	90.00	1600.00
PDT36	Pine dining tables	12	40.00	480.00
PWD44	Pine wardrobes	6	250.00	1600.00
		Goods value		3680.00
		VAT @17.5%		544.00
		Amount due		**4224.00**

P U R C H A S E   O R D E R   F O R M

Ludlow Fashions
Mill Road
Ludlow
Shropshire
SW34 6SM

Telephone/Fax: 01875 254687
E-mail: Lulow sports centre@aol.com

Purchase Order Number:
Date: 13 November 2002
Delivery: to above address

Please supply:

Quantity	Description		Price (ex VAT)
		Total	

Delivery required:

Authorised signature   Date:

Making payments

Businesses make payments for the goods and services that they receive – which can include everything from raw materials to legal advice from a law firm. Businesses receive payments from customers to whom they supply goods and services. Two of the most straightforward ways of paying are with cash and by cheque. Other ways include credit transfer and direct debit (see pages 172–3).

Paying with cash

Sometimes customers or businesses like to pay straightforwardly, with notes and coins. Being paid in cash offers businesses several advantages.

- A business receives the payment immediately, without having to wait for a bank to transfer money into its account. This enables the business, if it so chooses, to use the money immediately.
- Payment in cash ensures that a business does get paid. Other forms of payment such as cheques are more open to fraud.

Payment in cash also has its disadvantages.

- A business paid large sums of cash will to have to arrange to move the money to a bank. This may involve the expense of using a security firm to prevent the money from being stolen in transfer.
- A business that is paid just in cash can only sell direct to its customers. For example, cash payments cannot be made for goods sold on the internet or by mail order.

STOP & THINK

Why might a market trader such as the one shown above prefer to be paid in cash?

JOINED-UP THINKING

We looked at cheques in some detail on pages 164–5. The features of a cheque and how they are used to make payments were explained there. Re-read these pages to remind yourself of how cheques work.

STOP & THINK

Can you think of ways in which information technology might help customers to pay businesses?

STOP & THINK

A business or person having a bank account may also have a paying-in book and a cheque guarantee card. When and how might these be used?

Paying by cheque

A cheque acts as an instruction to a bank to take money out of the drawer's account and put it into the payee's. Businesses frequently use cheques to pay invoices from other organisations. Generally, shoppers prefer other forms of payment, especially credit cards, because it takes time to write a cheque out.

Payment by cheque has certain disadvantages.

- Sellers of products will not receive their money immediately. It can take about five working days for the payment to enter their bank account. Meantime they may need that money to pay their own invoices.
- In some circumstances, the seller might not receive payment because the cheque 'bounces'. This means that the purchaser does not have enough money in his or her bank account to pay the cheque.
- Some banks charge buyers a fee for each cheque that they write, and charge sellers fees for paying cheques into their bank accounts. All banks will charge customers fees and interest if they overdraw. Overdrawing is when the bank pays out more money on someone's behalf than that person has in his or her account at that time.

The extra money paid out by the bank is called an overdraft.

However, there are also advantages to paying by cheque.

- Buyers may have bank guarantee cards. These guarantee that the amount on the cheque will be paid into the seller's bank account. However, most bank guarantee cards only support cheques of up to £100.
- Buyers know that writing out a cheque means that the money will not leave their bank account for several days. This means that they may receive a few extra days' interest on the money.

CASE STUDY

Sound Experience

Ella Marsh owns and manages 'Sound Experience', a nightclub in Ipswich. But she has only had the business for two months and knows little about managing the place. It is not making profits and Ella has little cash at the moment. However, she is due to receive some money in a few days.

Ella has just received a large electricity bill. She has enough cash (just) to pay this bill, but is not sure whether to pay with cash or by cheque.

Tasks

1 State **one** advantage and **one** disadvantage of paying by cash.
(2 marks)

2 Would you recommend that Ella pay the bill by cash or cheque? Give two reasons for your decision. (8 marks)

Popular alternatives to cash

Credit and debit cards are the most popular methods of payment in Britain, apart from cash. Over 90 per cent of British adults, and most businesses, have one or more credit cards.

Debit and credit cards are an electronic method of paying. They use a system called Electronic Transfer of Funds at Point Of Sale (EFTPOS). This is a computer network linking businesses and banks. It allows businesses to transfer money from the buyer's bank account to their own as soon as the sale is made.

Credit cards

Although there are many different types of credit cards, they are similar in many ways.

- They are plastic payment cards that allow the cardholder to make payments.
- The holder can use the credit card to borrow money up to a limit agreed with the bank or building society that issued the card.
- All cards charge interest on money that is borrowed; some charge a yearly fee as well.
- Cardholders have to make a payment on their card each month. They can pay a small part of what they owe or pay the entire amount.
- If a cardholder pays the entire debit they have built up each month, they are not charged any interest.

KEY CONCEPTS

Credit cards are a type of borrowing. They are issued by banks and building societies and can be used to buy goods and services up to an agreed limit.

Debit cards are not a type of borrowing. They are a means of paying with money that is already in the buyer's bank account.

Interest is a charge made to a borrower for a loan. Interest is normally calculated as a percentage.

STOP & THINK

The numbers of purchases made using different methods of payment are shown in **A**. Which methods are most likely to be used to pay for expensive items, such as a foreign holiday, and which for very cheap items, such as a bar of chocolate?

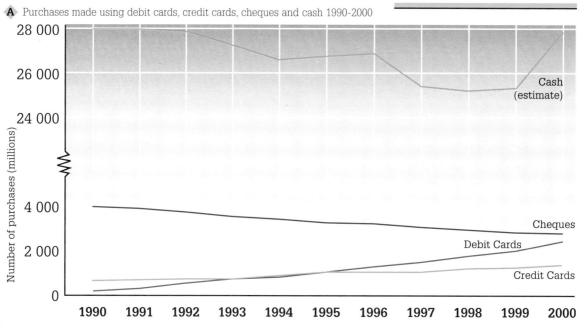

A Purchases made using debit cards, credit cards, cheques and cash 1990-2000

Source: www.apacs.org.uk/about

STOP & THINK

Why do you think a jeweller might be happy to accept payment by credit card? Can you think of any other businesses that might also be pleased to accept credit cards?

ADVANTAGES

- For purchasers, credit cards are an easy method of borrowing money.

- Credit cards are accepted by most businesses and can be used in many foreign countries.

- Buyers can borrow money without being charged any interest for up to four weeks.

DISADVANTAGES

- Sellers have to pay a fee to the credit card each time one of their customers uses a card. This is about 2 per cent of the amount spent.

- Some credit card companies charge very high rates of interest on credit cards. They can be very expensive way of borrowing money.

Advantages and disadvantages of payment by credit card

Debit cards

Debit cards may look very similar to credit cards, but there are important differences.

- Debit cards cannot be used to borrow money.
- They are linked to a bank or building society account. Cardholders must have money in their accounts to be able to use their debit cards.
- Debit cards provide sellers with an immediate payment. Money is moved from the buyer's bank account to the seller's account as soon as the card is used.

Many businesses prefer to receive payment by debit card, as they do not have to pay a fee to the bank or building society that issued the card. Buyers who do not want to bother writing out cheques every time may also like using debit cards.

OVER TO YOU

Carry out a survey in your local high street. Make a list of the businesses that are willing to accept credit and debit cards (they will have stickers in their windows). Also write down the names and types of businesses that do not accept cards.

1 What types of businesses
   - are happy to accept credit and debit cards?
   - prefer to be paid in cash?

2 Suggest why some businesses prefer to be paid in cash.

Modern payment methods

Direct debits and credit transfers are modern methods of making payments. Both happen automatically. They are carried out on behalf of buyers by banks and building societies.

Direct debits

Direct debits allow customers to pay regular bills automatically. A direct debit is an agreement under which a business selling goods and services can take money from the customer's bank account. For example, a small garage might sign a direct debit agreement to pay for its gas, shown in **A**.

A How a direct debit works

Brown's Garage buys its gas from the Eastern Gas Company. Brown's has agreed to pay by direct debit, paying £50 on the first day of each month. Both Brown's and Eastern Gas have bank accounts with Broadland Bank.

Paying by direct debit has its advantages for both buyers and sellers.

- Direct debits are free: buyers do not have to pay to use this method of payment.
- Buyers do not have to remember to pay regular bills. The direct debit scheme does this automatically.
- Sellers know that they will receive payment on time.
- Sellers can save time and money, as they do not have to pay cheques into their bank accounts or send out invoices or reminders to customers.
- Sellers usually receive payment promptly, so they are less likely to need to borrow money to pay their own invoices.
- The direct debit scheme offers customers a guarantee. If a mistake is made and too much is taken from a bank account, an instant refund is guaranteed.

Almost 32 million people pay bills using direct debits. They are very popular for paying certain types of bills. For example, in 1999 more than three-quarters of all mortgages in the UK were paid by direct debit, as shown in **B**.

KEY CONCEPTS

Credit transfers allow businesses and individuals to make electronic payments into bank or building society accounts.

Direct debits operate when customers allow businesses to take sums of money from their bank or building society accounts regularly.

JOINED-UP THINKING

Direct debits can help a business to manage its cash flow. You will learn more about cash flow on pages 176–9.

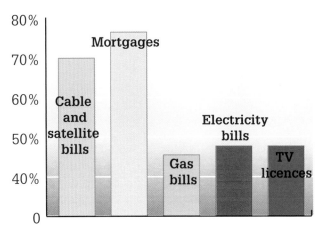

A security company at work

B Percentages of different bills paid by direct debit in the UK in 1999
Source: www.directdebit.co.uk/facts

Credit transfers

Credit transfer is also called 'direct credit'. It is method of payment that allows money to be moved directly from one bank account to another. Electronic transfer of this kind is used by businesses in different ways.

- Many businesses pay their employees each week or month by credit transfer. Over 70 per cent of employees in Britain are paid using credit transfer.
- Increasing numbers of businesses pay their suppliers using credit transfers.

Credit transfer offers businesses a number of advantages.

- It reduces the costs of paying wages. For example, if employees are not paid in cash, no administrative staff are needed to count out wages and prepare wage packets.
- It is secure. As there is no cash involved, it cannot be stolen.
- Payment can be made immediately. Money can be transferred from one bank account to another instantaneously.

In 2000, the largest 1,000 companies in Britain all used credit transfers to pay their employees' wages.

STOP & THINK

Why do you think that nearly half of all gas and electricity bills are paid by direct debit?

STOP & THINK

List as many costs as you can that a business may have to meet if it pays its employees in cash.

C A S E   S T U D Y

East Ham Clothing

Jacek Brant owns and manages a factory making clothing in the East End of London. Jacek employs 212 workers, most of whom are paid weekly. Jacek pays his workers in cash every Friday. However, he has been told that there are better methods of paying wages.

Tasks

1 State **two** other methods of payment Jacek could use to pay his workers.   (2 marks)

2 Explain **two** disadvantages of paying workers each week in cash.   (6 marks)

3 Suggest how Jacek should pay his workers. You should justify your answer.   (7 marks)

The previous six pages introduced you to the different methods of making and receiving payments. You need to know:

- the different methods of payment (cash, cheque, credit and debit cards, direct debit and credit transfer)
- how each payment method works
- the costs involved in each method of payment
- the time taken by each method of payment.

EXAMINER'S TIP

Unit 3 is assessed very differently from the way that Units 1 and 2 are assessed. It is important that you practise answering examination-style questions. You should attempt all the questions in the revision sections, such as those set out below. Your teacher will have the answers.

You should also complete the Unit 3 revision at the end of this unit. These review most topics within the unit and are similar to the type of questions you will have to answer in your examination.

Finally, it is very important that you attempt some of the past papers for the Unit 3 examination for your particular awarding body (AQA, Edexcel or OCR).

Revision exercises

1 Enterprise Service Station

The garage shown in **A** sells petrol and second-hand cars in a small village. The owner of the business, Harry Rowbory, has to pay suppliers for goods such as oil and petrol, and sweets and sandwiches for the garage's shop. He pays all of his suppliers each month.

Questions

(a) State **two** ways in which Harry might pay his suppliers.   (2 marks)

(b) Use your answer to (a). Explain **one** advantage and **one** disadvantage to Harry Rowbory of paying his suppliers in **each** of these ways.   (8 marks)

(c) Which method payment do you think the suppliers would prefer? Explain your answer.   (4 marks)

(d) Harry has two employees working at the garage. Suggest and justify the method Harry should use to pay his employees.   (6 marks)

Total = 20 marks

KEY WORDS AND PHRASES

Explain the meaning of the following words or phrases:

- an overdraft
- interest
- cheques
- cash
- invoices.
(2 marks per definition)

What is the difference between:

- credit cards and debit cards
- direct debits and credit transfers?
(4 marks per distinction)

You should refer back if you are unsure about the meaning of any of these words or phrases.

A A small country service station

2 Buckingham Gallery

Gill Nolan is the proud owner of the Buckingham Gallery, a shop in the centre of a busy town. Gill sells paintings and pottery made by local artists. Her shop is very popular and attracts large numbers of customers. Gill's paintings and pottery sell for high prices. It is not unusual for customers to buy items for £5,000 or more.

Gill has just agreed to sell a painting of a local church to a customer for £6,000. The customer has not decided on which method of payment to use.

Questions

(a) State **two** methods by which the customer could pay for the painting. (2 marks)

(b) Refer to your answer to question (a). In each case, explain **one** advantage and **one** disadvantage of the method of payment to the **customer**. (8 marks)

(c) What method of payment do you think that **Gill** would prefer? Explain your answer. (6 marks)

Total = 16 marks

3 Broadland Bank

You are an employee of Broadland Bank. Your boss has asked you to advise a local business about using credit transfer to pay its workers. The local business, Chalfont Garden Centre, has 29 employees working in three different towns. At present, Chalfont Garden Centre's workers are all paid monthly.

B Chalfont Garden Centre

The owner of Chalfont Garden Centre is thinking about using credit transfer to pay the business's workers.

Questions

(a) State **two** other ways in which Chalfont Garden Centre could pay its employees. (2 marks)

(b) Explain how credit transfer might be used to pay Chalfont Garden Centre's workers. (5 marks)

(c) Explain **two** advantages to Chalfont Garden Centre of using credit transfer to pay its workers. (6 marks)

(d) Do you think that Chalfont Garden Centre's workers would prefer to be paid by credit transfer? You should explain your answer. (7 marks)

Total = 20 marks

Cash flows

The money entering or leaving a business is called cash flow. Cash inflow is the money that the business receives. Cash outflow is the money that the business pays out.

Cash inflows

Cash inflows may be caused by a number of factors.

- **Sales revenue.** Firms receive money for selling goods and services. Payment from customers is a cash inflow for the business.
- **Loans from banks.** All businesses borrow money from the bank at some time. Such a loan is a cash inflow for the business.
- **Grants from the government.** The government gives grants to businesses if they create jobs in areas of the country where many people are out of work. This is an important cash inflow for new and growing businesses.

Cash outflows

Cash flows out of a business for several reasons.

- **Buying raw materials.** Manufacturing businesses spend large amounts on raw materials and components. This is a major cash outflow for these businesses.
- **Paying wages.** This causes a major outflow of cash for all businesses, but particularly businesses providing services.
- **Rent.** If a business leases its premises, it will pay rent, causing a regular outflow of cash.
- **Interest on loans.** Whereas a bank loan leads to an inflow of cash, paying interest on the loan leads to a regular cash outflow.
- **Telephone.** All businesses suffer a regular outflow of cash when they pay for telephone services.
- **New machinery.** Businesses need machinery, whether

KEY CONCEPTS

Cash flow is the money that enters and leaves a business as it makes and receives payments.

A **cash flow forecast** states the inflows and outflows of cash that managers expect over a future time period.

A **cash inflow** takes place when a business receives money.

A **cash outflow** occurs when money leaves the business.

STOP & THINK

The cash flows that Vicki Leverett, the owner of the new Cathedral Bookshop, expects in the first four months of trading are shown in **A**. Which of Vicki's outflows do you think are one-offs (that is, she doesn't have to pay them regularly)?

A Expected cash flows for a new bookshop

	JANUARY	FEBRUARY	MARCH	APRIL
Cash inflows +	• Loan from bank £35 000 • Sales revenue (sales of books) £4800	• Sales of books £6000	• Sales of books £8500	• Sales of books £10 500
Cash outflows −	• Buying stock of books £36 000 • Wages £2000 • Interest on bank loan £350	• Three months rent £10 000 • Wages £2000 • Interest on bank loan £350	• Purchase of computer £1500 • Wages £2200 • Interest on bank loan £350 • New stock of books £1500	• Telephone bill £750 • Wages £2200 • Interest on bank loan £350 • Purchase of extra bookshelves for shop £2500

production-line robots, computers or photocopiers. Buying new machinery can cause a large outflow of cash.

■ **Taxes.** Businesses have to pay sales taxes and taxes on profits, both of which cause cash outflows.

Cash flow forecasts

The inflows and outflows of cash that are expected by business managers are called cash flow forecasts. The cash flow forecast for the first four months of Vicki Leverett's new Cathedral Bookshop is shown in ◆B◆.

■ The cash inflows are normally recorded first and added together to give a Total Cash Inflow (A).

■ Cash Outflows are also added together as Total Cash Outflow (B).

■ The row called Net Cash Flow (C) shows the balance between cash outflows and cash inflows over the month. It is calculated by subtracting the Total Cash Outflow from the Total Cash Inflow.

■ The amount of cash held by the business at the start of the month is shown by the Opening Balance figure (D).

■ The amount of cash the business has at the end of the month is shown by the Closing Balance figure (E). Closing Balance is calculated by adding together Opening Balance and Net Cash Flow.

■ The Closing Balance for one month becomes the Opening Balance for the next month.

		JANUARY (£)	FEBRUARY (£)	MARCH (£)	APRIL (£)
Cash Inflows					
Vicki's savings		12 500	0	0	0
Bank loan		30 000	0	0	0
Sales revenue from books		4800	6000	8500	10 500
Total cash inflow (A)		47 300	6000	8500	10 500
Cash outflows					
Purchase of stocks of books		36 000	0	15 000	0
Wages		2000	2000	2200	2200
Interest on bank loan		350	350	350	350
Rent (for three months)		0	10 000	0	0
Telephone charges		0	0	0	750
New machinery, eg computers		0	0	1500	2500
(B) Total cash outflow		38 350	12 350	19 050	5800
(C) Net cash flow		8950	−6350	−10 550	4700
(D) Opening balance		0	8950	2600	−7950
(E) Closing balance		8950	2600	−7950	−3250

Closing balance is calculated by adding net cashflow to Opening balance

Net cash flow is calculated by subtracting Total cash outflow from Total cash inflow

The closing balance for one month is the opening balance for the next

B Cash flow forecast for the Cathedral Bookshop

STOP & THINK

Looking at The Cathedral Bookshop's cash flow forecast shown in **B**, what will be the opening balance for May?

CASE STUDY

The Cathedral Bookshop

Vicki has decided to extend her cash flow forecast into May and June. She has estimated the following figures:

■ sales revenue for May, £15, 000
■ wages for May and June, £2,200 in each month
■ rent for three months (paid in May), £10, 000
■ interest on bank loan, £350 in May and £350 in June
■ purchase of computer printer, £250 in May
■ sales revenue for June, £17, 500.

Tasks

1 What is the opening balance for The Cathedral Bookshop for May?   (1 mark)

2 Which of the items listed are cash inflows and which are cash outflows?   (6 marks)

3 Using **B** as a model, draw up the cash flow forecast for The Cathedral Bookshop for May and June.   (13 marks)

Managing cash flow

If a business does not have enough money coming in to pay its bills, it may not survive. If the business's suppliers do not receive payment on time, they may force the business to close down. Therefore it is very important for a business to manage its cash flow carefully.

Cash flow forecasts can help managers to:

- spot times when the business might be short of cash
- see the causes of cash flow problems
- decide whether to produce new goods or services or to stop selling existing product.

Vicki's cash flow problems

Vicki Leverett's cash flow forecast for her new Cathedral Bookshop was discussed on page 177. It is shown again here in **A** .

The graph in **B** shows Vicki's forecast of her business's cash flow. A negative figure in a cash flow can be shown in one of two ways:

- a minus sign (this is how a spreadsheet shows it)
- brackets around the figure.

You can see that during March Vicki expects that her business will have a cash problem. In March her cash outflow will be greater than her cash inflow. This means that her business will run out of cash. Vicki could overcome this problem in several ways.

- **She could arrange an overdraft.** This is a flexible loan that she could use during

	JANUARY (£)	FEBRUARY (£)	MARCH (£)	APRIL (£)
Cash Inflows				
Vicki's savings	12 500	0	0	0
Bank loan	30 000	0	0	0
Sales revenue from books	4800	6000	8500	10 500
Total cash inflow	**47 300**	**6000**	**8500**	**10 500**
Cash outflows				
Purchase of stocks of books	36 000	0	15 000	0
Wages	2000	2000	2200	2200
Interest on bank loan	350	350	350	350
Rent (for three months)	0	10 000	0	0
Telephone charges	0	0	0	750
New machinery, eg computers	0	0	1500	2500
Total cash outflow	**38 350**	**12 350**	**19 050**	**5800**
Net cash flow	**8950**	**–6350**	**–10 550**	**4700**
Opening balance	**0**	**8950**	**2600**	**–7950**
Closing balance	**8950**	**2600**	**–7950**	**–3250**

A Cash flow forecast for the Cathedral Bookshop

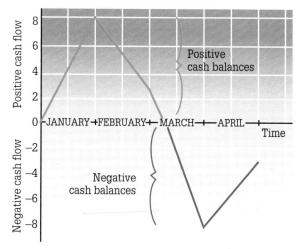

B Graph showing the Cathedral Bookshop's cash balance

the months when her business was short of cash. Banks encourage businesses to draw up cash flow forecasts and will give overdrafts.

- **She could try to reduce her costs.** For example, she might purchase fewer books to sell in her shop. This would reduce the cash outflow and would help with her cash problems.
- **She might try to increase her cash inflow.** If the Cathedral Bookshop could sell more books, the cash position of Vicki's business would improve.

◆ **C** Banks, such as Barclays, encourage businesses to draw up cash flow forecasts

The usefulness of cash flow forecasts

Most businesses draw up cash flow forecasts, usually for the next year. Cash flow forecasts help managers to make sure the business has enough cash to pay bills. They also help businesses in making important decisions.

- **Whether to go ahead with a new product.** A cash flow forecast might help Vicki to decide whether to proceed with opening her shop. If she thinks that the cash flow problems are too difficult to overcome, she might give up the idea.
- **Whether to invest in new resources.** For example, Vicki may decide not to buy a computer in March because of her business's poor cash flow position.
- **Whether to expand or reduce new activities.** If, for example, Vicki's cash flow position were stronger, she might decide to sell tapes and CDs as well as books.

	APRIL	MAY	JUNE	JULY
Cash Inflows				
Tom's savings	2500			
Bank loan	2500			
Sales revenue	2500	2750	2950	3150
Total cash inflow	**7500**	**2750**	**?**	**3150**
Cash outflows				
Purchase of materials	500	600	650	650
Wages	1500	1500	1500	1500
Interest on bank loan	125	125	125	125
Monthly rent	500	500	500	500
Telephone charges			250	
New machinery eg van	5000	850	0	0
Total Outflow	**7625**	**?**	**3025**	**2775**
Net cash flow	**?**	**–825**	**–75**	**375**
Opening balance	**0**	**–125**	**–950**	**–1025**
Closing balance	**–125**	**–950**	**–1025**	**?**

CASE STUDY

Tom's Dream

Tom Dix has dreamed for a long time of being his own boss. He has decided to start his own business repairing and cleaning cars. He has rented a garage to use as a workshop and also plans to visit his customers at their homes to work on their cars.

His cash flow forecast for the first four months is as shown above

Tasks

1 Complete Tom's cash flow by calculating and filling in the figures shown by a **?**
(4 marks)

2 Explain **two** problems that Tom's business might have with its cash flow? (6 marks)

4 Discuss **two** ways in which Tom could improve the cash flow position of his new business. (10 marks)

Producing cash flow forecasts on a spreadsheet

The spreadsheet program we will be using is Microsoft Excel. To draw up a cash flow forecast, first load the Excel program and open a new file (called a book). Each page of a spreadsheet is made up of rows (across the page) and columns (down the page). The columns are shown by the letters A, B, C etc. The rows are numbered from 1 upwards. In this way, every cell on the spreadsheet can be identified. For example, the top left-hand cell is A1.

Step-by-step instructions

Follow the steps set out here to construct a cash flow forecast, such as for the Cathedral Bookshop, using a spreadsheet, as shown in **A** .

1 Adding titles

The overall title should include the name of the business. The spreadsheet should have three main sections:

- **cash inflows**, setting out and showing the total cash entering the Cathedral Bookshop each month.
- **cash outflows**, stating the amount of cash leaving the Cathedral Bookshop each month. (This section will also show the net cash flow (that is, cash inflows less cash outflows.)
- **opening and closing balances**, setting out the Cathedral Bookshop's cash balances at the start and end of each month.

2 Entering data

Next, enter the cash inflow and outflow forecast figures for each month. Copy the figures from the cash flow forecast table for Vicki's bookshop on page 178.

Spreadsheets are computer programs used to calculate and display numerical information.

Spreadsheet formulae are typed in to tell the computer to carry out calculations such as addition and subtraction.

A Cash flow forecast spreadsheet for Vicki's Cathedral Bookshop

	A	B	C	D	E
1		JANUARY	FEBRUARY	MARCH	APRIL
2	Cash inflows				
3	Vicki's savings				
4	Bank loan				
5	Sales revenue from books				
6	Total cash inflow				
7					
8	Cash outflows				
9	Purchase of stocks of books				
10	Wages				
11	Interest on bank loan				
12	Rent (for three months)				
13	Telephone charges				
14	New machinery, eg computers				
15	Total cash outflow				
16	Net cash flow				
17					
18	Opening balance				
19	Closing balance				

3 Putting in formulae

Formulae tell the program to carry out calculations. The tinted cells in **A** indicate where the formulae should go.

- To find out the Total Cash Inflow, you need to add up all the cash inflows. First, click on the cell where you want the answer to appear. Start with the Total Cash Inflow for January, which will appear in cell B6.

- Begin writing a formula by typing = (equals sign). This tells the computer that it is a formula. Now, to add up, type **sum**, followed by, in brackets, the cells to be add up. So, in this case, our formula will read: **=sum(B3:B5)**. Type the formula, leaving no spaces, and press the enter button. The spreadsheet will perform the calculation for you.

- This formula can easily be copied for the other months. There is no need to write it in each time. Click on cell B6, where your have you answer for January, and a small black square will appear in the bottom right-hand corner. If you move the cursor over this square, the cursor will change to a +. Now, holding down the left-hand button of the mouse, drag the cursor across the squares where you want the formula to be copied. This action is called replicating.

- The same process can be used to add up the Total Cash Outflow.

- The figure for Net Cash flow for a particular month can be calculated by taking the Total Cash Outflow for that month away from that month's Total Cash Inflow. So, for January, we would write in cell B16 = **B6 – B15**. This formula can then be replicated to produce the Net Cash Flow for the other months.

- Finally, the Closing Balance for each month can be calculated by adding the Net Cash Flow to the Opening Balance. For January, we would type in cell B19 = **B16+B18**. This can be replicated to provide a closing balance for the other months.

- To give the Opening Balances, you need only set them equal to the closing balance for the previous month. For January, we would type in a figure as we do not have a previous month. For February's Opening Balance we would type in = **B19** (January's Closing Balance). This formula would be replicated for March and April.

The advantage of spreadsheets is that if you alter any figures, the program will recalculate the entire cash flow forecast. Thus, it is possible to see the effects of any changes in cash inflows or outflows.

OVER TO YOU

By now, you should have the Cathedral Bookshop's cash flow forecast on a spreadsheet. Make the following changes to it:

- increase the rent to £11,000 each three months

- reduce the interest on the loan to £300 each month

- change Vicki's sales figures to £10,000 in March and £12,000 in April.

What are the new closing balances for each month?

Preparing budgets

A budget is a short-term plan prepared by a business. Budgets are used by businesses to forecast:

- expenditure (on wages or raw materials, for example)
- revenue from sales of goods and services
- profits (by comparing revenues and expenditures).

A budget can cover a period of a few months or a few years. Most often, budgets cover a period of one year. The person with responsibility for a budget is called a budget holder.

KEY CONCEPTS

A **budget** is a financial plan showing expected revenues and/or costs.

STOP & THINK

When you get money from your parents or from a part-time job, do you plan your expenditure for each week or each month? What do you plan to spend next week's money on?

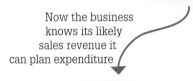

STAGE 1
The business draws up an income or revenue budget to forecast sales

Now the business knows its likely sales revenue it can plan expenditure

A The process of preparing a budget

STAGE 2
The business's managers can forecast its expenditure on wages and other costs

Now profits can be forecast

STAGE 3
By comparing revenue and expenditure budgets, profits can be forecast

Revenue or income budgets

The forecasts of the sales revenue that a firm expects to receive over some future time period are called revenue or income budgets.

We shall look at the example of Fryer Tuck's, a chain of fish and chip shops in Scotland. The company runs 14 shops and the company's managers are preparing their budgets for the next year. The managers start the process by forecasting the income expected from sales.

The information for Fryer Tuck's sales budget might come from:

- its sales over recent years
- market research among customers to discover whether sales are likely to increase or fall in the future.

	Jan – March	April –June	July – Sept	Oct – Dec	Total
	£	£	£	£	£
Sales of fish and chips	142 575	139 360	141 800	168 250	**591 985**
Sales of soft drinks	29 546	28 950	41 500	37 660	**137 656**
Total sales	**172 121**	**168 310**	**183 300**	**205 910**	**729 641**

B Fryer Tuck's sales revenue budget

Expenditure budgets

Once a business knows its expected sales, it can estimate expenditure. Fryer Tuck's can estimate the following costs:

- expenditure on wages, for example staff preparing and selling fish supper
- expenditure on fish, potatoes, oil and other materials
- rent and rates
- other costs.

Preparing an expenditure budget is helpful to businesses. It makes them think about what they spend money on and how spending might be reduced.

Fryer Tuck's fish and chip shop

	Jan – March	April – June	July – Sept	Oct – Dec	Total
	£	£	£	£	£
Wages	52 750	53 600	56 983	59 341	**222 674**
Fish, potatoes etc..	27 565	25 243	27 050	31 464	**111 322**
Rent & rates	44 905	44 440	43 838	44 345	**177 528**
Other costs	35 115	36 317	37 064	39 000	**147 496**
Total expenditure	160 335	**159 600**	**164 935**	**174 150**	**659 020**

C Fryer Tuck's expenditure budget

Profit budgets

Using budgets that show planned revenue and expenditure, a business's managers can forecast profits. This forecast can help managers decide whether, for example, a certain scheme is worth investing in.

We can see from **D** that Fryer Tuck's is forecasting a profit of £70,621 for the next year.

STOP & THINK

What costs do you think might have to be paid by a chain of fish and chip shops besides those listed under 'Expenditure budgets'?

The importance of budgets

	Jan – March	April – June	July – Sept	Oct – Dec	Total
	£	£	£	£	£
Total sales	172 121	168 310	183 300	205 910	729 641
Total expenditure	160 335	159 600	164 935	174 150	659 020
Profit	**11 786**	**8710**	**18 365**	**31 760**	**70 621**

D Fryer Tuck's profit budget

Budgets help businesses to manage their finances in three important ways.

- Budget holders are senior employees within a business. They are the only people with the authority to spend money. Having a few senior employees taking all spending decisions makes it easier for a business to ensure that it does not spend too much.
- Budget holders can prevent the business from spending money on unnecessary items, such as very expensive mobile phones for the sales force.
- Budgets prevent fraud. For example, budget holders make sure that employees do not buy items such as computers for their personal use.

The usefulness of budgets

Using budgets offers businesses several advantages.

- Budgets assist businesses in setting targets for revenues and profits.
- Managers can use budgets to decide if the business is performing as well as expected.
- By watching expenditure budgets, managers can check that a business does not spend more than it should.

Checking revenue budgets

Fryer Tuck's fish and chip shops' actual sales figures for the year are shown in  . The business has sold more than it forecast. The difference between the actual and budgeted figures is called a variance. The company's forecast sales were £591,985, whilst its actual sales were £604,814. This is called a favourable variance because it is good news for the business. Each of the variances shown in A has the letter 'F' after it to show it is favourable.

KEY CONCEPTS

A **budget** is a financial plan showing expected revenues and/or costs.

A **variance** is the difference between budgets for costs, revenues or profits and the actual figures.

A **favourable variance** occurs when actual sales are higher than expected, or costs lower than forecast.

An **adverse variance** occurs when actual sales are lower than expected, or costs higher than forecast.

STOP & THINK

Fryer Tuck's have sold more fish and chips and soft drinks than they expected. Why do you think this happened?

	Budget for the Year (£)	Actual Figures for the Year (£)	Variances (£)
Sales of fish and chips	591 985	604 814	12 829 F
Sales of soft drinks	137 656	137 942	286 F
Total sales	**729 641**	**742 756**	**13 115 F**

A Fryer Tuck's sales revenue budget

Checking expenditure budgets

Managers of businesses do not want costs to increase, because this may cause profits to fall. The budgeted costs and actual expenditure figures for Fryer Tuck's for the year are shown in **B** .

The variances for wages, raw materials (such as fish and potatoes) and rent and rates are favourable. This is because,

	Budget for the Year (£)	Actual Figures for the Year (£)	Variances (£)
Wages	222 674	220 543	2131 F
Fish, potatoes etc..	111 322	111 010	312 F
Rent & rates	177 528	174 388	3140 F
Other costs	147 496	148 775	1279 A
Total expenditure	**659 020**	**654 716**	**4304 F**

B Fryer Tuck's sales expenditure budget

STOP & THINK

State **two** reasons why Fryer Tuck's wages bill might have been lower than was forecast.

STOP & THINK

Marks & Spencer sets separate budgets for each of its stores. What advantages do you think the firm might gain from doing it this way?

in each case, the costs are lower than was forecast. Again, this is good news for the Scottish fish and chip shop chain.

However, some costs are higher than was forecast, and so the variance in these cases is not good news for the business. This variance is described as adverse. It is indicated by 'A' in the budget figures. Still, the variance for Fryer Tuck's total expenditure is favourable because the company's overall costs are lower than expected.

Checking profit (or loss) budgets

We can put together the budgeted figures and the actual figures to check the company's performance. We can see that whereas Fryer Tuck's forecast a profit of £70,621 for the year, its actual profit was £88,040. So the company's profit was higher than expected. This is good news for the business, and a favourable variance.

	Budget for the Year (£)	Actual Figures for the Year (£)	Variances (£)
Total sales	729 641	742 756	13 115 F
Total expenditure	659 020	654 716	4304 F
Profits	70 621	88 040	17 419 F

C Fryer Tuck's profit budget

CASE STUDY

The Spitfire Restaurant

Greg Garner's Spitfire Restaurant is one of the most popular in Manchester. He has just completed a very successful year's trading. In his budget at the start of the year he forecast total revenue of £246,000 and total expenditure of £206,000. However, his actual sales revenue for the year was £255,000, and his total expenditure £203,000. He thinks his business has enjoyed a good year.

Tasks

1 Calculate:
- the profit figure that Greg forecast (3 marks)
- the actual profits earned by the Spitfire Restaurant. (3 marks)

2 Calculate the variances for revenues, expenditure and profits for the Spitfire Restaurant. (6 marks)

3 Discuss whether Greg's restaurant has had a good year. (8 marks)

REVISION 4

The previous 10 pages introduced you to the cash flow and budgets. You need to know:

- the cash inflows and cash outflows that a business might experience
- how to complete a simple cash flow forecast
- how to use spreadsheets to complete cash flow forecasts and the advantages of using spreadsheets
- why businesses draw up budgets
- how to analyse budgets using variance analysis
- the benefits to businesses of using budgets.

Revision exercises

1 The Wherry Hotel

The Wherry Hotel is a popular hotel in Suffolk. The hotel has recently been bought by Mr and Mrs Wharton. One of the new owners' first actions is to draw up a cash flow forecast. Mrs Wharton uses a spreadsheet to complete this task. She enters the following data.

	APRIL	MAY	JUNE	JULY
	(£)	(£)	(£)	(£)
SALES REVENUE	46 000	51 000	62 500	67 500
Wages	11 450	12 450	14 200	16 000
Heat and light	6700	5 600	5750	6100
Food and drink	12 400	14 560	15 750	18 000
Other expenses	23 500	13 500	14 800	17 750

(a) Use the information given to complete the cash flow forecast shown in **A** on page 187. You should use a spreadsheet to perform this task. (15 marks)

(b) Give **one** reason why this cash flow forecast might be useful to Mr and Mrs Wharton. (3 marks)

(c) Study the completed cash flow forecast carefully. Will Mr and Mrs Wharton face cash flow problems at any time between April and July? Explain your answer. (5 marks)

(d) Suggest and justify **two** actions that Mr and Mrs Wharton might take to improve the cash flow position of their business. (8 marks)

(e) Mr and Mrs Wharton have negotiated a new wages policy such that the wages of the hotel staff will be £14,000 every month.

The Wherry Hotel

	APRIL	MAY	JUNE	JULY
Cash Inflows				
Sales revenue			62 500	
Total cash inflow			**62 500**	
Cash outflows				
Wages	11 450			
Heat & Light				
Food & Drink				
Other Expenses				
Total Outflow				
Net Cashflow				
Opening Balance	2500			
Closing Balance				

A Wherry Hotel's cash flow forecast

(i) Recalculate the spreadsheet including the new figures for wages. (6 marks)

(ii) Does this improve or worsen the business's cash flow position? (4 marks)

(f) Mr and Mrs Wharton are thinking about building an extension to their hotel. Evaluate whether the information in the cash flow forecast shows that this would be a good idea. (9 marks)

Total = 50 marks

2 Budgets at the Wherry Hotel

Mr and Mrs Wharton have decided to use budgets to help manage their new business. The budget and actual figures for the hotel's bars for the first four months are shown in the table **B**.

	Budget for April – July	Actual Figures for April – July	Variances
Sales Revenue (£)	39 675	41 300	?
Expenditure (£)	28 450	31 765	?
Profit or loss (£)	?	?	?

B Budget for the Wherry Hotel's bars, April–July.

(a) Complete the budget table in **B**. (5 marks)

(b) (i) Explain what a favourable variance is. (3 marks)
   (ii) State whether each of the three variances you have found is adverse or favourable. (3 marks)

(c) Analyse **three** advantages that Mr and Mrs Wharton might gain from using budgets to manage their new business. (9 marks)

Total = 20 marks

STOP & THINK

Do you think Mr and Mrs Wharton have made a good start to managing their hotel? You should explain your answer.

What is breaking even?

A business can make a profit only when its sales revenue is greater than its costs. If revenue is less than costs the firm will make a loss. Break even is a level of production (or output) at which revenue from sales equals the costs of the business. In this situation a business will not make a loss or a profit.

If total revenues are greater than total costs…	…the business will make a profit.
If total revenues are less than total costs…	…the business will make a loss.
If total revenues equal total costs …	…the business will break even

A Revenues, costs, profits and losses

Costs, revenue and the break-even point formula

To calculate break-even output, a business needs specific information both on types of costs and on revenues.

- **Fixed costs** are costs that do not change however much a business produces. Costs such as rent and insurance must be paid irrespective of output.
- **Variable costs** are running costs that depend on the business's level of production. If a business increases its production, variable costs, such as wages and the cost of raw materials, will also increase.
- **Variable cost per unit** is the variable cost of producing one unit of a good or service. Thus, if the variable cost of producing 100 DVDs is £75, the variable cost per unit will be 75p (£75 x 100).
- **Revenue** is income received from the sale of goods and services. It can be calculated by multiplying the selling

KEY CONCEPTS

Break-even is the level of production at which total costs equal revenue. This is sometimes called 'break-even point'.

Fixed costs are the costs of a business that do not change when the level of output rises or falls.

Variable costs are the costs that do change when a business raises or lowers its level of output.

Total costs are fixed costs and variable costs added together.

STOP & THINK

Give **three** examples of fixed costs and **three** examples of variable costs that a container ship business might have to pay.

A container ship in port

price by the number of units sold. If a market trader sells 50 pairs of jeans at £20 each, his revenue will be £1,000 (£50 x 20).

To calculate the level of production required for a business to break even, the following formula is used:

$$\text{Break-even point} = \frac{\text{fixed costs}}{\text{(selling price per unit of production minus variable costs per unit of production)}}$$

Calculating break-even – an example

Imogen Peace owns and manages one of Nottingham's most popular nightclubs. *Imogen's* is in the city centre and opens every night of the week, except for Monday. The place has a reputation for using top DJs and playing a variety of music. At weekends it usually gets very crowded.

Imogen has a number of costs to pay to keep her nightclub running.

- She pays rent and rates as well as insurance.
- She has to pay the wages of DJs, security staff and bar staff.
- Other costs include heating, lighting and telephones.

Imogen has calculated that her fixed costs each week amount to £3,000. She charges each clubber an admission fee of £4. The variable cost of each customer is £1.50. Imogen offers all customers a free first drink and has to hire extra security staff if large numbers of clubbers turn up.

The break even point for *Imogen's* each week is:

$$= \frac{£3,000}{(£4 - £1.50)} = \frac{£3,000}{£2.50} = 1,200 \text{ clubbers each week.}$$

So, Imogen has to have 1,200 clubbers in her nightclub each week if her business is to break even. If she gets more than 1,200 in a week she will make a profit. Fewer than 1,200 will cause her business to make a loss.

STOP & THINK

Suppose that Imogen increases her admission price to £4.50. How many clubbers will need to visit *Imogen's* each week for the nightclub to break-even?

CASE STUDY

Caroline's Café 1

Caroline's Café has only been open for three months. She sells a range of home cooked meals and freshly made cakes. Caroline is wondering if her business will make a profit. The café has the following fixed costs each month:

- rent and rates £500
- insurance £100.

Caroline knows that her customers spend an average of £10 each. But she has calculated that the variable cost of serving each customer is £6.

Tasks

1 How much are the fixed costs (in total) for Caroline's Café each month? (1 mark)

2 List **three** variable costs that Caroline might have to pay. (3 marks)

3 How many customers does Caroline need each month to break even? (6 marks)

4 Caroline is thinking of increasing her prices so that customers spend £12 each on average. Assuming her fixed costs and variable costs per customer do not change, how many customers will she need to break even? (6 marks)

Break-even chart

We saw on page 189 how break-even is calculated. It is also possible to draw a chart or graph to show the break-even point. A typical break-even chart is shown in **A**.

This chart is for Keith Young, who makes glass paperweights. His business has fixed costs of £7,500 a year. He sells his paperweights at £25 each and reckons that the variable cost of producing one is £10.

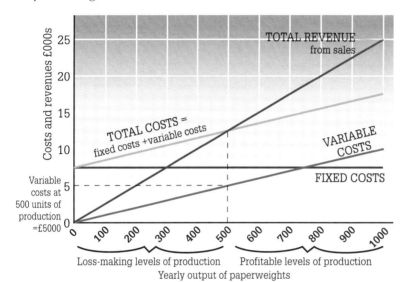

A Break-even chart for Keith Young's business

KEY CONCEPTS

A **break-even chart** shows a business's costs and revenues and the level of production needed to break even.

STOP & THINK

List five pieces of information that are needed to draw a break-even chart.

STOP & THINK

Use the information from the chart **A** to calculate the break-even point of Keith's business. What is the advantage of calculating break-even rather than drawing a chart?

STOP & THINK

What fixed costs have to be paid by Keith's business when he produces (a) 300 paperweights and (b) 800 paperweights?

A break-even chart such as **A** is made up of four lines: three representing costs, and one revenue.

- **Fixed costs.** Keith's business has fixed costs of £7,500 a year. These costs remain the same whether he makes 10 paperweights or 1,000 paperweights. That is why the fixed costs are represented as a horizontal line.
- **Variable costs.** These rise and fall directly with the level of production. At a higher level of output, Keith's business will have to pay higher variable costs. When he produces 500 paperweights, the chart shows that his variable costs are £5,000. The rise in variable costs is shown by the upward slope (from from left to right) of the variable costs line.
- **Total costs.** These are fixed costs and variable costs added together. For example, at a production level of 1,000 paperweights each year, the total costs of Keith's business would be £17,500. This figure is made up of fixed costs of £7,500 and variable costs of £10,000.
- **Revenue from sales.** This is also called total revenue. It is calculated by multiplying the level of output by the selling price of the product. Thus, Keith's business would have no revenue if it produced nothing and would have revenue of

£12,500 if it produced 500 paperweights (500 x £25). At an output of 1,000 paperweights the business's total revenue would be £25,000.

Imogen's nightclub break-even chart

Earlier we calculated the break-even point for *Imogen's* nightclub (see page 189). The fixed costs for *Imogen's* are £3,000 each week. Each clubber pays £4 to enter the nightclub, and Imogen reckons that the variable cost of each clubber is £1.50. The break-even chart for *Imogen's* is shown in **B**.

The chart shows that the break-even point is 1,200 clubbers a week. This confirms our earlier calculation. Imogen does not have to draw this chart by hand. If she uses a spreadsheet program such as Excel and enters the data, the program will produce a chart for her.

JOINED-UP THINKING

You can find out more about using computers to draw break-even charts on pages 180–1 and 202–3.

B The break-even chart for Imogen's nightclub

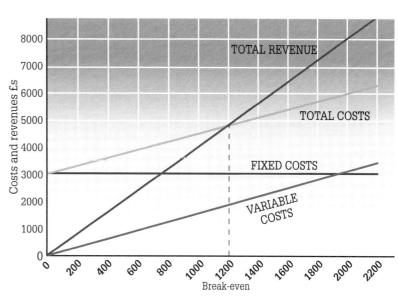

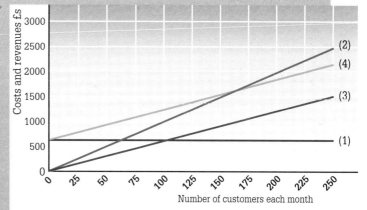

Break-even chart for Caroline's Café

CASE STUDY

Caroline's Café 2

Caroline has drawn a break-even chart for her café business but has not finished it. Complete the chart for her by answering the following questions.

Taskss

1 Caroline has just labelled the lines on her chart as 1, 2, 3 and 4. For each one, write down the proper label she should have used. (4 marks)

2 State and mark on the chart the break-even level of customers each month for Caroline's Café. (2 marks)

3 Over the last four months Caroline's Café had the following numbers of customers:

- November 146
- December 173
- January 153
- February 133.

For each month state whether she made a profit or a loss. (4 marks)

4 Analyse **two** ways in which this break-even chart might be useful to Caroline other than just calculating break-even point. (10 marks)

Break-even, profit and loss

Using a break-even chart offers several benefits for the managers of a business.

- They can read off how much profit or loss the business would make at different levels of production.
- If they are thinking about changing the price at which they sell goods and services, they can see the likely effects on profits or losses.
- In the same way, they can see the effects of any change in the costs paid by the business.

A **loss** is a situation in which a business's costs or expenses are higher than its revenues.

A **profit** is made when a business has sales revenue greater than its total costs.

JOINED-UP THINKING

We will look in more detail at profits and losses and how they are calculated on pages 196–7.

Reading a break-even chart

A break-even chart, such as ◆ , shows the profit or loss made by a business at each level of production. The variable costs line has been omitted, to make the chart easier to read.

- The amount of profit or loss is shown by the **vertical** distance between the total revenue line and the total costs line at any level of production.
- Production levels beyond the break-even point will create a profit for the business. Very high levels of production may result in large amounts of profit.
- Levels of production below the break-even point will cause a loss.

A Profits and losses on a break-even chart

The break-even chart for *Imogen's*

A break-even chart for *Imogen's* is shown in ◆ . We saw earlier that, if *Imogen's* charges every customer a £4 entry fee, the nightclub needs 1,200 customers each week to break even. In other words, 1,200 clubbers in a week will bring in just enough revenue for *Imogen's* to pay all its costs for that week.

The chart shows that if Imogen attracts only 800 clubbers in a week, her business will make a loss. This is to be expected since the figure is below the break-even point.

- If *Imogen's* attracts fewer than 1,200 clubbers, the nightclub's total costs are higher than its total revenue.
- The chart shows that, with fewer than 1,200 customers, the total revenue line is below the total cost line.
- With only 800 clubbers in a week, *Imogen's* takes only

£3,200 (800 x £4). This can be read from the chart.

- For 800 clubbers, Imogen's total costs are £4,200. As a result, the business makes a loss.

However, if *Imogen's* attracts 2,000 people a week the nightclub will make a profit.

- At this level of production, the total revenue line is higher than the total cost line, showing that the nightclub will be profitable.
- The total revenue with 2,000 clubbers is £8,000 (£4 x 2,000), as can be seen from the chart.
- *Imogen's* total costs will be £6,000, so the nightclub makes a profit of £2,000.

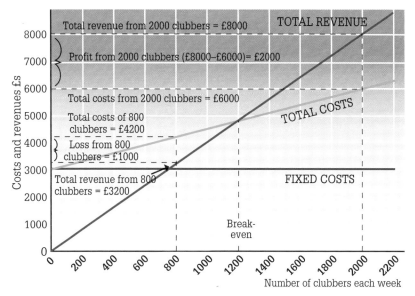

Decision-making with break-even charts

Break-even charts can help managers to take important decisions.

- They show the effects of any changes in prices. Thus, if Imogen Peace decided to increase the entrance fee to her club, she would need fewer clubbers each week to break even. If, for instance, she put up the price to £4.50, she would only need 1,000 clubbers a week. But if she dropped the price to below £4, she would need more customers than at present for her to break even.
- Rises in costs make it more difficult for businesses to break even. Higher costs mean that more customers are needed, whereas falling costs allow a business to break even with fewer customers.
- A break-even chart has its limitations. It assumes that a business will sell all of its product, which is unlikely, for a new, little-known business. Also, costs may rise or fall unexpectedly, making the chart inaccurate.

STOP & THINK

How much profit or loss will *Imogen's* make if 1,400 clubbers go there in a week?

B Break-even chart for *Imogen's*

A busy night at *Imogen's*

STOP & THINK

Can you work out why *Imogen's* total costs are £6,000 if it has 2,000 clubbers during the week?

The previous six pages introduced you to break-even. You need to know:

- the differences between fixed costs, variable costs and revenue
- the meaning of break-even
- how to calculate break-even point
- how to read a break-even chart to see the profit or loss made at different levels of production
- the effects of changes in prices or costs on a break-even chart.

EXAMINER'S TIP

It is easy just to concentrate on calculations when revising for your Unit 3 examination. However, it is important to concentrate on other things too when revising. The following list of questions may be helpful.

- What advantages and disadvantages might there be in using techniques such as budgets, break-even analysis and cash flow forecasts?

- How can techniques like these help the owners and managers of businesses to make decisions such as increasing prices or reducing the level of production?

- In what ways might information technology help businesses to plan, record and analyse their finances? Are there any drawbacks to using IT in these ways?

- Are you sure you know the meaning of all the important terms used in Unit 3? Drawing up a glossary might be useful.

KEY WORDS AND PHRASES

Explain the meaning of the following words or phrases:

- break-even.
- a break-even chart
- total costs
(2 marks for each definition)

What is the difference between:

- fixed and variable costs
- revenue and costs
- a loss and a profit?
(2 marks for each distinction)

You should refer back if you are unsure about the meaning of any of these words or phrases.

Revision exercises

1 Chet Tours

Chet Tours runs a cruiser called *The Loddon Princess* on the beautiful river Chet. The cruiser can take up to 50 passengers on a trip and each customer is charged £8. The fixed cost of operating the cruiser for each trip is £210. The variable costs of each passenger are low. The cruiser's owner, Caron Hughes, estimates that they work out at £1 per passenger.

Caron is interested to know how many customers she will need on each trip in order to break even.

(a) Explain what is meant by the term 'break-even'.

(3 marks)

(b) Caron wants to calculate the break-even number of passengers for a trip on *The Loddon Princess*. What information would she need to do this? (3 marks)

(c) Calculate the number of passengers needed to break even. (4 marks)

(d) Explain two ways in which a break-even chart might help Caron to manage Chet Tours? (10 marks)

2 Chedgrave Clothing

Simon Harris owns Chedgrave Clothing. The company produces designer T-shirts. These have sold well in both Britain and the United States. Simon has recently looked at the costs of running Chedgrave Clothing and is thinking about changing the price at which he sells his T-shirts.

Cost or Revenue	£
Fixed costs	450 000
Variable cost per T-shirt	10.00
Selling price per T-shirt	25.00

A Chedgrave Clothing's costs and revenues

(a) Name three variable costs that Chedgrave Clothing might have to pay. (3 marks)

(b) Write down the formula used to calculate break-even point. (3 marks)

(c) Using the information in **A**, calculate the break-even point for Chedgrave Clothing. (4 marks)

(d) State whether Chedgrave Clothing will make a profit or a loss if it produces the following numbers of T-shirts each month:
- 20,000
- 40,000? (2 marks)

(e) Complete the break-even chart **B** by doing the following:
- writing the correct names for each of the numbered lines on the graph
- marking on the break-even point for Chedgrave Clothing.
- filling in the missing label on the graph. (5 marks)

(f) Read off from **B** the level of Chedgrave Clothing's profit or loss if the company produces:
- 55,000 T-shirts a year
- 15,000 T-shirts a year. (4 marks)

(g) Simon is thinking about increasing the price of his T-shirts to £30. If he did this, what would be the new break-even point? (4 marks)

STOP & THINK

What fixed costs might a clothing factory have to pay?

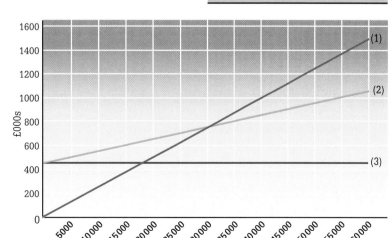

B Break-even chart for Chedgrave Clothing

Producing a profit and loss account

A profit and loss account shows the following information for a business over a period, normally one year:

- sales revenue earned by the business
- costs of production that the business has paid
- profit earned by the business.

All profit and loss accounts are drawn up the same way. The sections that make up a business's profit and loss account are shown in **A**.

A profit and loss account has five sections.

- **Sales revenue.** This is simply the income received by a business from selling its goods and services over a period of time. Profit and loss accounts usually cover a one-year period.
- **Cost of sales.** These are mainly variable costs. The main costs making up cost of sales include:
  - raw materials
  - fuel
  - wages of employees directly involved in production.
- **Gross profit.** This is sales revenue minus the cost of sales. A corner shop selling groceries would calculate its gross profit as follows:

Gross profit = sales revenue (the income received from selling food and other products to customers) minus cost of sales (the cost of buying in food and other items as well as employees' wages).

- **Overheads.** These costs do not vary along with the level of production. They include items such as the wages of administrative staff and marketing costs. Interest paid by a business on its loans is also included as an overhead. These costs are sometimes called expenses and are mainly fixed costs.
- **Net profit.** This is what is left of a business's sales revenue once all its costs have been paid. Thus, net profit is the money left to a business from a year's trading when it has paid its fixed and variable costs.

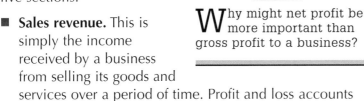

STOP & THINK

Why might net profit be more important than gross profit to a business?

KEY CONCEPTS

A **profit and loss account** is a financial statement listing a business's revenues and expenditures, and also its profit or loss, over a period of time.

Cost of sales is the costs of materials and labour used in production.

Gross profit is sales revenue minus cost of sales.

Net profit is the sales revenue of a business less all the costs of producing goods or services.

Overheads are costs that relate to the whole business. Examples include rent, security costs and the wages of administrative staff.

SALES REVENUE

less

COST OF SALES

equals

GROSS PROFIT

less

OVERHEADS

gives

NET PROFIT

A Structure of a profit and loss account

196

Profit and loss account – an example

Henry Shaw runs a small business making wooden furniture for gardens. Henry has run his business for three years. His benches and patio sets are very popular. Many garden centres near to Henry's home sell his furniture.

Henry has just written down all the costs and revenues for his business during the last year.

- expenditure: wood and other raw materials £17,900
- sales revenue for the year £67,550
- wages £34,000
- marketing costs (mainly adverts in local papers) £5,250
- accountant's fees £1,000
- interest on bank loan £3,500

From these figures, he produces the profit and loss account for his business, shown in B .

Henry has made a profit of £11,150 for the year.

A display of wooden garden furniture

	£
Sales revenue	67 550
Cost of sales (costs of wood and other raw materials as well as wages)	51 900
Gross profit	**15 650**
Overheads (Accountant's fees and interest on bank loan)	4500
Net profit	**11 150**

 B Henry Shaw's profit and loss account

STOP & THINK

Henry Shaw's business made a net profit of £11,150 last year. How do you think Henry might use this money?

CASE STUDY

Thorntons plc

Thorntons sell chocolate and the company's shops are found in most towns and cities in Britain. Some important financial information for the company during the year 1 July 2000 to 30 June 2001 is as follows.

	(£m)
• cost of sales	76.72
• sales revenue	159.92
• overheads	73.05

Source: Adapted from Thorntons Plc Annual Report and Accounts, 2001

Tasks

1 Thorntons' cost of sales was £76.72 million for the year. List **three** costs that the company might have to pay as part of its cost of sales. (3 marks)

2 Thorntons spend a lot of money each year on advertising their shops and chocolates. Where might this cost be included on the company's profit and loss account? (1 mark)

3 Calculate Thorntons' profit and loss account for the year. Use the structure diagram in A to help you. (6 marks)

How a balance sheet works

A balance sheet records the assets and liabilities that a business has on a particular day. It shows how a business raised its money and how that money has been used. The structure of a balance sheet is shown in **A** .

Balance sheets contain the following information about a business.

- **Assets** are items owned by a business. Businesses need to hold two types of assets.
  - Current assets are items that the business expects to have for only a short time (normally less than one year). Examples include cash and stocks of raw materials. Current assets (especially cash) are used by the business to settle debts.
  - Fixed assets will normally be kept by a business for many years. Examples of fixed assets include factories and machinery. Fixed assets are used to create an income for the business and to earn profits.
- **Liabilities** are a business's debts. As with assets, these fall into two categories.
  - Current liabilities are debts that a business will pay within a year. Overdrafts and money owed to suppliers are examples.
  - Long-term liabilities are debts that will be paid back over many years. Loans from the bank or a loan to buy property (called a mortgage) are examples of this type of liability.
- **Shareholders' funds** are that part of the company's money that belongs to shareholders. If a company stops trading and sells off all its assets (stock, property and vehicles, for instance) this will raise a large sum of money. That money will be used to pay all the company's liabilities (its debts). The money that is left, once this is done, is shareholders' funds. If the business is not a company (for example, if it is a partnership) this item is called 'capital'.

A balance sheet is so called because the value of the assets owned by the business (less current liabilities) equals the money put into the business by its owners. So

Net assets employed = Shareholders' funds.

If, for example, the owners put in more capital to buy new premises, then the value of the business's assets and the money put in by shareholders will increase by the same amount. The top of the balance sheet shows how money is used by the business; the bottom shows the source of the money. Thus, a balance sheet will always balance.

FIXED ASSETS
e.g. property

plus

CURRENT ASSETS
e.g. cash

minus

CURRENT LIABILITIES
e.g. money owed to suppliers

minus

LONG-TERM LIABILITIES
e.g. mortgage

equals

NET ASSETS EMPLOYED

and this equals

SHAREHOLDERS' FUNDS

These two figures are the same (they balance). This is why this financial statement is called a balance sheet.

A Structure of a balance sheet

STOP & THINK

Suppose a company borrows £10 million from a bank to purchase new machinery. Which **two** parts of the balance sheet would be affected by this action?

A company balance sheet – an example

A balance sheet for Thorntons plc is shown in **B** . Thorntons, like all other companies in Britain, must produce a balance sheet each year.

	£ million
Fixed assets	96.747
Current assets	25.519
Current liabilities	34.242
Long-term liabilities	38.797
Net Assets Employed	**49.227**
Shareholders' Funds	**49.227**

Thorntons has total assets (fixed plus current) equal to £122.266 million. The company's liabilities are £25.519 million plus £34.242 million = 73.039 million. The company's net current assets are calculated as follows:

		£ million
	Total assets	122.266
less	Total liabilities	73.039
	Net assets	49.227

If Thorntons sold all its assets and paid its liabilities, the company would have £49.227 million remaining with which to pay to its shareholders. Thus the company's shareholders' funds are £49.227 million. This confirms that Net Assets Employed equal Shareholders' Funds.

STOP & THINK

Thorntons is famous for selling chocolate. What fixed assets might this company have?

B Balance sheet for Thorntons plc 30 June 2001

CASE STUDY

Breckland Farms Ltd

Bob Mizon is about to draw up the balance sheet for Breckland Farms Ltd. Breckland Farms own 57 farms in Cambridgeshire and Suffolk. The company supplies major British supermarkets such as Sainsbury's and Waitrose with fruit, vegetables and meat products.

Bob has gathered together the following information shown below. All figures are in £000s.

- Cash 47.5
- Stock of raw materials 426.9
- Overdraft 299.3
- Money owed to suppliers 150.7
- Mortgage 2520.1
- Other long-term loans 1000.0
- Land and property 6786.0
- Vehicles and machinery 2345.6
- Shareholders' Funds 5635.9

Tasks

1 Which of Bob's list are:
  (a) current assets
  (b) fixed assets and
  (c) current liabilities
  (d) long-term liabilities? (8 marks)

2 Using the balance sheet **B** as a guide, construct the balance sheet for Breckland Farms Ltd. (10 marks)

3 How might Breckland Farms' balance sheet change if the value of the company's 'land and property' increased to £7,786,000? Explain your answer. (6 marks)

Stakeholders and business accounts

'Business accounts' is a term used to describe the following:

- the profit and loss account
- the balance sheet.

These accounts, which are sometimes called financial statements, will be of interest to stakeholders. There are six main types of stakeholder, which are shown in .

1 The **Inland Revenue** collects taxes on behalf of the government. This stakeholder will be interested in the business's profit and loss account. The amount of tax that a business pays to the Inland Revenue depends upon the level of that business's net profits.

2 **Banks** will be interested in a business's accounts because they may have lent money and will want to see whether the business is able to pay it back. A bank may be especially interested in how much profit the business has made over the year.

3 **Shareholders** will want to see how much profit the business has made. They will also want to know the value of their 'stake' in the company, which is shown by shareholders' funds.

4 **Employees** will want to see how much profit the business has made. If the business has made high levels of profits, employees may be looking for wage increases. Also, high profits may mean that employees' jobs are more secure.

5 **Suppliers** will be interested in whether the business can pay for its supplies on time. The business's balance sheet will give suppliers this information.

6 **Customers** want to know if a business is financially sound. They will not want to place orders, or pay deposits, to a business that might not be able to continue trading.

KEY CONCEPTS

Business accounts
include important financial statements such as the balance sheet and the profit and loss account.

A **stakeholder** is any individual or group with an interest in a business.

STOP & THINK

Explain two differences between the profit and loss account and the balance sheet.

STOP & THINK

Why might Customs and Excise be interested in a company's business accounts?

A   Business accounts and stakeholders

What can be learned from business accounts?

A stakeholder can learn several important things about a business by looking at its balance sheet and profit and loss account.

■ **Whether the business can pay its debts.**
Stakeholders will look at the amount of current assets that a business has and compare them to its current liabilities. If current liabilities are much higher than current assets, they may think that the business is not financially sound. Suppliers may ask for cash when they deliver goods, and refuse to give the business credit.

■ **Whether the business will be a profitable investment.** Shareholders and banks invest money into businesses and will want to know whether the business will earn enough profits to give a good return on their investment. If the business is not very profitable, they may decide to invest elsewhere.

■ **Whether the business is financially secure.**
Few stakeholders will want to be involved with a business that has borrowed too much and may not be able to pay its debts. Banks, customers, employees and suppliers will want to know that the business is secure. They will look at the profit made by the business and will see from the balance sheet how much money the business has borrowed. Businesses with large, long-term liabilities may be regarded as risky because, if interest rates rise, they will have to pay higher interest on their loans.

To see whether key figures such as sales and profits are rising or falling, it is necessary to compare a company's balance sheets and profit and loss accounts over several years.

B Important features of balance sheets and profit and loss accounts

What is the difference between current assets and current liabilities?

Giving a friend advice...

A friend of yours called Chris is considering buying £10,000 worth of shares in a particular company. He has asked you to help him decide whether this would be a good investment.

Tasks

1 Name **two** financial statements that Chris could usefully read. (2 marks)

2 Explain **two** features of these financial statements that would be important to a shareholder. (6 marks)

3 Explain **one** reason why Chris should look at financial information about the business over a period of several years. (6 marks)

JOINED-UP THINKING

Earlier we looked at spreadsheets and how they are used to write cash flow forecasts. You may find it useful to re-read pages 180–1 before continuing.

Computers and business applications

Nowadays most businesses produce their financial documents on computers. Big companies such as Vodafone plc and a sole trader running a corner shop can both use computers to keep their financial records.

Computers and business applications software can be used in a number ways to help businesses manage their finances.

- **Recording all the sales and revenue.** Thus businesses can automatically calculate sales revenue for a year.
- **Calculating costs.** A business can record all of its costs on a computer. Software such as spreadsheets can total up a business's costs and separate costs into cost of sales and overheads.
- **Calculating net and gross profit.** Profits can be calculated each month and for the whole financial year.

Businesses can also use computer applications to:

- calculate the amount of VAT they have to pay
- identify customers who are slow to pay
- draw up break-even charts.

Benefits and drawbacks

Using spreadsheets and other software to record and calculate profit and loss accounts has a number of advantages.

- **Calculations are performed automatically.** Many people who run businesses do not understand how to construct profit and loss accounts. Spreadsheets do all the work for them and give immediate answers.
- **Monthly profit and loss accounts are easy to produce.** This helps managers to see how a business is performing. Problems, for example falling profits, can be spotted at an early stage.
- **Changes in costs and revenues are easily accommodated.** Computers are ideal for carrying out calculations when data changes. If, for instance, prices change, the computer can change budgets and cash flow forecasts easily and quickly.

However, using business applications software may also have its drawbacks.

- **Software can be expensive.** For example, some software for calculating a business's accounts might prove costly to small businesses.
- **Training may be needed.** Some computer applications are quite complicated, and training may be essential before a business can use it.
- **Computer systems can break down.** This can be very disruptive when businesses rely heavily on computers to provide financial information.

KEY CONCEPTS

Computer applications are software used, for example, to record and calculate profit and loss accounts.

Spreadsheets are computer programs for displaying and calculating numerical information.

Spreadsheet formulae are used to tell the computer to carry out calculations such as addition and subtraction.

	January	February	March	Total
Sales revenue	4900	5250	6200	16 350
Cost of sales	3750	4025	4660	12 435
Gross profit	**1150**	**1225**	**1540**	**3915**
Overheads	395	450	500	1345
Net profit	**755**	**775**	**1040**	**2570**

An extract from Henry Shaw's profit and loss account.

STOP & THINK

Look at Henry Shaw's profit and loss account opposite, where might Henry have used formulae if he had been using a computer spreadsheet?

STOP & THINK

Sage plc produces a variety of software to help small and medium-sized businesses manage their financial affairs. What advantages might Sage get from using its website to sell its products?

CASE STUDY

Little Wonders

Little Wonders is a traditional toy store established in 1997 by Trudi Goulding and Mark Roake. Since their business began, the couple have used Sage Instant Accounting, a software accounting package for start-up and small businesses

Mark, a former City banker, says: 'We chose Sage because of the excellent reputation of its products, particularly Instant Accounting. I find its features really easy to use. It allows me to present information graphically at the touch of a button.'

Source: Adapted from www.uk.sage.com/products

Tasks

1 List three ways in which Sage's computer software might help Mark and Trudi to run Little Wonders. (3 marks)

2 Sage plc sells software that records and calculates financial information. Explain two reasons why this might be useful to a small, newly established business. (6 marks)

3 Many small firms decide not to use computers to record and calculate financial information. Suggest and explain reasons why they might take this decision. (9 marks)

The previous eight pages introduced you to balance sheets and profit and loss accounts. You need to know:

- the structure of a profit and loss account
- how a business calculates profits and losses
- the advantages and disadvantages of computer applications to calculate profit and loss accounts
- the structure of a balance sheet
- why business accounts are important and why stakeholders are interested in them.

EXAMINER'S TIP

Make sure that you are properly prepared when you start your Unit 3 examination.

- You **will** need a calculator – it is impossible to complete the Unit 3 examination without one.

- You must make sure that you have a watch, so you can manage your time properly.

- Make sure you take several pens into the examination room in case one or more of them stops working.

Revision exercises

1 The Natural Choice

Clare Richards is feeling very pleased. Her business, The Natural Choice, has just had a really successful year. Her business has been trading for four years. Clare has one shop selling organic foodstuffs in Blackburn. Now that the financial year is over, Clare has collected the following information:

- Cost of sales   £47,000
- Sales revenue   £72,500
- Overheads   £15,000

Clare is about to construct her profit and loss account.

Questions

(a) Complete the following statements.
 (i) Sales revenue – cost of sales = ...
                                    (1 mark)
 (ii) .... – Overheads = Net profit.(1 mark).
(b) Clare's business sells organic foods. Give **two** examples of costs that might be paid as part of her 'cost of sales'.
                                    (2 marks)
(c) Construct the profit and loss account for The Natural Choice.   (4 marks)

KEY WORDS AND PHRASES

Explain the meaning of the following words or phrases:

- profit and loss account
- balance sheet
- shareholders' funds
- business accounts
- overheads
- cost of sales.
(2 marks for each definition)

What is the difference between:

- gross and net profit
- assets and liabilities
- profit and loss?
          (4 marks for each distinction)

You should refer back if you are unsure about the meaning of any of these words or phrases.

Computers being used in a small business

STOP & THINK

Explain **two** possible disadvantages to a small business of using computers to record and calculate profit and loss accounts.

(d) Explain **three** advantages to Clare of using a computer to record and calculate her profit and loss account. (9 marks)

(e) Suggest and justify two reasons why the profit and loss account is a very important document for the stakeholders of The Natural Choice. (8 marks)

Total = 25 marks

2 Goldstar Cleaning

Goldstar Cleaning plc is one of the largest cleaning companies in Britain. The company's accountants have drawn up the balance sheet for the year that has just ended. The following information is available:

	£ millions
Fixed assets	96.75
Current assets	25.52
Total assets	?
Current liabilities	34. 24
Long-term liabilities	38. 80
Net Assets Employed	?
Shareholders' Funds	49. 23

The balance sheet for Goldstar Cleaning 31August 2001

Questions

(a) Give **two** examples of fixed assets and two examples of current assets. (4 marks)

(b) Complete Goldstar Cleaning's balance sheet by filling in the spaces. (2 marks)

(c) Identify **two** stakeholders who might be interested in Goldstar Cleaning's balance sheet. In each case, explain why the stakeholder would be interested. (6 marks)

(d) Explain **two** indications on a balance sheet that would show that the business was financially strong. (8 marks)

(e) 'Banks decide whether to lend money to businesses by looking at their latest balance sheet'. How far do you think this is true? (10 marks)

STOP & THINK

What information can you find out from a balance sheet that you cannot discover from a profit and loss account?

Raising finance

Finance (or money) for businesses comes from two major sources:

- inside the business – known as internal sources of finance
- outside the business – known as external sources of finance.

Internal and external sources of finance are shown in A. Businesses using these sources of finance are said to be 'raising finance'.

Businesses may need to raise finance for a number of different reasons. The money may be needed to:

- start up a business
- expand the business, for example buying a new factory
- investigate new products through research and development
- pay for an advertising campaign
- buy new equipment (such as up-to-date computers).

Internal sources of finance

Using internal sources of finance has its advantages.

- A business avoids paying high interest charges.
- Other people and organisations, such as banks, do not have a say in how the business is run.
- Finance can be arranged quickly.

Several internal sources of finance are available to a business.

1 **Owners' funds.** This is money put into the business by the owners. It is normally invested when the business is first established. It is a major source of finance for sole traders and partnerships, which cannot issues shares.

2 **Retained profits** This is profit made in earlier years. Businesses often save their profits until these are needed. One big advantage of using retained profit, rather

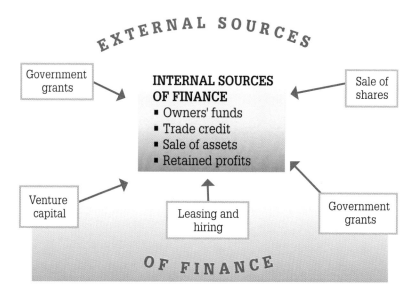

A Internal and external sources of finance

EXTERNAL SOURCES

Government grants

INTERNAL SOURCES OF FINANCE
- Owners' funds
- Trade credit
- Sale of assets
- Retained profits

Sale of shares

Venture capital

Leasing and hiring

Government grants

OF FINANCE

than borrowing money, is that no interest is charged. But this source of revenue is available only to successful firms. Moreover, the owners of the business may be disappointed if profit is kept within the business and not paid to them.

3 **Delaying paying bills and chasing up customers.** Businesses can raise small amounts of finance by making their suppliers wait for payment. This 'free' source of finance is really a short-term loan with no interest charges. At the same time, a business may be able to persuade its own customers to pay sooner. Both of these are important sources of short-term finance for a business.

4 **Selling assets.** This can be done in two ways:
   - selling assets such as vehicles, equipment and premises for cash
   - sale and leaseback. A business sells an asset to another business and receives money for the sale. The business then leases back the asset. Many retailers (Woolworth's, for example) have sold their shops to property companies and then leased them back to continue using them as shops.

▲ **A** A Sainsbury's supermarket .

STOP & THINK

The supermarket giant Sainsbury's has used money raised through sale and leaseback to finance the company's growth. Explain **one** advantage and **one** disadvantage of raising finance in this way.

Choosing an internal source

Businesses will take into account several factors when choosing an internal source of finance.

- **The time that the business has been established.** New businesses will not be able to use retained profits or sell assets to raise finance. Instead they will have to rely on owners' funds. However, it is more likely that new businesses will use external sources of finance. (These are considered on pages 208–9).
- **The amount of profit made by the business.** A more successful business will have more profits from the current and previous years. These profits can be an important source of finance.
- **The business's reputation.** Businesses will find it easier to negotiate trade credit with suppliers if they have a reputation for paying bills on time. If a business has paid late, or not paid at all, suppliers will be unlikely to offer trade credit.

C A S E   S T U D Y

Clemence Photographers

Nick Clemence, who owns two photography shops in Birmingham, has decided to expand his company. Nick's company has eight shareholders, including himself. Nick is the only shareholder involved in managing the business. The company's shops sell equipment for photographers as well as a wide range of professional photographic services. Nick's business has been very successful in recent years, earning high profits. Nick is a now a wealthy man and has decided to use internal sources of finance to expand his business.

Tasks

1 List two internal sources of finance that Nick might choose to use.   (2 marks)

2 Nick has decided to use some retained profits from his business to buy a new shop. Explain one advantage and one disadvantage of raising the money in this way.   (4 marks)

3 Explain why you think that Nick might have preferred to use internal sources of finance?   (9 marks)

External sources of finance

Few businesses can manage without raising some finance from external sources such as banks or building societies. There are many different external sources for businesses to choose from.

1 **Loans.** These can be arranged for different periods: a mortgage may last twenty years or an overdraft one year. The rate of interest paid on the loan might be fixed or variable. Businesses find it easier to plan when interest payments on loans are fixed. That way, the cost of the loan does not change. Businesses with large loans can suffer if interest rates rise. Banks may also ask for collateral – that is, something that can be sold if the business does not repay the loan.

2 **Hire purchase and leasing.** These sources of finance mean that a business does not have to raise large sums of money.
   - Leasing allows businesses to rent assets such as vehicles and photocopiers. The business never owns the asset, but does not have to find a large sum of money to buy it.
   - Hire purchase is a method of purchasing assets by paying in instalments. A business will own the asset, but not until it is completely paid for.

3 **Government grants.** The government and the European Union offer a wide range of grants. Normally, firms can claim these if they create new jobs in areas of high unemployment.

4 **Issuing shares.** Only companies can sell shares. They sell the shares to start or expand their businesses. The shareholders, who buy the shares, become owners of the business. Public companies can sell shares through the Stock Exchange. However, if a business sells too many shares, the current shareholders may lose control of the company.

KEY CONCEPTS

External source of finance is money that is available from outside the business, for example a bank loan.

Hire purchase is a type of borrowing where a business pays for an asset over a period of time.

Leasing is the hiring of items such as machinery and vehicles for some period of time.

Venture capital is money lent to high-risk businesses. Businesses lending venture capital normally buy some shares in the business borrowing the money.

STOP & THINK

Can you think of **two** differences between an overdraft and a mortgage?

STOP & THINK

The Bank of England sets interest rates, and these affect businesses throughout Britain.

How might a rise in interest rates affect a public limited company planning to raise a large sum of money?

The Bank of England, London

TYPE OF BUSINESS ORGANISATION	POSSIBLE SOURCES OF FINANCE	KEY ISSUES
Sole Trader	Owner's funds, government grants and loans	Banks may be unwilling to lend to a small business. Sole traders have few internal sources of finance.
Partnership	Partners' savings, banks, government grants, hire purchase and leasing companies	Partnerships often do not have enough collateral. Partners may disagree.
Private Limited Company (Ltd)	Suppliers, banks, leasing and hire purchase companies, government grants and loans, venture capital, private share issues	Larger private limited companies may find it easier to borrow. Loss of control by existing shareholders Existing shareholders may not agree to the company selling more shares.
Public Limited Company (plc)	Suppliers, banks, leasing and hire purchase companies, government grants and loans, venture capital, share issues on the Stock Exchange	Ability to move to area receiving government aid Recent financial performance of the company Reputation of company and senior managers

5 **Venture capital.** This is a source of finance for businesses that are a risky investment. Venture capital firms lend money to small, high-risk companies. They may make a loan or buy some shares in the company. Venture capital providers usually lend relatively small sums of money. It is unusual for them to provide more than £500,000.

A Sources of finance for different types of businesses

C A S E   S T U D Y

A Step Ahead

A Step Ahead is one of Britain's largest manufacturers of shoes and boots. The business is a public limited company. A Step Ahead has been profitable recently and has seen sales of its footwear rise steadily.

The company has decided to build a new factory to meet the increasing demand for its shoes and boots. The new factory will cost £20 million. The directors of the company are unsure as to the best way to raise the money. However, most of it will be raised from external sources.

Tasks

1 Name three sources of external finance that A Step Ahead could use to raise the £20 million it needs. (3 marks)

2 Some of the company's managers want to pay for the new factory through a loan. Explain one disadvantage of using this source of finance. (4 marks)

3 How do you think that A Step Ahead should raise the money it needs? Justify your answer. (8 marks)

The importance of financial plans

Financial plans are estimates made by businesses about the next 12 months. These are important, but difficult to forecast accurately. They include the following elements, which are summarised below.

- **Sales forecasts.** These are the start of the financial planning process. A business may use market research or look at past sales figures to forecast sales. A business will also draw up a marketing plan to explain how it is to achieve its sales forecasts.
- **Sales budgets.** These state the revenue that a firm expects to receive if it meets its sales targets. They will be set out monthly and will normally cover the year ahead.

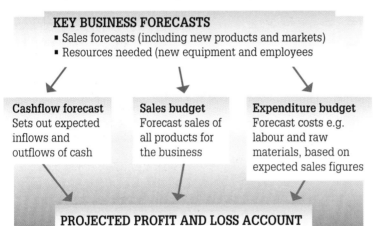

KEY BUSINESS FORECASTS
- Sales forecasts (including new products and markets)
- Resources needed (new equipment and employees

Cashflow forecast Sets out expected inflows and outflows of cash

Sales budget Forecast sales of all products for the business

Expenditure budget Forecast costs e.g. labour and raw materials, based on expected sales figures

PROJECTED PROFIT AND LOSS ACCOUNT

- **Expenditure budgets.** Once a business knows its expected sales, it can work out the amount of labour and raw materials it will use. This allows the business to forecast its expenditure on wages, raw materials, fuel and other costs.
- **Cash flow forecasts.** When a business knows the revenue it expects and the costs it will have to pay, it can draw up a cash flow forecast. This states the times at which the business expects to receive and pay out money.
- **Forecast profit and loss account.** The information from the sales and expenditure budgets can be used to draw up an expected profit and loss account for the coming year. This helps the business to set itself targets for profits.

How they help businesses

Drawing up financial plans can help businesses in different ways.

1 **To prepare for expansion.** A business that is growing will need to plan how much extra finance will be required to purchase raw materials and other resources. Banks will be

more willing to lend money if businesses can show that they have planned their finances carefully. Drawing up a cash flow forecast will help a business to persuade banks to lend money.

2 **To plan for unexpected costs.** Businesses may face costs that they did not expect, if, for example, sales fall suddenly. The business may then have to spend more on advertising than it had planned. Expenditure budgets will help a business decide on the best way to obtain this money.

3 **To plan reductions in costs.** If, for instance, a business plans to save costs by reducing its workforce, cash flow forecasts and expenditure budgets will be important in making these plans. Expenditure on wages will fall, but the business will have to pay compensation to employees who lose their jobs.

Who makes use of them?

Financial plans are used by different groups within businesses or having an interest in a business.

- **The whole business.** The managers of the business can see in advance if the business is likely to make a loss or to run out of cash. Financial problems can be settled before they become too serious.
- **Departments within a business.** Financial plans help each department within a business to make a contribution to the success of the business. For instance, the research and development department of a drug company will try to keep within its expenditure budget, while the sales department will try to achieve its sales budgets.
- **Investors in a business.** Businesses that show that they plan their finances carefully are more likely to attract investors, who will see those businesses as less risky.
- **Suppliers who lend the money to business.** Suppliers may be particularly interested in a business's cash flow forecast. This will tell suppliers whether the business will be able to pay its debts on time.

STOP & THINK

In 2002, Ford ended car production at its Dagenham factory, with the loss of hundreds of jobs. How might the closure of the factory have affected the company's cash flow plan?

CASE STUDY

Starting a business

Jane Earthy is about to open a small hotel in Brighton. She intends to offer low-priced, good-quality accommodation to families. Jane has not run a business before, and needs a loan from her bank. She is not sure what information they might expect her to provide, and has turned to you for help.

Tasks

1 Name three pieces of financial information the bank might want before lending Jane money. (3 marks)

2 How might financial planning help Jane persuade her bank to lend her money? (6 marks)

3 Where might Jane get the information she needs to draw up her sales budgets and expenditure budgets? (6 marks)

The previous six pages introduced you to sources of finance and financial planning. You need to know:

- the internal and external sources of finance available to a business
- the factors that might affect a business's choice of source of finance
- the reasons why firms engage in financial planning
- the financial documents used in financial planning.

Revision exercises

1   Identify the best source or sources of finance in each of the situations below.
   (a) A business wishes to buy 40 new cars for its sales force.
   (b) A company wants to build a major new factory costing £50 million.
   (c) A small business needs to pay suppliers now but its customers are not expected to pay for a further two months.
   (d) A large public limited company wishes to finance the development of a new range of products.
   (e) A company wishes to install a new IT system but is aware that the technology is changing rapidly.
   (f) A business wishes to invest a substantial sum, but anticipates steady profits over the next few years.
   (g) A business wishes to raise £50,000 to invest in a high-risk project.
   (h) A business is planning to build a new factory in an area of high unemployment.
   (i) A company with head offices in central London wants to build a new head office in Wales.

2   **Bankrupt Clothing Company**
   In 2000 the Bankrupt Clothing Company collapsed. The company had seven shops in the south of England selling jeans and other fashion clothes. Despite heavy advertising, the company had never achieved high levels of sales. The company's managing director said that he was disappointed sales had not been as high as he had expected.

   Questions

   (a) Name **two** budgets that the Bankrupt Clothing Company might have prepared as part of its financial planning.   (2 marks)
   (b) Explain how financial planning might have helped the Bankrupt Clothing Company.   (8 marks)

KEY WORDS AND PHRASES

Explain the meaning of the following words or phrases:

- owners' funds
- collateral
- venture capital
- financial plans
- retained profits.
(2 marks for each definition)

What is the difference between:

- internal and external sources of finance
- an expenditure budget and a sales budget
- leasing and hire purchase
- a profit and loss account and a projected profit and loss account?
                    (4 marks for each distinction)

You should refer back if you are unsure about the meaning of any of these words or phrases.

3 Severn Valley Farm

Salmon has become much more popular in Britain over the last few years. The Severn Valley Farm is one of the largest suppliers of salmon to shops and restaurants in England and Wales. The farm is owned by two partners and has a reputation for supplying high-quality products. It has not been able to supply enough fish to meet its customers' demands.

Helen Godbolt, one of the farm's owners and its manager, has decided to create a new lake at the farm and stock it with salmon. This will allow the company to supply 20 per cent more fish within three years. However, she is worried about raising the £30,000 needed to carry out her plans.

(a) Name **three** sources of finance that Helen would **not** be able to use. (3 marks)

(b) Severn Valley Farm has been very successful over the last few years. Explain how this might help the business to raise the money it needs. (5 marks)

(c) What source or sources of finance do you think that Severn Valley Farm should use to pay for the new lake? Explain your answer. (7 marks)

STOP & THINK

A very large company such as BP Amoco can use many sources of finance. Which of these sources would not be available to a sole trader that had just started trading?

One of BP Amoco's drilling platforms

Unit 3 contains a number of important themes. These are highlighted in **A** – **E** and tested in the corresponding Stop & Think exercises.

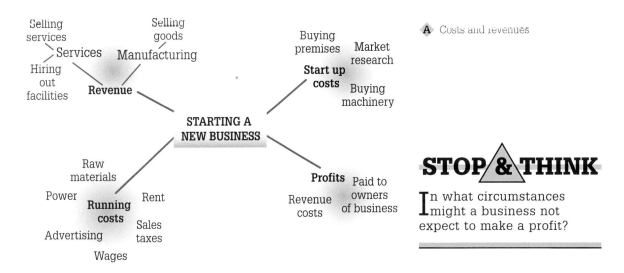

A Costs and revenues

STOP & THINK

In what circumstances might a business not expect to make a profit?

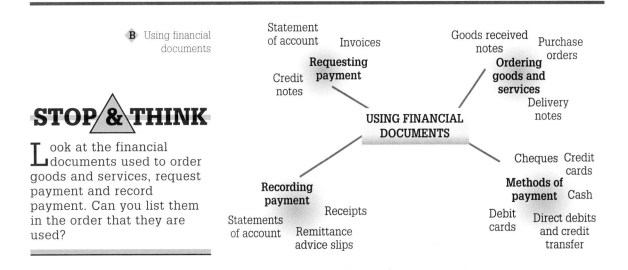

B Using financial documents

STOP & THINK

Look at the financial documents used to order goods and services, request payment and record payment. Can you list them in the order that they are used?

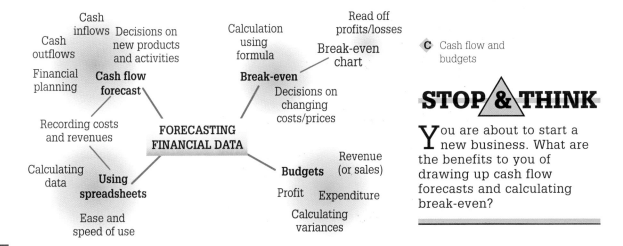

C Cash flow and budgets

STOP & THINK

You are about to start a new business. What are the benefits to you of drawing up cash flow forecasts and calculating break-even?

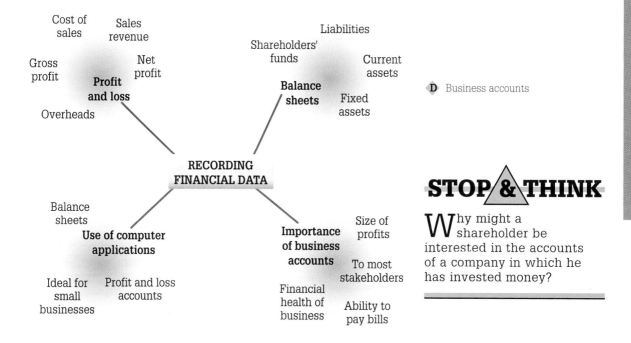

Cost of sales

Sales revenue

Gross profit

Net profit

Profit and loss

Overheads

Liabilities

Shareholders' funds

Current assets

Balance sheets

Fixed assets

D Business accounts

RECORDING FINANCIAL DATA

Balance sheets

Use of computer applications

Ideal for small businesses

Profit and loss accounts

Importance of business accounts

Size of profits

To most stakeholders

Financial health of business

Ability to pay bills

STOP & THINK

Why might a shareholder be interested in the accounts of a company in which he has invested money?

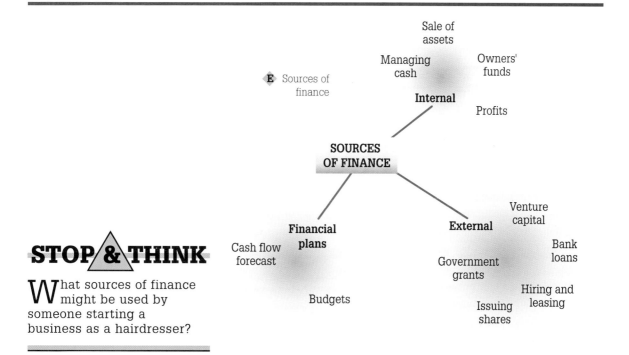

E Sources of finance

Sale of assets

Managing cash

Owners' funds

Internal

Profits

SOURCES OF FINANCE

Financial plans

Cash flow forecast

Budgets

External

Venture capital

Government grants

Bank loans

Issuing shares

Hiring and leasing

STOP & THINK

What sources of finance might be used by someone starting a business as a hairdresser?

Unit 3 is assessed through an examination. The examination will last 1 hour and 30 minutes. The examination paper will be made up of a series of questions similar to the ones that follow. Completing these questions will help you prepare for your Unit 3 examination. Good luck!

The questions all refer to ToyBox, a manufacturer of wooden toys for children. ToyBox is a private company run by a husband and wife team, David and Sarah James. The business was established three years ago and is now beginning to grow rapidly. Sarah has looked after the financial side of the business while David has concentrated on making the toys.

It is important for the business to keep accurate financial records. However, Sarah has had an invoice returned to her by an angry customer because it has several mistakes.

Question 1: The angry customer

(a) Identify **three** errors in Toybox's invoice on the right. (3 marks)

(b) Calculate the invoice correctly. (6 marks)

(c) Describe **two** problems that ToyBox might face if the company sends out inaccurate invoices such as this one. (8 marks)

(d) Sarah wants to use IT to produce all of ToyBox's financial documents. Explain **one** advantage and **one** disadvantage of using IT in this way. (8 marks)

Question 2: End of year

It is 31 December. Sarah and David are about to draw up the profit and loss account for ToyBox. They have the following information for the financial year:

Overheads/Expenses

Rent	£ 50 000
Insurance	£ 25 000
Sales revenue	£505 000
Cost of sales	£325 750

INVOICE

ToyBox
12 Bridge Street
Banbury
OX12 9PT

Telephone 01234 756123
Fax 01234 756398
VAT Reg. Number 132 78275123
Invoice number: 65/2309

The Toy Shop   **Date: 9 August 2002**
97 High Street
Bicester

Product	Quantity	Price	Value
Pine train sets	20	89.99	1799.80
Jigsaws	12	7.50	80.00
Puppets	6	15.99	95.94

Goods value	**£1870.74**
VAT @17.5%	**£345.75**
Amount payable	**£2216.49**

	£		£
Sales revenue			
Cost of sales			
Gross profit			
Overheads/expenses			
		Total overheads/ expenses	
Net profit			

(a) Use the financial information to complete ToyBox's profit or loss for the year ending 31 December, by completing the tinted boxes. (9 marks)

(b) David and Sarah also have to draw up the business's balance sheet. List **four** items that they might include in the balance sheet for ToyBox. (4 marks)

(c) (i) Name three stakeholders who might be interested in ToyBox's balance sheet and profit and loss account. (3 marks)

   (ii) In each case, explain why the stakeholder might be interested in ToyBox's balance sheet and profit and loss account. (6 marks)

Question 3: The business grows

ToyBox has been very successful. David has decided that he needs a new piece of machinery to make a larger range of wooden toys. The company needs to raise £15,000 to buy the machinery.

(a) State two possible ways in which ToyBox might raise the £15,000 it needs to buy the machinery. (2 marks)

(b) David has just agreed to buy wood from a new supplier. He has to pay £100 each month for the wood.
(i) Select a method of payment that could be used to pay for the wood. (1 mark)
(ii) Explain the reason for your choice. (3 marks)

(c) Sarah is worried because ToyBox's customers often take several weeks to pay. How might a cash flow forecast be useful to ToyBox? (5 marks)

Question 4: Will Sarah's new idea break even?

Sarah has suggested that ToyBox should rent out some of its toys to local schools and playgroups. David thinks this is a good idea, but is worried that they will not have enough customers. Sarah decides to calculate the break-even point for the new idea.

She has the following information:
- fixed costs per week   £750
- rent for each toy per week   £3
- variable costs   £1.50

(a) Calculate the number of toys that ToyBox will need to rent out each week to break even. (4 marks)

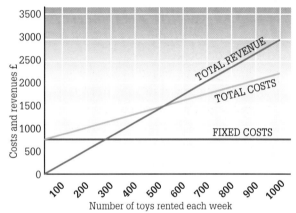

The break-even chart for ToyBox's rental scheme

(b) Look at the break-even chart that Sarah has drawn.
(i) State the total costs if 600 toys are rented out each week. (1 mark)
(ii) State the profit or loss made if ToyBox rents out 800 toys each week. (1 mark)

(c) David thinks that a price of £3 per week is too high. He thinks that £2.50 would be better. What would be the break-even point if his price were used? (4 marks)

(d) Explain how using a break-even chart might help David and Sarah to decide whether or not to go ahead with renting out toys to local schools and playgroups. (7 marks)

WEBSITE ADDRESSES

Websites are an important source of information for you and should prove especially useful for Units 1 and 2 assignments.

Unit 1

www.ons.gov.uk contains statistical information relating to many different business activities.

www.statistics.gov.uk is possibly an even better website for government statistics.

www.dti.gov.uk/search there is muchthat can be learnt about British businesses on this site. It also has a search engine.

www.companies-house.gov.uk provides information about all British companies, as well as answers to questions about different types of companies.

www.milfac.co.uk/bisindex.html is a useful site with a database containing basic details of over two million British businesses, which you can search either according to the type of business or its location.

www.british-franchise.org.uk gives a fascinating insight into how franchises work and looks at the operation of a number of real-world franchises.
.

www.bat.com is the website of British American Tobaccos, which is a large, international business involved in a variety of industries.

www.bpamoco.com the BP Amoco website.

www.unilever.com is the website of Unilever, one of the UK's largest businesses.

www.bized.ac.uk is a student-friendly site containing a variety of useful features. It is especially worth looking at for company facts and information about the functions of business.

www.marketingcouncil.org contains good case study material. It is also worth looking at the research and innovation pages.

www.bbc.co.uk/education/work/life/ you will find a package of worksheets on the 'World of Work' available here, offering an insight into real workplace issues.

www.tesco.com/customerservices provides a good example of the customer services department of the UK's largest retailer.

www.mcdonalds.co.uk/company/asp/ci_HR this is part of a recruitment campaign for McDonald's, but it does give an insight into the work of a human resources department.

www.shell.co.uk is an interesting website. It is particularly worth looking at the company performance pages to see how Shell has responded to environmental issues.

www.britishairways.com/responsibility looks at British Airways policies with respect to protecting the environment.

www.bluecircle.co.uk have a look at Blue Circle's environmental report. The compnay produces cement and other products for the construction industry.

Unit 2

ww.businessbureau-uk.co.uk is a site containing a section on contracts of employment.

www.virgin.com is the website of one of Britain's most popular companies. It is a useful site for finding job descriptions.

www.tiscali.co.uk/jobs/selfemployment is a very readable website offering an introduction to self-employment.

www.teleworking-survey.co.uk is an excellent site on teleworking, which is easy to follow and offers basic information.

www.telegraph.co.uk/search provides a top class archive, where you can search the last few months' issues of the newspaper. Using the search word 'productivity' should produce some interesting and relevant articles.

www.acas.org.uk gives general information about the ACAS's work. It also explains how arbitration works, and has some interesting statistics. It also has information sheets on a variety of employment matters.

www.bbc.co.uk/news is a useful site for business studies' subjects. It has a search engine and an A–Z of European organisations, which includes the European Court of Justice.

www.cre.gov.uk is the Commission for Racial Equalitywebsite. The CRE may be involved in workplace disputes where racial discrimination is said to have occurred.

www.employmentservice.gov.uk is a government website to help employers find employees, and employees to find jobs. It advertises over 400,000 jobs across the UK. An important source of information for human resources departments.

www.careers-gateway.co.uk is an enormous website, offering advice to job applicants, particularly helpful for first-time job seekers.

www.bbc.co.uk/education/work/life is an extensive website, which includes plenty of advice on all aspects of work, including what it is like being at the workplace. Essential reading!

www.jratech.co.uk/jobs/appform is a really good website of a company whose human resources department makes effective use of technology.
Look at the online application form.

www.iipuk.co.uk is the Investors in People website. It explains how the scheme works and gives details of the benefits this can bring. A number of interesting case studies are included.

www.nationaltrainingawards.com contains case studies of both businesses and individiuals. It is the website of the National Training Awards.

www.bized.ac.uk/listserv/companies/comlist.htm is a helpful web page on the Bized website with links to the 100 largest companies in the UK. It shows how these businesses use their websites as part of their customer services.

www.tesco.com/customerservices is a useful website for comparison. Go to the Tesco home page and look under 'Today at Tesco'. There you'll find good ideas to help you decide how good another company's customer service is.

www1.sky.com/skycomHome is another interesting website, but very different from Tesco's. It also has some good ideas on customer services that may be compared with those of other companies.

www.tradingstandards.gov.uk is a central site for the Trading Standards Institute, the organisation that looks after consumers and ensures that consumer legislation is enforced.

www.purchasing-consultants.co.uk is a large website covering a range of consumer protection issues. It also contains advice for consumers and links to other useful sites. Excellent for finding out about consumers' rights.

INDEX

Published by HarperCollins*Publishers* Limited
77–85 Fulham Palace Road
Hammersmith
London
W6 8JB

www.CollinsEducation.co.uk
Online support for schools and colleges

© HarperCollins *Publishers* Limited 2002
First published 2002

10 9 8 7 6 5 4 3 2

ISBN 0 00 713808 3

Malcolm Surridge asserts the moral right to be identified as the author of this work.

British Cataloguing in Publication Data
A cataloguing record for this publication is available from the British Library

Almost all the case studies in this book are factual. However, the persons, locations and subjects have been given different names to protect their identity. The accompanying images are for aesthetic purposes only and are not intended to represent or identify any existing person, location or subject. The publishers cannot accept any responsibility for any consequences resulting from this use, except as expressly provided by law.

Series commissioned by Graham Bradbury
Series design and cover by Patricia Briggs
Book design by Kim Bale, Visual Image
Cover picture by The Stock Market © Thierry Cariou
Pictures researched by Thelma Gilbert
Cartoons by Jerry Fowler
Index by Patricia Baker
Project managed by Michael March/Bender Richardson White and Kay Wright
Production by Jack Murphy
Printed and bound by Scotprint, Haddington

www.fireandwater.co.uk
The book lover's website